NATIVE MEN REMADE

Ty P. Kāwika Tengan

NATIVE MEN REMADE

....

Gender and Nation in Contemporary Hawai'i

Duke University Press   Durham and London   2008

© 2008 Duke University Press

All rights reserved

Printed in the United States of
America on acid-free paper ∞

Designed by Heather Hensley

Typeset in ITC Galliard by
Keystone Typesetting, Inc.

Library of Congress Cataloging-in-
Publication Data appear on the last
printed page of this book.

IN MEMORY OF DAVID CARVALHO JR.

CONTENTS

....

ILLUSTRATIONS

....

E nā kupa o ka ʻāina, mai ka hikina a ka lā i Haʻehaʻe a i ka mole o Lehua; I greet you with aloha. What follows is my analysis of the gendered and cultural transformations occurring as Hawaiian men remake their identities as warriors and as members of a men's house called the Hale Mua. I write as a member of the Hale Mua, an indigenous scholar, and an anthropologist. I see my project as both an intellectual and a political one, and thus I have some comments on language and terminology.

I do not italicize Hawaiian words, and I usually define them upon first usage only (though there are a few exceptions). I have thus provided a glossary for those who are unfamiliar with the Hawaiian words I use in the text; most words (though not all) are defined there. The revitalization of Hawaiian language terms and names has been an important part of the remaking of Hawaiian identity that I seek to analyze and enact in my writing.

The more common vernacular used in the islands and by most of the men in the Hale Mua is called Pidgin, officially Hawaiʻi Creole English (HCE). Emerging from the plantation camps and from the need to communicate across language barriers, Pidgin has become a marker of "local" (typically nonwhite, working-class) identity for people who were raised in Hawaiʻi, and for men a similarly ethnic and "tough" vision of masculinity. Pidgin has acquired a number of valuations, many of them negative (e.g., Pidgin as "broken" or "bad" English) (Sato 1991; Tamura 1996). However, Pidgin is a legitimate language, and a number of scholars and writers have put enormous effort into validating and maintaining its integrity (Da Pidgin Coup 1999; Hargrove et al. n.d.). Most of the men I spoke with used Pidgin to varying degrees, reflecting the HCE continuum today (Sato 1993). For those who spoke Pidgin in interviews, I used an "eye dialect" spelling approach, which is a modified English writing system (the alternate is the Odo orthography, which is a phonetic spelling system).

The terminology used to reference Hawaiians as a group is a particularly complex and politically charged topic. The term "kanaka," which literally means "people," has historically referred to aboriginal Hawaiians. Under American occupation, kanaka came to be associated with the derogatory adjectives "stupid" and "lazy" (among others). Following the language revitalization and cultural nationalist movements, Native Hawaiians have reclaimed kanaka as a source of pride, especially when framed as the original metaphor for self-identification when used in modified form as Kanaka Maoli (Real People) and Kanaka ʻŌiwi (People of the Bone) (Ayau and Tengan 2002; Blaisdell 2005). Noenoe Silva notes that these terms, which were commonly used in the writings of nineteenth-century Hawaiian authors, evoke "linguistic and familial relationships with people in Oceania" (2004a, 13); for example, the indigenous people of New Zealand/Aotearoa are called Tangata Māori, and their tribes are called iwi. (As will become apparent in the text, the comparison with the Māori is of particular importance for the ways in which men in the Hale Mua have come to think of themselves.) The terms "Kanaka Maoli" and "Kanaka ʻŌiwi" signal a political and cultural identification as indigenous people, and though their usage is more common in activist and intellectual circles, they have also found their way into popular discourse.

Similarly, the various meanings of "Hawaiian," with and without the various qualifiers of "native," "Native," "aboriginal," and "indigenous," have been the subject of intense debate for a range of reasons, including divergent framing strategies within the nationalist movement as well as appropriations by non-Hawaiians. As Kauanui (2005a; 2007) has detailed, native Hawaiian (with a small "n") comes from the 50 percent or more blood quantum definition established in the Hawaiian Homes Commission Act of 1920, whereas "Native Hawaiian" (capital "N") refers to those Hawaiians with any degree of aboriginal ancestry. While usually synonymous with Native Hawaiian, the term "Hawaiian" has also been used by nonethnic and ethnic Hawaiians alike for contradictory purposes of arguing for a color-blind society. On the one hand, those who oppose the political and historical claims of Native Hawaiians feel that "Hawaiian" (like "Californian") should apply equally to all residents of the state, regardless of race; frequently proponents of this idea are politically conservative and right wing. On the other hand, independence activists claim that "Hawaiian" only properly refers to subjects (nationals) of the Hawaiian Kingdom, and they reject both American citizenship and American models of racial thinking. They often prefer the term "aboriginal" (found in Kingdom laws) to refer to Native Hawaiians, and some go as far as to say that using the labels "native" or "indigenous" is harmful, as it validates U.S. authority by accepting the mantle of being "colonized" (which the political category of "indigenous peoples" assumes).

Aware of this diversity, I nonetheless use the terms "Kanaka 'Ōiwi," "Kanaka Maoli," "Kanaka," "Hawaiian," and "Native/indigenous/aboriginal Hawaiian" interchangeably to refer to ethnic Hawaiians with any degree of ancestry. I also use the term "indigenous" as it articulates with the larger transnational indigenous rights movement that many Hawaiians identify with. My use of these terms reflects the understanding of and usage by most in the men in the Hale Mua, though the terms "Hawaiian" and "Kanaka Maoli" are perhaps most prevalent there.

ACKNOWLEDGMENTS

....

Many hands and voices have coproduced the experiences, knowledge, and text found in this book. I owe a great debt of gratitude to the individuals, groups, and communities that have helped me along the way, and I apologize to any I fail to mention by name here.

I would like to first mahalo ke Akua, nā 'aumākua, nā kini akua, a me nā kūpuna for all the guidance, inspiration, and fortitude to ho'omau in this ha'awina. My family has been the most direct conduit of the strength, love, and support flowing from these sources, and so mahalo to my grandparents Carol and George Tengan, Margaret Kamaka and David Carvalho; to my parents Wendell Tengan and Davelynn Carvalho Tengan; to my brother Michael John Tengan; and to members of the Reyes 'ohana.

Mahalo to the men of the Hale Mua, who became something of a second family to me beginning in 1997. Thank you for all you have given and taught me, and I hope that this book helps to repay your generosity and maintain the relations of reciprocity that have been established with your gifts. I would like to thank especially those who have given me important feedback on this and other versions of the text: Sam Ka'ai, Kyle Nākānelua, Kamana'opono Crabbe, Keawe'aimoku Kaholokula, Kūkona Lopes, Richard Bissen, Cliff Alakai, Kāwika Ramos, Keoki Ki'ili, Kāwika Davidson, Puka Ho, Pākī Cabatingan, Kamika Nākānelua, Wiliama Smith, Greg Nee, and Glen Gibson (with Delaina Thomas). In particular I would like to thank Kāwika Ki'ili, who served as an informal research assistant in 2006–07, recording and transcribing follow-up interviews, gathering data, corresponding with research participants, and critiquing my writing. Mahalo also to all the men of the Hale Mua o Kūali'i for suffering my absence as I wrote this book.

Mahalo to the core groups and leaders of Nā Papa Kanaka o Puʻukoholā, including Nā Alo Aliʻi, Nā Waʻa Lalani Kahuna, Nā ʻElemākua, Nā Koa, and Nā Wahine, as well as Kanu o Ka ʻĀina Charter School, Nā Aikāne, and the civic clubs. Thanks to John Keola Lake for the years of spiritual leadership and for taking the time to talk story with me; also helpful was park superintendent and ceremonial participant Daniel Kawaiʻaeʻa. A special mahalo goes out to Keʻeaumoku Kapu and ʻohana, and Nā Koa Kau i ka Meheu o Nā Kūpuna, who challenge us each year to go to the next level.

Numerous colleagues have read and commented on my work, and I would like to thank them: Deborah Elliston, Keith Camacho, Lori Pierce, Puakea Nogelmeier, Vilsoni Hereniko, Ben Finney, Christine Yano, Noenoe Silva, Keone Nunes, Houston Wood, Vicente Diaz, J. Kēhaulani Kauanui, Margaret Jolly, Roderick Labrador, Pensri Ho, Nandita Sharma, Vernadette Gonzales, and the two anonymous readers who reviewed the book for Duke University Press. Special thanks go to Davianna McGregor, Hōkūlani Aikau, John Charlot, Stephen Boggs, and Geoffrey White for their extensive reviews, suggestions, comments, support, and guidance throughout.

Much of my research was initially supported by fellowships and grants from the Ford Foundation and the Andrew W. Mellon Foundation, whom I thank for their assistance. I would also like to thank everyone at Duke University Press, especially Ken Wissoker for his guidance and advice; others who have helped me along the way include Anitra Grisales, Mandy Earley, Emma Boyer, and Molly Balikov.

Finally, mahalo to my wife, G. Kuʻulei Reyes Tengan, my son, Kauilaonālani Tengan, and my daughter, Liʻuakalaʻikamakua "Plum" Tengan. You all carried burdens that I left behind when I disappeared into my office for hours, days, weeks, and months, and words cannot express my gratitude and love for you. Mahalo a aloha piha.

INTRODUCTION

....

Lele i Ka Pō

O ke au i ka huli wela ka honua	At the time when the earth became hot
O ke au i kahuli lole ka lani	At the time when the heavens turned about
O ke au i kukaiaka ka la	At the time when the sun was darkened
E hoomalamalama i ka malama	To cause the moon to shine
O ke au o Makalii ka po	The time of the rise of the Pleiades
O ka walewale hookumu honua ia	The slime, this was the source of the earth
O ke kumu o ka lipo, i lipo ai	The source of the darkness that made darkness
O ke kumu o ka Po, i po ai	The source of the night that made night
O ka lipolipo, o ka lipolipo	The intense darkness, the deep darkness
O ka lipo o ka la, o ka lipo o ka po	Darkness of the sun, darkness of the night
Po wale hoi	Nothing but night
Hanau ka po	The night gave birth
Hanau Kumulipo i ka po, he kane	Born was Kumulipo in the night, a male
Hanau Poele i ka po, he wahine	Born was Poele in the night, a female[1]

I stand on the precipice, and my world spins as the ocean crashes into the jagged rocks sixty feet below me. I am surrounded by people both living and not, and the pillars holding up the heavens call to us. I hear the voices of women behind me chanting and the explosions of men landing in the water below me. I call out to my ancestors to give me the strength, the courage, and the mana to jump into the Pō to be with them again, even though I am not entirely sure what that will mean. All sounds and sights freeze as my feet leave the edge and I fall . . . fall . . . fall . . .

The first Oceanic voyagers emerged out of the darkness, guided by stars as they plied their double canoes across oceans to land on the shores of Hawai'i some two thousand years ago. More canoes came later, and eventually a highly stratified chiefdom was established; yet once Hawai'i was put on the global imperial map with Captain James Cook's arrival in 1778, change was much more rapid. Despite the establishment of a monarchy (1810) and international recognition of the Hawaiian Kingdom's independence (1843), the nation suffered an overthrow (1893) backed by the U.S. military and annexation (1898) — both done illegally. White American sugar barons and missionary descendants thereafter ran the Territory like a plantation, as Hawaiian leaders worked to reverse the population collapse that saw some 90 percent of their people swept away by epidemics. World War II brought further changes, including the empowerment of second-generation Japanese American veterans and labor leaders who secured statehood in 1959 and led the political economic shift from agribusiness to militarism and tourism.

Native Hawaiians, dispossessed and debased, renewed their cultural pride and political consciousness during a period of renaissance and protest in the 1970s, and by the 1980s, a native nationalist movement flourished. A protest march and rally in downtown Honolulu attended by fifteen thousand people and an apology from President Bill Clinton and the U.S. government marked the centenary of the overthrow. The return of lands and sovereignty seemed imminent. However, in 2000 a U.S. Supreme Court ruling fueled a backlash of lawsuits aimed at dismantling the few remaining Hawaiian programs, entitlements, and rights. While U.S. Senator Daniel Akaka pushed forward a bill to protect against these attacks by redefining Hawaiians as a nation, about eight hundred men, women, and children on the island of Maui marched to affirm that Hawaiians would not be pushed back. At the end of the march, Hawaiian men wearing only malo — loincloths — jumped from the top of an ocean cliff to display their courage and dedication to move forward, ma mua. . . .

On March 4, 2001, I marched and jumped with the Hale Mua, a grassroots organization that strives to develop a cultural foundation for Hawaiian men to become strong leaders and community members. With a membership of approximately forty men drawn from various backgrounds and ages (though mostly middle-class and middle-aged), the Hale Mua provides a space for the teaching, learning, and practicing of Hawaiian traditions and histories. In particular we focus on the fighting arts and philosophies of warriorhood, and in the context of the struggles over Hawaiian identity, we respond to the call. We were one of two warrior groups that served as marshals for the Keepers of Aloha march, which went through Maui's tourist hub of Lāhainā to disturb (if only momentarily) the carefully cultivated image of a trouble-free paradise. When we arrived at our final destination of Pu'u Keka'a, a leaping point for the spirits of the departed, we stripped off our street clothes, girded our malo, and prepared for the Lele I ka Pō Leap into the Heavens ceremony we would perform. We gave chants and performed dances honoring the ancestors and recalled the courage of the eighteenth-century Maui chief Kahekili, who would dive from that spot in times of famine to inspire his people and to petition the gods for life. As we jumped into the Pō, the night and the realm of the ancestors, the people gathered once again to lift up a prayer for the power and strength needed as they found themselves in a familiar fight for all they had, a future in their past.

Into the Pō: Transformations of Self and Society

The central project of this book is to describe and theorize the ways in which individuals create meaningful identities in relation to larger political forces, and how these identities are themselves productive of new social practices and relations. I am particularly interested in the formations of masculine and indigenous subjectivities as they develop within a historical context in which race, class, gender, and colonial domination—including global touristic commodification—have played major roles. As a consequence, many indigenous Hawaiian men feel themselves to be disconnected, disempowered, and sometimes emasculated. In response, the men I write about have remade Hawaiian masculine identities within a group called the Hale Mua (the Men's House). I explore their transformations of self and society as they occur in practice through narrative and performative enactments. In the process I also consider the possibilities and problematics these reformulated identities hold for social and political change. More generally, this ethnography seeks to create a space in which various theories and methodologies of indigeneity (and anthropology) articulate new forms of knowledge and understanding of sociocultural process.

This is a story about Kanaka 'Ōiwi Maoli[2] men jumping into the Pō — the

FIGURE 1. Men from the Hale Mua (on the left) join other participants at a predawn "Hāʻule Lani" ceremony (see chapter 3) at Puʻukoholā, Hawaiʻi, 2005. PHOTO BY SHANE TEGARDEN.

darkness, the night, the realm of the gods. In the cosmogonic chant Kumu-lipo (see the epigraph to this chapter), the Pō represents the time when the world was created, a time before people walked the land (Beckwith 1972). It is seen today as a source of empowerment and guidance for modern Kānaka who seek escape from the constant glow of their mass-mediated lives. Yet it is also a place where people stumble and trip as they grope their way along in a darkness utterly unfamiliar to them. When the ground disappears from under their feet, the duration of the fall and the impact of the landing is anything but certain.

The story of the Hale Mua begins with the commemoration of the heiau (temple) called Puʻukoholā on the island of Hawaiʻi in 1991 (see figure 1). Two hundred years prior, Kamehameha dedicated it to his family god Kūkāʻilimoku in fulfillment of a prophecy that said all of Hawaiʻi would be his and war would end with its construction and consecration. In an effort to once again petition the heavens for Hawaiian unity, a committee led by the Maui carver and storyteller Sam Kaʻai conducted new ceremonies on the heiau and assembled a group of men called Nā Koa, "the Warriors" or "the Courageous Ones." Taking up the production of carved weaponry and the practice of martial arts, these warriors for the nation would embody the aggressive posturing of identity that came out of the cultural nationalist movement. On Maui, a group of Nā Koa led by Kyle Nākānelua, a firefighter and practitioner of the Hawaiian fighting arts, returned to Puʻukoholā each year to conduct ceremonies of rededication, renewal, and re-membering. This group evolved into the Hale Mua, and I found myself in their ranks in 1997. In this ethnographic study I trace the historical, political, and cultural milieu in which the Hale Mua emerged and continues to transform itself.

More important, I analyze the gendered formation of Hawaiian identity and masculinity in the Mua and in the larger context of the Hawaiian cultural nationalist movement. The Keepers of Aloha March brings into high relief a number of complex social dynamics: uniting people in resistance to the continued exertion of U.S. colonial power; developing various strategies of political, cultural, and spiritual re-empowerment rooted in reclamations and practices of place and space; asserting identities within and against competing discourses of culture and nation put forth by Kānaka on the one hand, and the state (e.g., tourism) on the other; and renewing a warrior tradition that itself is reworking notions of gender and embodied action/performance, especially for men.

Standing in the parking lot of the Sheraton Maui, the luxury resort that now stands on Puʻu Kekaʻa, the spiritual leader Kaponoʻai Molitau addressed the men who were about to jump. Molitau is also a product of the Puʻukoholā ceremonies — in addition to warriors, priests and ritual specialists were also established there. He told us that when he was first asked to come and offer prayers, he was ambivalent. He asked himself, "Why are you guys doing that? Just because it's the 'manly' thing to do?" He said he finally came to see (or perhaps he was trying to make everyone else see) that this was not about proving one's manhood but about honoring Kahekili and all our kūpuna, those elders in attendance that day and the ancestors who had gone before us.

I have pondered Molitau's words ever since that day. Though he saw the jump as being more about spiritual dedication than about gender performance, I wonder how true that was for the men assembled there. Indeed, I would argue that culture, place, and gender are deeply intertwined and cannot be separated from one another. A number of the men who had gathered that day have told me in other conversations that Hawaiian men in general have lost their place and role in society. Often they linked this to the loss of the old ways — the religious formations, political systems, cultural practices, and relationships to the land that our ancestors knew. With the arrival of colonialism, Christianity, and modernization, all of these configurations of knowledge and power were radically transformed; some say they were lost to the Pō. Many Kanaka Maoli men in the various movements today argue that they need to restore these structures and reclaim their traditional roles and kuleana (rights and responsibilities) as men; indeed, that was precisely what led to the formation of the Hale Mua in the first place, and what led many of these men to Lele i Ka Pō. Thus this jump was every bit as much about being a *man* as it was about being *Hawaiian* or, more specifically, a *Hawaiian man*.

Into the Pō(stcolonial)

Current political and cultural developments demand more than ever new ways of understanding the world. Both inside and outside the academy, there is deep uncertainty about the current historical moment. The theme of the annual meeting of the American Anthropological Association in 2002, "(Un)Imaginable Futures," indicates the perils and possibilities that anthropologists and indeed all people face when trying to make sense of a world characterized by war, global commodity flows, unequal access to and distribution of technological innovations, and the politics of nation-states contending with strong trans- and subnational collectivities. The Hawaiian movement has been steadfast in its adherence to nonviolence, and its cultural warriors have not taken up arms in the pursuit of sovereignty. Indeed, it was the very establishment of the Kingdom under Kamehameha that brought an end to the actual practice of warriorhood; consequently, the current efforts to reformulate both warrior and nationalist subjectivities have relied heavily on memory work and adaptation to contemporary realities.

At the same time, a renewed patriotic nationalism pervades the United States in response to the events of 9/11, evidence that older models of masculinist nation-state power—epitomized in Bruce Willis's heroic struggles against the world's most deadly terrorists—"die hard." The "war on terror" prompted the largest military landgrab in the islands since World War II as the army moved to transform its twenty-fifth infantry into a Stryker (light armored vehicle) brigade. When President George W. Bush occupied Iraq, Hawaiian warriors were once again called to serve their nation. Militarized masculinities were forged in jingoism, and Kanaka men (and women) found themselves in contradictory positions as foot soldiers in a war to reaffirm and reassert American colonial power, the same power that Hawaiians have been fighting since 1893. Indeed, it has historically been military service that filled the void for Hawaiians seeking to be warriors, leading Hawai'i to have the highest rate of men killed in the Vietnam War. During the second Iraq War, the sniping death of army Lt. Nainoa Hoe, leader of a Stryker platoon, received national attention; at home, men from the Hale Mua joined other modern and ancient warriors at his funeral to send him back to the Pō.[3]

Yet visitors do not come to Hawai'i to hear about war or young Hawaiian men dying. They come to escape such harsh realities and find renewal in paradise before returning to the day-to-day grind of their own lives — 7.4 million of them in 2006. Voted twelve years in a row "the best island in the world" in *Condé Nast Traveler* magazine, Maui absorbs about a third of that number, despite (or perhaps due to) the fact that it accounts for only 11 percent of the state's total residents. The embodied disparities are even more pronounced for the thirty-four thousand Kanaka 'Ōiwi who, already a minority at 24 percent of the Maui's population, are further engulfed by the forty-eight thousand tourists who are present on any given day. Not surprisingly, poll after poll has shown that the majority of the state's population feels that the islands are being run for the benefit of tourists at the expense of locals, these sentiments being most strongly expressed by 'Ōiwi on Maui.[4]

This story is my personal narration of a history being rewritten by many, a story of the struggle people face when trying to at once reconnect with, recreate, and defend traditions and other sources of life and identity. Inundated by the images and gazes produced by the global tourist apparatus, challenged by military and private interests that seek to take Hawaiian lands and resources, and burdened by the need to maintain indigenous practices and knowledge in an ever-expanding web of transnational capital and violence, Kanaka 'Ōiwi Maoli today often feel like they are falling into an eternal night.

Yet with every Pō, there is an Ao, a time of day, light, and life. It is with the hope for a new day and a new era of Kānaka that the people give themselves to the Pō. There they reinvigorate a mana that exists in all, in its many gendered, classed, and racialized forms. Here I explore the Pō(stcolonial) space of the Hawaiian cultural nationalist movement, a space in which 'Ōiwi Maoli incorporate ancestral knowledge practices into projects of re-empowerment in the world of neocolonial global capitalism. If nothing else, I seek to shed some light onto the darkness, and some darkness into the light.

How are the meanings of being a Hawaiian man (re)defined and enacted in the Hale Mua? Against the legacy of colonialism and its concomitant discourses of death and disappearance, the Hale Mua has endeavored to build strong, culturally grounded men who will take up their responsibilities as members of their families and the larger Kanaka 'Ōiwi Maoli community. The processes through which the men of the group come to define, know, and perform these kuleana articulate with the larger projects of cultural revitalization, moral regeneration, spiritual/bodily healing, national reclamation, and the uncertain and ambiguous project of mental and political decolonization.

In Hawai'i, attempts to reconnect with and to reassert a Maoli—a "real," "authentic"—cultural and political identity have been closely tied to issues of gender, class, race, place, and spirituality, to name a few. While all of these are central to understanding subjectivity and identity in Hawai'i, I focus primarily on the ways in which projects of nationalism, decolonization, revitalization, and reclamation produce new subjectivities of culture and gender, reworked by Hawaiian men.

One of the primary discursive formations I explore is that of the "emasculated Hawaiian male," whose loss of land, tradition, authenticity, culture, and power stems from the historical experience of colonialism and modernity. This discourse is produced on a number of levels and for various ends. As a number of feminist scholars have shown, the touristic commodification of culture and land in Hawai'i proceeds most notably (and profitably) through the marketing of a feminized and eroticized image of the islands as the hula girl; meanwhile, men are either completely erased from the picture, relegated to the background as musicians for the female dancers, or portrayed in similarly sexualized fashion as the surfer, beach boy, or Polynesian fire-knife dancer whose body and physical prowess are highlighted in an economy of pleasure (Desmond 1999; Ferguson and Turnbull 1999; Trask 1999). An example of such a figure in film is the character of David Kawena in Walt Disney's *Lilo and Stitch* (2002). Clumsy, awkward, and generally unimportant to the plot, David's only redeeming quality is that he knows how to surf, "hang loose," and earn his keep as a fire-knife dancer (though a hopelessly inept one until the very last scene of the movie, at which point he finally manages to avoid setting himself on fire).

Alternatively, movies such as *North Shore* (1988) and *Blue Crush* (2002) and the reality television show *Boarding House: North Shore* (2003) represent Hawaiian male surfers as irrational and senselessly ruthless (Walker 2005), depictions that are understood by the viewing audience not as assertions of agency and resistance to colonial incursions (cf. Ishiwata 2002) but as evidence of the innate savagery and violence of native men and the threat they pose to the touristic order (Tsai 2003). These images articulate with another discourse of emasculation that posits Hawaiian men as unable to survive in the modern world and trapped in a cycle of substance abuse, violence, and criminal activity.

Nunes and Whitney (1994) expressed this view in a *Honolulu* magazine article entitled "The Destruction of the Hawaiian Male." Keone Nunes, a Hawaiian man renowned as an instructor of hula and tattoo artist, and Scott Whitney, a haole (white) freelance writer known for his controversial pieces on Hawaiian culture, argued that "Hawaiian men have been marginalized and disempowered by the loss of their own place in the traditional culture" and that "Hawaiian men have suffered the most" (1994, 43). People have told me in conversation that the authors were severely criticized for some of the views they expressed, especially those that seemed to implicate Hawaiian women as part of the problem. Others thought the essay accurately reflected the reality of Hawaiian men's situation today and supported its assertion that modern society would "benefit from the re-examination of *maoli* wisdom about the roles of men and women" (60). Pūlama Collier (2002) states that this argument holds true in her study of the role of male teachers in the Hawaiian language immersion program on Maui, three of whom she observed enacting a specifically Hawaiian cultural and gendered mode of relating to the male students; this dynamic was typically absent in the immersion classroom, where 81 percent of the teachers were women (2002, 12).

Nunes and Whitney make a number of questionable claims, such as the conjecture that Hawaiian women's participation in the early sex trade contributed to their "head start" in learning about Western currencies, banks, retail goods, prisons, courts, and hospitals (60). The attempt to invoke traditional gender roles is problematic on a number of levels. First, we need to ask how "traditional" roles are defined, by whom, and for what purposes (Hoskins 2000). Gender scholars have also critiqued the very premises of "sex role theory" (Messner 1998). Connell (2005b, 26) argues, "In sex role theory, action (the role enactment) is linked to a structure defined by a biological difference, the dichotomy of male and female—not to a structure defined by social relations. This reduces gender to homogenous categories, betrayed by the persistent blurring of sex differences with sex roles." Another major problem with sex role theory is that it does not require an analysis of power and the ways in which masculinity is formed as a process, not merely a set of norms that one does or does not internalize (ibid., 25).

On the other hand, ancestral knowledge can be a powerful tool for addressing contemporary problems. Having been a part of the immersion community that Collier described, I can attest to the importance of Hawaiian male role modeling for the adolescent boys I taught, some of whom came from broken homes and experienced violence regularly outside of my classroom. It was also important that I contest dominant images of Hawaiian men, for as Nunes and Whitney cogently lay out, numerous representations of health, education, crime, history, and tourism incessantly speak to and actively create the "destruction of the Hawaiian male."[5]

Similar to the experience of indigenous peoples elsewhere, local popular, literary, and scholarly depictions of Hawaiian men often highlight the negative stereotypes associated with the ills of colonization: high incidence of suicide, incarceration, and domestic, alcohol, and drug abuse, disturbing health and life expectancy statistics, and poor job and academic accomplishment (Blaisdell and Mokuau 1994; Cook et al. 2005; Crabbe 1997; Kamauʻu 1998). Within the Hawaiian community, many have noted the strong leadership of ʻŌiwi women in the fields of politics, scholarship, literature, education, arts, dance, and other cultural productions (Kameʻeleihiwa 1999; Kauanui 1998; McGregor 2003; Trask 1999). While men have also held prominent positions of leadership in these areas, feminist scholars such as Trask criticize them for their patriarchal and misogynistic brand of activism (Trask 1984) and for their political collaborations in the power structures of the colonial state (Trask 1999). While such representations of Hawaiian men are based in a reality experienced by many, they quickly become pernicious when combined with the larger historical narratives of vanishing natives.[6] They also obscure the numerous instances in which Hawaiian men have shown strong leadership or otherwise contributed to the Hawaiian community. I do, however, argue that such discourses are productive of a socially emasculated and ineffectual Hawaiian male subjectivity, and that these ideas exert pervasive influence in the public consciousness.

A number of Kanaka Maoli artists and performers have wrestled with this issue explicitly in their work. Māhealani Kamauʻu, a poet and the director of the Native Hawaiian Legal Corporation, has poignantly written about the violence and incarceration of Hawaiian men as well as their effects on the family, which she knows from personal experience (Hartwell 1996, 173–91; Kamauʻu 1996, 1998, 2002). In a newspaper article on Native Hawaiian inmates (Meskin 1997), Kamauʻu stated, "The things we value are emasculating our men. They don't have a place anymore, the way they fit into society is being redefined. In more traditional societies men can be warriors, but it means different things in modern society (cited in Marshall 1999, 264)." In *Kāmau Aʻe,* the playwright Alani Apio explores the possibilities and implications of forming a nationalist warrior masculinity through the transformation of Michael Mahekona, a young ʻŌiwi man who spent his time in prison learning about the sovereignty movement from activist "educators" visiting Hawaiian inmates. Upon his release, he expresses his frustration to his cousin's haole wife, "Lisa, I tell you, all ouwa warriors stay in jail. Hard for rebuild da nation when the warriors behind bars" (Apio 1998, 10–11). Ernie Cruz Jr., Hawaiʻi Academy of Recording Arts 2002 Male Vocalist of the Year, echoes this concern in his widely popular song "Where Are the Brothers?" written by his sister Ernelle Downs. Calling all men to join the struggle for sovereignty, he sings, "Too many brothers fill our jails, live their lives in hopeless hell/You must think first and do right, we need you all to win this fight" (Cruz 2001).

These calls for a renewed Hawaiian warriorhood are heavily gendered ones. Though women warriors have stepped forward as well, the "call to arms" is directed specifically at Hawaiian men (see figure 2). This is part of a larger project of reclamation and remasculinization that ties claims of cultural and political re-empowerment to the reclamation of traditional male roles and practices. At the risk of oversimplifying, I tentatively characterize some of the main traits of this new-old Hawaiian masculinity as strong, healthy, heterosexual, working- or middle-class, between twenty and fifty years old, possessing "local" Hawaiian sensibilities, styles, and looks, educated and knowledgeable in some cultural practice, nonviolent to women and children, responsibly providing for one's family, respectful of one's elders, having a tangible relationship with the land and sea, exhibiting spiritual facilities and mana, courageous and ready to fight for the people — a modern-

FIGURE 2. Peter "Lupe" Vanderpoel looks back at other members of Nā Koa, "the Courageous Ones" or "the Warriors," who served as ceremonial guards at a 1998 centennial march and rally protesting the illegal annexation of Hawaiʻi by the United States in 1898, ʻIolani Palace, Oʻahu, 1998. PHOTO BY MAKANI ORTOGERO.

day warrior chief. Many of these qualities obviously apply to both genders and thus speak as much to the formation of Hawaiian personhood and maturity as to masculinity. It is not my intention here to reify a model of masculinity; rather, I wish to highlight some of the terms and ideals employed by Hawaiian men involved in this ethnography.

Just as men are being implored to be more Hawaiian, so too are Kanaka practices being made more manly. Counter to the feminized constructions of tourism, which draw upon and reproduce the image of the hula maiden, the nationalist discourse articulates more masculine traditions such as the fighting arts, sacred dance, tattooing, kava drinking, and heiau rituals. Though by no means inherently the sole province of men, these spheres have come to be dominated by men and figured as masculine (which itself may be more indicative of Western views on masculinity than of indigenous ones).

Many of these practices have been heavily influenced by, if not directly borrowed from, other Polynesian traditions; foremost among them are the Māori of Aotearoa / New Zealand, whose resistance to settler colonialism has inspired many Hawaiians. The Hawaiian language instructor and scholar

Leilani Basham notes that Kānaka Maoli have modeled certain revitalization projects, especially those of language and ritual greetings, after Māori traditions precisely because these traditions represent a strong, vibrant, living culture that was able to survive colonization in ways that Hawaiian ones could not (Basham 2003; see also Wong 2002). Moreover, strength becomes gendered as *masculine* and coupled with authenticity, by men and women alike. Kīhei Nāhale-ā, a musician and Hawaiian language instructor at Hilo Community College, related an experience in which a group of Hawaiian language teachers returned from a trip to New Zealand. One of the women in the group was so impressed with the strength and ferocity of Māori greeting ceremonies that she told Kīhei, "You Hawaiian men need to be more like them!" (Nāhale-ā 2002). Here we see the ways in which gendered configurations of nation and culture that operate in colonial projects often reproduce themselves in anticolonial ones: masculinity is identified with the strong and authentic — Māori / Maoli — traditions of precolonial Polynesian society that were able to resist the perceived death, weakening, feminization, and emasculation colonization exacted on Hawaiian culture. As Harper (1996, ix) notes in regard to black men, claims to an "authentic" identity "are largely animated by a profound anxiety about the status specifically of African-American *masculinity.*" At least for some Kānaka Maoli, these anxieties are resolved by reconnecting with the masculinity of their ancestors and their Polynesian brothers.

However, these same ideologies of gendered power and authority have come under heavy critique by indigenous women from Hawai'i and New Zealand (Hoskins 2000; Trask 1984). In their view, the articulation of masculine power and authority with sovereignty and self-determination represents a double colonization for indigenous women, as both white society and their own men work to marginalize them. They highlight the need to recognize that assertions of patriarchy reproduce the same structures of oppression and hierarchy that disempower individuals along the lines of race, class, gender, sexuality, age, body, and so forth. However, statements such as "male leaders in our movement . . . are not the most visible, the most articulate, nor the most creative" (Trask 1999, 94) often evoke such a visceral and emotional reaction that men do not hear the important feminist insights of the critique. Instead, comments such as these often provoke masculinist ones that go beyond the level of "men need to do their part" to the extreme of "men need to reclaim their rightful places as the leaders and women need to take a back seat."

Formations of Culture, History, Nation, and Gender

Taking such feminist critiques seriously, I explore what it means to remake a Hawaiian masculinity, in whose interests such projects are carried out, and which individuals benefit and how. Through critical reflection and ethnographic work, I seek to move beyond conjecture and commentary to examine in close detail the ways in which these gendered dynamics of culture and nation are worked out in practice, talk, and performance on the ground. I look especially at how discourses of culture, history, nation, and gender are inscribed, embodied, and remade in the Hale Mua.

Recent theorists have examined the cultural bases and structures of feeling that make nationalism such a powerfully "imagined community" (Abu-Lughod 2005; Anderson 1991; Foster 2002; Kelly and Kaplan 2001). Discourses of the nation and national belonging reconstitute subjects along such lines as culture (Anderson 1991; Dominguez 1992), gender and sexuality (Enloe 1990; Parker et al. 1992), race and ethnicity, class, and place (Gupta and Ferguson 1997; Morley and Chen 1996). In the Hale Mua, men take up and transform identities in their actions, highlighting the fluidity and creativity of the categories at play. James Clifford (2001) offers Stuart Hall's reworking of Antonio Gramsci's notion of articulation (Morley and Chen 1996) as a useful approach to understanding this sort of indigenous dynamism: "In articulation theory, the whole question of authenticity is secondary, and the process of social and cultural persistence is political all the way back. It is assumed that cultural forms will always be made, unmade, and remade. Communities can and must reconfigure themselves, drawing selectively on remembered pasts. The relevant question is whether, and how, they convince and coerce insiders and outsiders, often in power-charged, unequal situations, to accept the autonomy of a 'we'" (Clifford 2001, 479). Like other groups engaging in similar projects within the Kanaka Maoli and in other indigenous movements, the remaking of the ʻŌiwi self and society proceeds through the reconnection with and retelling of moʻolelo — legends, histories, personal stories, and narrative accounts of events. The Hale Mua does this by contesting the dominant narratives of neocolonialism, modernity, and global capitalism; re-membering lāhui (collectivity as a people/

nation) through the commemoration and reliving of indigenous histories; carrying out ritual practices that (re)utilize, (re)consecrate, and (re)create sacred sites and spaces; embodying the stories and legends of the ancestors in dance and martial arts while also rewriting and reforming the body as a site of personal and collective strength; and reforming subjectivities through the telling and hearing of life stories that are shared in ceremonies, weekly meetings, and in the interviews I conducted as a member, group historian, and university anthropologist.

In theorizing the production of masculinities in the Hawaiian movement, I am concerned with the ways in which particular visions and ideals of what it means to be a proper or successful man are being reworked, for these figurations in turn work to naturalize and maintain systems of gendered, raced, and class-based oppression and domination. Many theorists influenced by Gramscian–Marxist feminist theory have examined the ways in which "hegemonic masculinities" (those dominant ideals of what men should be and how they should act) legitimate patriarchal structures and subordinate femininities and other "marginalized masculinities" along the multiple lines of ethnicity, race, class, property, age, sexuality, the nation, and so on (Connell 2005b; Cornwall and Lindisfarne 1994).

While these constructs are useful in highlighting the power dynamics of gender, they are easily reified. Hegemonic masculinities and subaltern masculinities should not be seen as two homogenous, discrete productions that are separated by distinct boundaries. To do so would be to replicate the debilitating dichotomies upon which colonial hegemonies and authority rest as well as to miss the complexities of what actually takes place "on the ground" (Elliston 2004, 628). We need to see gendered social actors as complexly situated, located, and positioned in multiple settings and historical contexts. In so doing, we can attend to the ways in which men and women have access to different points of privilege and subordination through such positionings (Anzaldúa 1987; Haraway 1991; Sandoval 1991). Hegemonies are always incomplete, allowing interplay between structure and agency—an interplay that involves and transforms indigenous ideologies of gender and power. Such an approach to hegemonic power relations allows us to explore the ways in which men and women who are complexly situated in multiple contexts can draw upon dominant gender constructs for contradictory and even subversive purposes.

In *Making Gender,* Ortner utilizes a "practice theory" approach to high-light the ways "that human action is made by 'structure,' and at the same time always makes and potentially unmakes it" (1996, 2). My explorations of the (re)making of Hawaiian masculinities emphasizes the ways in which cultural and gendered formations emerge through discursive practices, both at the macrosocial level of power-laden institutions that produce "regimes of truth" (Foucault and Gordon 1980; Foucault and Rabinow 1984), and at the microlevel where agents internalize, reproduce and transform these orders through everyday practice (Bourdieu 1977; Certeau 1984). Elliston (1997) employs such an approach in her study of gender and nationalism in Tahiti. Rather than relying on an identity construct, which leaves unexamined a problematic theory of subjectivity, she develops a "discursive practices of difference" analytic. Tacking between "ideological and symbolic differences which people use and elaborate on" and "the social practices in and through which those differences are instantiated," the discursive practices approach "references the dynamic, dialectic, and productive relationship which holds between, on the one hand, the material practices through which life is lived and, on the other hand, the ideologies which people deploy to explain, contest, and reshape the practices through which they live their lives" (Elliston 1997, 14).

In this book I examine a range of discourses that include touristic and news media representations, filmic and literary depictions, international and domestic laws, Western and indigenous histories, and ethnographic and personal accounts. I link various narrative and performative enactments of the Hale Mua, including storytelling, life history narrative, and ritual-ceremonial performance, with these other forms of mediation as the men work to negotiate the contradictions of defining self and nation. One of the contributions this book offers is a look at an identity politics from the vantage point of local (and personal) practices, complementing the tradition of research focusing on media and documentary representations (Anderson 1991; Morley and Chen 1996).

Discursive practices of gender are relational, fluid, and historically contingent processes that are (re)defined and embodied in social interaction (Cornwall and Lindisfarne 1994; Lamphere et al. 1997; Ortner 1996). By "embodied," I mean to highlight the ways in which bodies are inscribed by and themselves produce meanings and ideas through performance and action. I find Connell's notion of "body-reflexive practices" useful, for it sees bodies as "both objects and agents of practice, and the practice itself forming the structures within which bodies are appropriated and defined" (Connell 2005b, 61). The discursive processes of which I speak—those related to ideas, language, texts, knowledge, and representations—are understood, experienced, and produced in very important and immediate ways in and through the body. Likewise, bodily processes produce new forms of knowledge that exist and work in ways that both complement and go beyond the contemporary understandings of culture as symbolic system (Farnell 1999). It is this quality of embodied discursive action—the active signification, enactment, and production of identities through bodily movements and engagements—that makes groups such as the Hale Mua such potent sites for identity and self-formation.

As anthropologists have long noted, multiple layers of symbolism, meaning, and emotion are effected and affected through the ritual process (Turner 1969). In chapters 2 and 3, I detail the ways in which rituals create a context for men to both separate from the dominant structures of neocolonial society and reestablish indigenous structures of knowledge, power, and embodiment—even if only for a short time. Importantly, these processes are both inscribed on the body and enacted through bodily performances and actions. Thus the dances, martial art forms, dress, and tattoos that are sited on the men's bodies and in their performance tell stories and communicate messages about identity which are negotiated and understood by other Hawaiian men in the group and in the community (Wendt 1999).

Perhaps the most fundamental and meaningful of such acts occurs when the men of the Hale Mua don their malo during cultural and political events (see figure 2 on page 12 and figure 3). In precolonial times, the malo was the basic garment worn by men and was bestowed upon them as young boys when they were initiated into the hale mua—the men's eating and worship house that has come to serve as a cultural model for the group I write about (see chapter 1). The majority of Hawaiians today wear clothes typical of Western industrialized nations (if, perhaps, with an "island" flair), and the malo has become valued, in both the tourism industry and the nationalist movement, more as cultural signifier than as everyday attire. Most of the men in the contemporary Hale Mua had never worn a malo before they joined the group, and they struggled to overcome both bodily inhibitions

FIGURE 3. Men of the Hale Mua and Nā Koa Kau i ka Meheu o nā Kūpuna engage in a sparring demonstration at Puʻukoholā, Hawaiʻi, 2006. The malo that the men wear have one flap in the front and none in the back. PHOTO BY SHANE TEGARDEN.

and historical ignorance as they learned to wrap a single strip of cloth ten to twelve inches in width and four to five yards in length over their genitals, between their buttocks, and around their waist to end with a short flap extending to just above the knee. Moreover, they did this in order to participate in highly visible rituals that lay bare their strengths and weaknesses before audiences of family, friends, and strangers. As Richard Bissen related, such moments led him to understand modern Hawaiian warriorhood as the courage to "wear a malo in public" and not be ashamed of what he stood for — his culture and his people (see chapter 4).

Members of the group frequently recall such experiences and understandings when they speak of personally significant events, and thus I also look at linguistic discourse by analyzing life stories narrated by the men of the Hale Mua (see below and chapter 5). Whether through the creation of coherence in disrupted cultural or psychological models or the healing of individual and collective memories, the telling and hearing of life stories is a shaping event that allows for a redefinition of identity through interaction with others (Cain 1991; Ginsburg 1989; Linde 1993; Mattingly 1998; Ochs and Capps 1996; Peacock and Holland 1993; Swora 2001). My purpose is to look at the pragmatics of life stories and at the transformative effects of language and performance, specifically the ways in which various kinds of narrative and ritual practice rework emotions and self-understanding. Karen Ito observed that her Hawaiian "lady friends" living in Honolulu during the 1970s participated in "talk story," a relaxed conversation involving a search for shared feeling (Boggs 1985) to engage in *emotional exchange* that reaffirmed and reproduced the ties of affect that bound Hawaiian communities and represented "the heart of Hawaiian culture" (Ito 1999, 9). I too recognized this naturally occurring mode of talk among men in the Hale Mua and focus on that in a number of related contexts ('awa circle talk, for example) as well as in my interviewing, which extends and modifies talk story styles of speaking by eliciting narratives of personal and collective histories through nondirective interviewing techniques.

Like the Hawaiian families Ito describes, the Hale Mua maintains its "ties that define" through the sharing of affect-rich life stories in a variety of contexts of formal and informal talk story. The Hale Mua becomes a safe space where 'Ōiwi men heal themselves and the other men suffering the historic pain of colonization by re-membering self and society through the sharing of mo'olelo and rebuilding and reconstituting a community of men bound by their words.[7] The narrative structures and therapeutic functions of life story telling in the Hale Mua bear resemblance to those found in Alcoholics Anonymous meetings (Cain 1991; Swora 2001). As I lay out in chapter 4, Kamana'opono Crabbe, a clinical psychologist and the "talking chief" for Kyle Nākānelua, first implemented the model of the Hale Mua as a culturally based form of treatment for Hawaiian men suffering from substance abuse and domestic violence in a Hawaiian community on O'ahu. Many of the men who come to the Hale Mua have experienced physical violence and alcoholism to varying degrees as well as the more discursive acts of violence visited on them through the mainstream representations of Hawaiian men.

Mo'olelo, as fragments of narrated life experiences, also place speakers and listeners alike in a succession of personal, social, historical, and spiritual events and thereby actively form individual and group subjectivities in the Hale Mua. Through the mo'olelo, the men I interviewed both contextualize their participation in the Hale Mua and actively work out issues of identity that extend into other areas of their life. As the men relate their reasons for

FIGURE 4. Kamana'opono Crabbe (right) and Ke'eaumoku Kapu (left) flank Sam Ka'ai, who pours 'awa (kava) into a cup held by Lono during an 'awa ceremony at the East Maui Taro Festival in Hāna, Maui, 1997. Such formal events honor dignitaries — in this case the crew of the *Hōkūle'a* voyaging canoe — and frequently feature oratory and the telling of life stories. PHOTO BY MASAKO CORDRAY.

joining, the timing in their lives at which this occurs, and the desires that preceded and serve as the context for their experiences in the Mua, they create individual subjectivities that feed back into larger discourses on Hawaiian masculinity and identity. During my interviews, a number of the men stated that they did not actually know what was missing until they found it in the Hale Mua. By learning to place their stories in a larger context of talk (and history) the men come to a new understanding of their subjectivity.

The life story of Kamana'opono Crabbe (see figure 4) illustrates the multiple layering of discursive practice I follow throughout this book, and it provides something of a road map of the larger themes I cover here; I summarize his mo'olelo here on the basis of my formal interviews with him (in 1999 and 2006) and of informal talk story during the years we were neighbors (2001–05). Crabbe was born on O'ahu in 1964, the second youngest of seven children. His father was a fire captain and his mother an airlines cabin service employee. After graduating in 1982 from Kamehameha, a school for Native Hawaiians (see chapter 1), he joined the U.S.

Army Reserve (100th Battalion 442nd Infantry) and slowly began to learn Hawaiian language at the community college and from his uncle, a retired prison guard and warden for the local correctional facility who was a native speaker. While enrolled in the clinical psychology graduate program at the University of Hawai'i in 1991, he heard Sam Ka'ai give a speech calling for Hawaiian men to assemble as ceremonial warriors at the upcoming commemoration at Pu'ukoholā (see chapter 2). Crabbe had already been meeting with other Hawaiian men in the Army Reserves and National Guard to talk about "Hawaiian things" and cook pigs in the imu (traditional underground oven), yet he felt like they were "struggling" and "wanted to learn" more. He thus flew to Hawai'i in August of 1991 to attend Pu'ukoholā, an experience that brought him "closer culturally and spiritually" to his heritage. Importantly, he narrated his personal transformation, which occurred in the ritual process and in relation to the other Hawaiian men he saw, as the outcome of his own family history and quest for identity:

Ever since I was young, my father used to give us boxing gloves, I used to fight my addah two braddahs, take karate, play sports. So to me, that's more my 'ano [style], my more physical kind of path. But then . . . I noticed that throughout my childhood, my teenage years, and growing up into my early adult years, you know I really had this desire to do something Hawaiian, but I never knew what it was. So I was always searching . . . looking for my place. For me, Pu'ukoholā was a significant event in my life. It created an experience that I saw. I saw kāne [men] I could identify with. . . . I saw Sam Ka'ai, I saw Kyle Nākānelua [and others]. You know like, "Wow, dese kine guys I wouldn't mind being like." . . . I saw Keone Nunes ovah there, he was an inspiration to me too. All dese addah kāne dat I saw was sort of role models for me to aspire to, to fulfill my own identity, but an identity that I comfortable with, not somebody placing on me (Crabbe 1999).

At the time, Crabbe, like many others, associated the cultural nationalist movement only with women leaders, and so the sight of Hawaiian male role models he could identify with served as his entry point into the world of Kanaka 'Ōiwi cultural politics. He also embodied a new Hawaiian male subjectivity when he wore a malo and took up a carved spear to stand as a member of Nā Koa, the Warriors or the Courageous Ones (see figure 8 on page 82, third figure from far right wearing fishhook necklace). In 1993, another rebirth in traditional warriorhood occurred when a group of experts in the previously secret fighting art of lua began to teach a new generation of students (Paglinawan et al. 2006). Crabbe became a student in the lua school and developed a strong bond with Kyle Nākānelua and Keʻeaumoku Kapu, two of the advanced students who would later go on to form their own groups of Nā Koa (see chapters 3 and 4).[8] He eventually joined Nākānelua and Kaʻai to create the Hale Mua, and he completed his Ph.D. in clinical psychology in 2002.

In 2006, Crabbe's cultural and professional trajectories converged as he and a committee of Native Hawaiian community leaders successfully organized a Native Hawaiian men's health conference attended by approximately five hundred men. Health was defined broadly to include physical, psychological, spiritual, cultural, and political well-being — pono — that emerged in the restoration and balance of proper relationships between individual, family, and community. Significantly, his welcome message framed the event as one that would involve the production of community through the sharing of stories that linked individuals to community and nation (lāhui): "We gather this weekend in unity as native sons and fellow companions to share our knowledge of cultural traditions, experiences as males, strengths within our communities, and hopes for the future of our *lāhui* and homeland we know as Hawaiʻi" (Crabbe 2006). This, in essence, is the goal of the Hale Mua, and it is the struggle to achieve it through narrative and ritual production of moʻolelo that I examine in this book.

Discursive Battlegrounds

Such discursive practices (of identity) have become increasingly salient not only in Hawaiʻi but throughout the Pacific in areas where nationalist struggles for decolonization, sovereignty, and self-determination produce new articulations of traditional culture and strong assertions of indigeneity and identity. Clifford (2001, 475) notes that in Oceanic decolonization efforts, "traditions articulate, selectively remember and connect pasts and presents. . . . Very old cultural dispositions — historically rerouted by religious conversion, formations of race or ethnicity, communication technologies, new gender roles, capitalist pressures — are being actively remade."

As scholars in the early 1990s increasingly set their gazes on political constructions of culture (termed "inventions of tradition") in Native struggles (Jolly and Thomas 1992; Keesing 1989; Linnekin 1992; Linnekin and

Poyer 1990), the Natives gazed back and brought their politics to bear on the academy. A much-cited exchange between Roger Keesing and Haunani-Kay Trask serves as a reminder that all discourses — especially those *about* discourses — produce power differentials (Keesing 1989; Linnekin 1992; Tobin 1994; Trask 1991). Commenting on the invention of tradition literature, Briggs (1996) insightfully noted that both anthropologists and indigenous people stake claims to moral, political, and intellectual authority in ways that are not altogether different. What *is* different is the access to discursive and economic resources enjoyed by the various parties, and it is this differential that privileges the anthropologist's formulations.

As Noenoe Silva (2004a, 16–23) has argued for the case of Hawai'i, the claims to discursive authority have further proceeded through a near-total neglect of Hawaiian language materials (which stems from the colonial oppression of our language) and a reliance on the partial, fractured, and even mistranslated texts and the dominant colonial histories typically written by Anglo historians who could not access the indigenous archive. One particularly relevant example highlights not merely an omission, but also a clearly biased addition. Writing in the Hawaiian language newspaper in 1867, the historian Samuel Kamakau detailed a gendered division of labor in which women beat the tapa cloth used for pillows, mats, sheets, and clothing, while men did most of the heavy outdoor work, including farming, fishing, cooking, and house building, and provided women with everything they needed for their material production.[9] This practice varied from island to island, and he notes (with some disdain) that on Hawai'i and Maui the women worked outdoors just as hard as the men; the norm, however, was for men to do the laborious work. Another exception, as it appears in the English translation and collection *Ruling Chiefs of Hawai'i*, reads, "Men who were disinclined to follow manly pursuits were taught to be experts in making loincloths and women's skirts and were called 'dyers and printers of Ehu'" (Kamakau 1992, 238). The Hawaiian text it was based upon read, "'O nā kāne nō ho'i kekahi po'e loea ma ke 'ano hana malo a me ka pā'ū wahine. He po'e hapa nō na'e ka po'e i a'o 'ia ma ia 'ao'ao; ua kapa 'ia lākou 'o ka po'e ho'olu'u a kāpalapala a 'Ehu" (Kamakau 1996, 233), a more literal translation of which is, "The men in fact were also some of the people expert in the making of loincloths and women's skirts. The people trained as such were a minority, however; they were called the dyers and printers of 'Ehu" (my translation). Though Kamakau says that these men were a "hapa nō" (minority), nowhere does he assert that they were "disinclined to follow manly pursuits." One can speculate as to what Kamakau *may* have thought, but to add morally loaded phrases that were not present steals mana from the work. This holds grave implications for people who are looking to these texts as the sources of "traditional roles." If we Kanaka Maoli scholars and intellectuals are seeking to develop strategies for decolonization, healing, and reempowerment based on the indigenous archive, it behooves us to make sure we are rooting our projects in the Maoli — that which is *real*.

Recognizing these dynamics and the need to assert a more proactive cultural politics in the academy, a number of indigenous and nonindigenous scholars in the Pacific have attempted to retheorize and renarrate Oceanic experiences and lives (Borofsky 2000; Diaz and Kauanui 2001; Hauʻofa 1993; Hereniko and Wilson 1999; Smith 1999). For example, the symposium and publication *Native Pacific Cultural Studies on the Edge,* co-convened and co-edited by Vicente Diaz and J. Kēhaulani Kauanui, offers an important intervention in conceptualizing indigeneity. Diaz and Kauanui draw upon the seafaring and island-based sensibilities characteristic of Pacific peoples to address current contests over Pacific indigeneity. Turning to indigenous navigational concepts used for voyaging, they offer "triangulation as a native style of analysis and mode of politics" (Diaz and Kauanui 2001, 316; see also Diaz 2006). They state, "As a technique for successful travel, whose urgent stakes are the peoples' survival and stewardship of place, triangulating among moving islands in a fluidic pathway involves a clear and unambiguous sense of one's place at all times. The islands may move, but one must always know their location at any given time, as indexed by their signs in the natural and supernatural worlds. To lose one's place, to not know where one's island is, or to no longer be possessed by that island, is to be perilously lost at sea" (317).

This approach to indigenous struggles in academia as well as in native communities is both liberating and empowering for its ability to recognize that rootedness in land and place persists despite — and even because of — the fluidity that comes with histories of travel and tidal change. These voyaging traditions are reproduced in the Hale Mua's annual trips to Puʻukoholā (chapter 3) and the visit to Aotearoa/New Zealand in 2004 (conclusion). Individually, though, many of the men had already experienced a great deal of mobility in their lives, which created in them ambivalences of disconnection from land and community that were worked out in the telling and hearing of life stories in the group (chapter 5). The ritual performance of genealogical chants and moʻolelo of ancestral figures, gods, chiefs, and places (see Sam Kaʻai's discussion of the navigator's song in chapter 2) also served to create identities that remained rooted (in history) while also routed (in geography) (Clifford 1997, 2001).

On Being an ʻŌiwi Anthropologist

In this book, I both document and produce such discursive practices of personal and social narration as I triangulate my work as an ʻŌiwi anthropologist. The term "ʻŌiwi" means "indigenous/native" and literally roots indigeneity in the iwi (bones) by identifying the people with the kulāiwi ("bone plain" or native land) where they bury the iwi of their ancestors, the same land that feeds their families and waits for their bones to be replanted by their descendants (Ayau and Tengan 2002). As an ʻŌiwi, I have a special kuleana (right and responsibility) to nurture and maintain the genealogical connections between place, people, and gods. I also seek to tell new moʻolelo (using both English and Hawaiian) that shed light upon our ability to traverse the borders of insider/outsider, indigenous/foreign, colonized/decolonized, global/local, and modern/traditional. This orientation is especially salient given that Kānaka encounter otherness on the inside as much as on the outside of Hawaiian communities today. Yet this very diversity of experience and positionality is a strength when understood as broadening and enlarging the spaces of indigeneity and the possibilities of transformation (Clifford 2001; Diaz and Kauanui 2001; Hauʻofa 1993).

One way I have sought to articulate indigenous and anthropological practices has been to use Hawaiian language texts and concepts not only for the information they provide, but also for the theoretical insights they offer into the ways knowledge and meaning are created. For example, I draw upon a genealogical chant to interpret Sam Kaʻai's narration of his life story (chapter 5). Wherever possible I have also included original quotes of Hawaiian text from the writings of nineteenth- and early twentieth-century ʻŌiwi intellectuals, followed by my own translations and interpretations (see chapter 2).

Taking up such a position, I work to bring change not only in my community, but also in the discipline of anthropology and the academy in general.

Ever since (in fact, even before) anthropologists first began wrestling with the disciplinary "crisis" of the mid-1980s (Marcus and Fischer 1986), the call to redirect cultural critique inward has been accompanied by an increased focus on the problematics and possibilities of doing "native," "indigenous," "insider" and "halfie" anthropologies, "auto/ethnography" and other forms of "homework" (Abu-Lughod 1991; Fahim 1982; Manalansan 2003; Mankekar 1999; Peirano 1998; Reed-Danahay 1997; Teaiwa 2004; Visweswaran 1994). Lanita Jacobs-Huey argues that although the position of the indigenous anthropologist is as partial, negotiated, and problematic as any other identity one claims, the act of self-identifying as a native ethnographer is not done as "a noncritical privileging endeavor. Instead, foregrounding *native* in relation to anthropology, or oneself as a *native* anthropologist, can act as an empowering gesture and critique of the positioning of natives in the stagnant slot of the Other" (Jacobs-Huey 2002, 800). Like Jacobs-Huey, my efforts at decolonization are mobilized for not only the people I write about, but also the people I write for; in both cases, these communities are located inside and outside the academy. It is thus that I seek to practice "anthropology as an agent of transformation" (Harrison 1997), and one that responds to the politics of reception by challenging audiences (Lederman 2005).

As the Māori educator Linda Tuhiwai Smith (1999, 137) points out, critical reflexivity must underpin every step of the research project, for indigenous and other "insider" researchers "have to live with the consequences of their processes on a day-to-day basis for ever more, and so do their families and communities." This has been particularly important counsel for me to follow as my participation both predates and extends beyond my anthropological relations to the Mua and to the Hawaiian community. I joined the Hale Mua in 1997 upon the invitation of Richard Bissen, at the time the chief prosecutor on Maui. He knew me through my mother, who was a deputy prosecutor under him, and through my participation in the Hawaiian language immersion program, which his children were a part of (though not my students). Our families also shared a deeper connection, as my grandmother and his parents grew up in the same community, Piʻihana, and buried their loved ones in the same cemetery, Mahalani. Admittedly I was initially drawn by the prospect of learning lua and becoming initiated into a warrior clan; it turned out that the group was something quite different, as will become apparent in the following pages.

I initially resisted the urge to write about the group because I was aware of the dangers that came with being an indigenous anthropologist: reconciling competing obligations to community and to academia; determining what level of discussion and critique was appropriate; producing work that was accessible to multiple audiences; encountering unforeseen constraints as an insider; and wrestling with my own multiple positionalities and identities, which also made me an outsider. Most important, I was afraid of alienating myself from the group by objectifying and analyzing everything said and done there. Then I started to see that the stories shared and experiences created needed to be told to others. I was in the group for a purpose, and that was to write.

After receiving guidance and approval from Kyle Nākānelua, Sam Kaʻai, and Kamanaʻopono Crabbe, I took my ideas for writing an ethnography to the larger group in 1999 and asked them both for permission and for suggestions. Some individuals were very invested in seeing the project come to fruition, for as a written document it would validate the group's efforts and serve as a tangible source of information not only for themselves and their families, but also for other Hawaiian men. Others were eager to sit down and tell their story to me because they had never had a chance to reflect on their lives and tell of their experiences, let alone to someone who would record it (cf. Myerhoff 1982). Many saw the interviews as an extension of the sharing of moʻolelo in the Hale Mua, and so it was not a major issue for them. In the same vein, a number of men shared stories that were meant to teach *me* a lesson about being a Hawaiian man and what responsibilities I carry. Some of the older men told me how proud they were of me, saying that I am doing what all young Hawaiian men should be doing: getting an education, practicing the culture, and taking care of my family. Most of the guys just wanted to help out in any way they could; that's what the Hale Mua was established for, to help men go forward. Above all, they trusted me and were confident I would tell their story in a pono way, and that it was my kuleana.

Much to my regret, I unwittingly broke that trust. As I have discussed elsewhere (Tengan 2005), some of the things I wrote in an earlier draft, though never intended to harm, hurt one individual so deeply that he was prepared to fight. There was a sad irony there, for it was precisely the issue of male violence I had hoped my writing would address. Fortunately we were able to talk things out and make them right and pono again — an affirmation that the Hale Mua's focus on sharing moʻolelo to develop community could work. It also brought to light the ways in which class and status differentials (which turned out to be a major issue in my representations of him) underpin many of the tensions we need to resolve when we come together as Hawaiian men, both in and out of the Hale Mua. Sometimes we succeed, sometimes we fail. Thus I was reminded of my responsibilities to the group and of the fact that my writing was both a part and a product of the intersubjective formations and relationships we created and worked constantly to maintain.

Striving toward a more collaborative ethnography (Lassiter 2005), I have continued the process of consultation and discussion throughout. Some occasions dictated that I participate rather than record, despite my preference to record. At other times I chose to discard the anthropological hat when in fact I didn't need to. I was surprised at times to see other members recording with digital video and still cameras for their own purposes and with more tenacity than I was showing; this has produced another important archive and resource for both myself and others, and it illustrated the fact that I was not the only one interested in ethnography. I have also received insightful critique on my writings and learned from the ways that others have theorized the group's development and growth. Finally, I have had the joy of being able to teach what I know about anthropology to Kāwika Kiʻili, a fellow member who indicated some interest in learning ethnographic methods through practice and thus assisted with interviews, transcriptions, and analysis. Indeed, this is the direction the Hale Mua is taking — teaching the young ones (though Kiʻili is only four years my junior). As we seek to pass on knowledge to the new generation, I write with them in mind.

Although I have tried my hardest to incorporate the words (through interview transcripts) and ideas (from feedback on earlier drafts) of the other men in the Mua, as well as the guidance of my ancestors, this ethnographic account represents my own style of articulating these multitudes of voices. The Hale Mua means something different to everyone involved, and thus my own narration of it should not acquire a special authority that overshadows the viewpoints of the men who see it as a social club or those who see it as their entire life. For me, it is both more and less, and it is constantly in flux for myself and for the others. Such is the nature of a living culture and a living people.

Ma mua: Moving Forward

In chapter 1, I look at Hawaiian men's engagements with modernity as they relate to changes in notions of lāhui (nation), kingdom, territory, state, and sovereign nation. In particular, I have an eye to the ways masculinity is defined and redefined through the macrosocial changes that produce a particular gendering of nation, but also to how this plays out in men's lives as impacted by work and militarism. I end with some reflections on the ways in which the Hawaiian cultural renaissance and sovereignty movements have shifted the terms for identifying men and their contributions to culture and nation.

Chapter 2 presents a history and an analysis of the Hoʻokuʻikahi commemoration and ceremonies at Puʻukoholā in 1991 that created Nā Koa, which later became the Hale Mua. Here I lay out my approach to discursive practices of history, memory, body, and ritual process that I follow throughout the rest of the book. In chapter 3 I develop an ethnographic account of later ceremonies as viewed from the perspective of the Hale Mua, with a close focus on the event of 2002. I also point to the tensions that emerge at Puʻukoholā when the multiple projects of cultural reclamation, nationalist imagining, touristic appropriation, and gender empowerment converge on site.

Chapter 4 presents an overview of the development of the Hale Mua and its use of carving, ritual, and training to address the ambivalences men bring with them to the group, ambivalences regarding cultural identity, status differentials, violence, and gender politics. I also begin to incorporate life stories and moʻolelo to highlight the ways in which these issues are worked out in narrative practice. The close examination of talk story narrations and the work they do is the subject of chapter 5. Here I analyze the pragmatics of moʻolelo used to form a sense of self as a Hawaiian man connected to and defined through a community of Hawaiian men.

I conclude with a description of a trip our group took to Aotearoa/New Zealand in 2004 to visit our "younger brothers." Cultural genealogies that linked us to Māuiakamalo (Māui of the loincloth) were renewed as our similarities in language and culture recalled our shared connections as part of the larger Polynesian diaspora, formed by the remarkable story of voyaging and settlement of Oceania (Finney 1994). For many it was our "graduation" and final validation of being Maoli. I end with a contemplation of the lessons learned from the men's stories.

Sighting/Citing Islands

Just as this study is itself situated within the various intellectual, political, social, and personal currents discussed above, so too does it offer cultural theorists and workers a new site for retriangulating knowledge and practice (Wood 2006). Given Hawai'i's unique Oceanic position, island-based formations speak to developments in multicultural, ethnic, and Native studies in the United States, the Pacific, and Asia. The separation of "Native Hawaiian and other Pacific Islanders" from "Asian Americans" in the 2000 Census and a related debate over attempts to change the name of the Association for Asian American Studies (AAAS) to include the "P" (for Pacific) call attention to the importance of Pacific Islander experiences for rethinking race, ethnicity, and indigeneity in America (Diaz 2004; Kauanui 2004). Even further shifts may occur if legislation currently being put forth in the Congress by Senator Akaka (the Akaka Bill) succeeds in establishing a process for the federal recognition of Hawaiians as an indigenous group with rights to self-determination and self-governance; such a move would dramatically alter the discursive and material conditions of Native nationhood in the United States and the Pacific (Kauanui 2005a).

The Hawaiian case offers a particularly useful lens through which to view American imperialism in the past and present. A growing body of literature has critically reread the history of land tenure (Kame'eleihiwa 1992; Kirch and Sahlins 1992; Linnekin 1990; Stauffer 2004), government and law (Merry 2000; Osorio 2002), regimes of truth and knowledge (Buck 1993), race and diaspora (Hall 2005; Halualani 2002; Kauanui 2000, 1998), tourism (Desmond 1999; Imada 2004), militarism (Ferguson and Turnbull 1999), religious formations (Aikau 2005), and national identity and sovereignty (Merry and Brenneis 2003; Osorio 2001; Silva 2004a, 2004b; Trask 1999; Young 2004) in Hawai'i with a keen eye to the transformations brought on by U.S. colonial policies. Such scholarship has taken important cues from the gains made by Hawaiian activists, a number of whom are now further challenging the terms of the debate by reframing the American presence not as

FIGURE 5. *Left to right:* Kyle Nākānelua, Keʻeaumoku Kapu, and Kamanaʻopono Crabbe prepare to greet the crew of the *Hōkūleʻa* in Hāna Bay, Maui, 1997. PHOTO BY MASAKO CORDRAY.

one of colonization, but instead as one of belligerent occupation that has distinct parallels with the situation in Iraq (Sai 2004). Whichever approach one takes, there are important lessons that scholars in the United States and beyond may take from Hawaiʻi as the world braces itself in the age of American empire, an undertaking that found its sea legs one hundred years ago when the United States claimed Hawaiʻi, Puerto Rico, Guam, and the Phillipines.

This book seeks to bring an ethnographic grounding to others' readings of history and politics in Hawaiʻi, one that reveals the emotional nature and human face of individuals engaged in the process of identity and nation making (see also McGregor 2007) as well as the importance of reading gender in these intimate and personal spaces (cf. Ito 1999; Manderson and Jolly 1997; Stoler 2002). The individuals featured here thoughtfully reflect on their lives, mourn their perceived alienation from their culture and society, struggle with their forced acceptance of American values and citizenry, ambivalently comment on women's leadership, and proudly claim a new place as men in a nation groping toward recognition. The further intricacies of their lives and endeavors are laid out in detail throughout the book, and therein one will glimpse a subjectivity-in-process that is underrepresented in studies of Hawaiian and other Native communities. Here subjects negotiate the multiple discourses that impinge on their lives, often at a purely visceral, physical level, where the traces are found only in the strained notes of a ritual chant or a misstep during a ceremonial dance. Thus this ethnography may serve as a navigational site, even a point of departure, for new voyages of world- (and academic-) enlargement through anthropology, politics, history, and ethnic and gender studies. Last, I write this moʻolelo with the intent of reassuring the travel-weary that landfall is possible and that there are indeed more islands of hope than there are of despair.

ENGAGEMENTS
WITH MODERNITY

....

In the twentieth century, the institutions of work and the military have been particularly important in the production of ideologies and practices of Hawaiian masculinities, and indeed, these prove to be some of the major themes that emerge in the life stories of the men of the Hale Mua (see chapter 5). In this chapter, I situate changes in men's status and understandings of self in a larger history of nation making, which includes the establishment of lāhui, or people, nation, international recognition of the Kingdom, territorial occupation by the United States, admission as the fiftieth state, and reassertions of cultural and political identities of Hawaiian sovereignty. In the context of the present cultural nationalist movement, men's experiences with modernity have produced in some a feeling of acute alienation from indigenous history, culture, and community, and thus the Hale Mua has been constructed as a means of pushing men forward into a new understanding and experience of community that attempts to bridge the gap between modernity and tradition.

Masculinities, Nation, and Empire

Following Connell, I see masculinities, femininities, and trans- or third genders as social practices "organized in relation to a reproductive arena, defined by bodily structures and processes of human reproduction" (Connell 2005b, 71). Ortner (1996, 12–13) argues that gender is just one of the many "serious games" of social life played out in numerous arenas and by unevenly matched individuals and teams: "The effort to understand the making and unmaking of gender, as well as what gender makes, involves understanding the workings of these games as games, with their inclusions and exclusions, multiple positions, complex rules, forms of bodily activity, structures of feeling and desire, and stakes of winning, losing, or simply playing. It involves as well the question of how gender games themselves collide with, encompass, or are bent to the service of, other games, for gender is never, as they say, the only game in town" (19).

Hegemonic norms of gender, especially those of masculinity, work to naturalize inequalities and oppressions that are tied to the other "games" of race, class, nation, age, and sexuality, to name a few. Recognizing this, we must also attend to the ways that men and women access different points of privilege and subordination based on their positioning, engage in both hegemonic and marginalized practices in different contexts, and articulate new social and cultural forms over time. Gendered social actors are situated within larger sociocultural systems and structures of knowledge and power, which both shape and constrain the possibilities for action, as well as provide resources which individuals use to reproduce, negotiate, and transform those very systems (Lamphere et al. 1997; Ortner 1996).

Empire building (and dismantling) involves a reshaping of both local and global gender orders, which leads to a resituating of men and women in their relationships between and among each other (Connell 2005a; Lamphere et al. 1997). Nationalisms, whether colonial or anticolonial, tend to be structured by heteropatriarchy, configuring woman as the embodiment of tradition and mother of the nation that needs to be protected by militarized masculine men (a construction which also has no place for gay men) (Enloe 1990; Yuval-Davis and Anthias 1989). As Jolly has pointed out in Vanuatu, though, this does not preclude women from also being subjects of nationalism, though as objects and icons they are often represented as lying between tradition and modernity, albeit in different ways from men (Jolly 1997). Here, I am particularly focused on the ways in which men, as subjects and objects of the Hawaiian nation, localize macrosocial processes and discourses in their own lives and understandings of self. To do that, however, one needs some sense of what these processes are.

A New Era: Nation, Religion, and People

In 1810, with the peaceful cession of Kaua'i, the Hawai'i Island chief Kamehameha ended his twenty-eight-year campaign of conquest and became the first chief to bring the entire archipelago under control. Kamehameha established a monarchy and the lāhui of Hawaiʻi. The ritual system that enabled and legitimated his ascent was called the ʻaikapu, a religiopolitical set of laws that separated men and women during eating periods. More important, it separated the classes of aliʻi (chiefs) from makaʻāinana (commoners) and imbued the class of specialists known as kāhuna with powerful ritual authority that could direct the political and spiritual course of events in the islands (Kameʻeleihiwa 1992, 39). Within this system, a junior male chief endowed with the family god could usurp a higher-ranking aliʻi, which is precisely what Kamehameha did through war, marriage, and spiritual petition (guided by kāhuna) to the heavens on large-scale sacrificial heiau (temples).[1]

On all levels, the responsibility for feeding both the family and the gods fell on the shoulders of men. They prepared food in separate imu (underground ovens) and built separate eating houses: the hale mua (front or first house) for the men and the hale ʻaina (eating house) for the women and children. Certain foods (e.g., pig, coconuts, bananas, red fish) that represented the sexual power of the four major male akua (deities) — Kū, Lono, Kāne, and Kanaloa — were kapu (forbidden) to women. For the commoner men, who were primarily subsistence farmers and fishers, the hale mua served as the domestic temple, and family gods were fed along with the major deities.

The hale mua was an important site for the sustenance of life and the production of masculinities in the learning of skills and stories related to fishing, farming, cooking, canoe and house building, fighting, sailing, lovemaking, fathering, and providing for the family (Handy et al. 1972, 297, 301–2; Handy and Pukui 1972, 9; Malo 1951, 27–30; 1987, 20–23). Boys between the ages of five and seven were kā i mua, or "cast into the mua," and given their first malo in a ceremony that dedicated them to Lono, akua of fertility; from that day on, they would begin their growth into manhood (Handy et al. 1972, 316–18; Handy and Pukui 1972, 95–97; Malo 1951, 87–93; 1987, 64–66). Women too had their own separate work houses for beating tapa (hale kuku) and temple sites (Hale o Papa), where their own gender practices and ideologies were learned and enacted (Kameʻeleihiwa 1999; Linnekin 1990). The duality and complementarity of male/female (Kū/Hina), aliʻi/makaʻāinana, and Pō/Ao (realm of dead/realm of living) structured much of Hawaiian thought, and the balance of both created, at least ideologically, a state of pono, or well-being and balance.

In practice, though, throughout the late eighteenth century and early nineteenth this balance was becoming increasingly difficult to maintain. Since the arrival of James Cook in 1778, haole (foreigners) had been openly disregarding the ʻaikapu without penalty, spiritual or legal. The threat they posed militarily had also been established from the start, when Cook attempted to abduct Kamehameha's uncle and the ruling chief of Hawaiʻi Island, Kalaniʻōpuʻu,[2] an event that led to the British captain's (in)famous death. Finally, the venereal diseases and epidemics brought by his and others' crews were beginning to take their toll on the population; in 1804 alone, half the population died from a massive epidemic called maʻi ʻōkuʻu, which was either bubonic plague or cholera (McGregor 2007, 30).

When Kamehameha died in 1819, Kaʻahumanu, his most powerful wife and the prime minister after his death, orchestrated the overthrow of the ʻaikapu by convincing Kamehameha II Liholiho to ʻainoa (eat freely) with herself and his mother, Keōpūolani, at his installation as successor to the Kingdom. In large part this was done to prevent the rebellion of traditional rival chiefs. McGregor (2007, 31) explains, "By abolishing the traditional chiefly religion under which rivals could claim rank, prestige, and position, the Kamehameha chiefs consolidated political power under the control of their monarchy." The single effort to defy this move ended in the defeat at Kuamoʻo (Hawaiʻi Island) of Kekuaokalani, Liholiho's cousin entrusted with the dynastic god Kūkāʻilimoku. While this did not immediately put an end to the old religion, which carried on outside the reach of the new state for years, it did bring to a close the era in which junior male warrior chiefs could usurp status through battle. Ironically, this groundwork was laid in part by Kamehameha when he brought peace to the islands and subordinated all other aliʻi below him (Boggs, personal communication, 1/2/07).

Jocelyn Linnekin (1990, 72) argues that the ʻaikapu was already internally unstable owing to the fact that the ideological devaluation of women in the male sacrificial religion was at odds with their status as points of access to rank, land, and political power. "With the defeat of Kekuaokalani and the political strategy he symbolized, women became more important than ever" in this regard (ibid.). These same female chiefs subsequently embraced the American Calvinist missionaries, who arrived in 1820, as the new kahuna and Christianity as the new set of kapu. Linnekin notes, "In the aftermath of the *kapu* abolition women replaced men as the active, focal figures in the state religion. And perhaps correlatively, with the demise of the sacrificial cult that legitimated conquest, male Hawaiian *ali'i* seem to have lost some of their *mana,* their efficacy and directedness. In the nineteenth-century monarchy one sees fewer personally powerful and effective male chiefs, at least in the ruling line, and more of a tendency to psychological conflict, depression, and dissipation" (ibid., 73).

Linnekin rightly cautions that the 'ainoa was only one of many factors contributing to the "demoralization of male chiefs" (ibid.). Kame'eleihiwa argues that the attempt to "live as white men" and find a new path of life came about as a result of the inability of the older set of kapu and ritual to achieve the pono of the people and the society. Most profoundly, this was evidenced in the catastrophic loss of life (as high as 80 percent population loss in the forty-five years after contact) due to foreign diseases (Kame'eleihiwa 1992, 81–82).

The missionaries saw the drinking and prostitution associated with the sailors and merchants as clear evidence of the need of God's law, and thus they worked tirelessly to instill the Christian morality that would save the Hawaiians from both the heathen darkness of their past as well as the depravity of the docks. The Calvinists offered new life as the answer to the "great dying" they associated with the old heathen, pagan, barbaric, and savage ways. As Wende Marshall (1999, 110–11) argues, discourses of sin and tropes of ignorance and susceptibility to disease, criminality, and deviance worked to "narrate the myth of Hawaiian dissipation and extinction — a myth which worked to justify the encroachment on Hawaiian resources and the usurpation of Hawaiian power by an elite group of (mainly) American men." Kanaka 'Ōiwi were well aware of this. Writing in 1867, Samuel Kamakau noted "The reason for this misfortune and the decimation of the lāhui, it is understood, is that the haole are people who kill other peoples; and the desire for glory and riches, those are the companions of the devastating diseases" (quoted in Silva 2004a, 26; translation Silva's).

Capitalism, Law, and Gender in the Kingdom

In the early nineteenth century, Hawaiian society was undergoing widespread political and economic transformations brought on by an established mercantile capitalist economy, which at the time was fully engaged in the sandalwood trade. Relations between ali'i and maka'āinana, characterized by reciprocity and aloha in the past, were strained as growing debts to haole businessmen led to an ever-increasing pace of sandalwood extraction, always through the labor of the commoners and at the neglect of the taro patches and older subsistence economy (Linnekin 1990, 164–67). Linnekin notes that as new class relations began to displace the now distorted ones between chief and commoner, the mana and authority of the male chiefs were further undermined (1990, 170; see also Osorio 2002). The 'ainoa contributed to this state of affairs as men who were freed from household labor that women could now perform (e.g., cooking) gradually but progressively took jobs outside of the local extended family and increasingly in workplaces owned by foreigners (McGregor, personal communication, 4/14/07). Maka'āinana began to exercise their own autonomy from chiefs in this new economy, especially in the port towns, where fur traders, sandalwood merchants, and whalers purchased the labor and commodities of Kanaka men and women (Kame'eleihiwa 1992, 140; Ralston 1984). According to one source, there were four thousand Kanaka men on whaling ships in 1849, approximately 5 percent of the total population and 17 percent of males between the ages of eighteen and fifty-three (Linnekin 1990, 185). The Hawaiian foreign minister Wyllie went as far as to say it was "one of the causes of the depopulation of the islands" (Linnekin 1990, 184).

Amidst all this, the Hawaiian Kingdom was struggling to maintain its sovereignty against predatory imperial powers in the Pacific; Kamehameha III Kauikeaouli was keenly aware that the Treaty of Waitangi (1840) made New Zealand a British possession and that the French had claimed Marquesas and made Tahiti a protectorate (1842). As Merry (2000) and Silva (2004a) note, Hawai'i's acceptance by the world powers as an independent nation, which came in 1843 (Sai 2004; Silva 2004a, 37), required a display of properly masculine, modern civilization. Merry (2000) argues that laws creating new forms of marriage and new restrictions on sexuality were central to the civilizing process in nineteenth-century Hawai'i. The bourgeois family was constructed as the model to be emulated and was enforced by law. Masculinity was now defined by ownership and control of property, which included land, women, and children. This new regime was in stark contrast to precolonial practices, in which men were stewards of the land, women exercised autonomy in conjugal relationships, and the family unit was an extended rather than a nuclear one (Merry 2000, 230).

Another gendered contrast emerges in relation to the most significant and lasting transformations of property, namely, the privatization of land in the form of the Māhele, a legal process that spanned the years 1846–55. Linnekin (1990, 9) notes that for those commoners who did come to control land, inheritance patterns favored women (53 percent) in 1855, a significant break from precedent. This she attributes to an understanding that women were more stable on the land, a product of both the increased mobility of young men, who emigrated en masse to port towns and whaling ships to meet increased demands for taxes, as well as an already present symbolic association of women with the ʻāina and their high status in families as mothers and sisters (Linnekin 1990, 212–26). Thus even as an ideology of male dominance came to characterize the laws and representations of the monarchy, women's local status and authority increased in relation to men's.

At the level of public discourse, a need to present a masculinized image of the nation led to a celebration of the masculine heroism of the Kanaka past. As the biggest threat to the stability of the government and the king came from the cadre of elite American expatriate men living in the islands, Hawaiian men used nationalist newspapers to critique rising haole influence and, after 1887, dominance. The newspapermen published both political speeches and stories of male heroes like Kaweloleimakua. Kawelo was a legendary chief from Kauaʻi who embodied the exemplar of ʻŌiwi masculinity. A devout worshiper of his gods and generous leader, he was unparalleled in his prowess in fighting, farming, and dancing the hula. Importantly, he was also a chief from a junior line who defeated and usurped the power of his oppressive cousin who was ruler of the island; the allegorical parallels to the colonial situation were well understood by readers (Silva 2004a, 75, 83). They also published stories (especially around the turn of the twentieth century and early Territorial period) of powerful female deities such as Pele and Hiʻiaka, an indication that they did not feel threatened by women's mana and efficacy (Silva 2004b).

Some of the later monarchs sought to strengthen the monarchy through practices associated with Freemasonry (Karpiel 2000). As Karpiel (2000) notes, Alexander Liholiho (Kamehameha IV), Lot Kapuāiwa (Kamehameha V), King David Kalākaua, and his sister successor, Queen Liliʻuokalani (through her brother and husband), all drew upon Masonic practices of ritual and fellowship, which resonated with indigenous ones, to increase their spiritual power and prestige and to facilitate coalition building with influential foreigners. In 1865, Kamehameha V drew upon Masonic and other European traditions when he created the Royal Order of Kamehameha, a fraternal organization that rewarded individuals for their service to the Kingdom (Karpiel 2000, 380–81). As I discuss in chapters 4 and 5, the modern-day Royal Order has had some very direct articulations with the shaping of the Hale Mua on Maui.

Huliau: Time of Overturn

Despite these interventions, some of which were more subversive than others, the racialized and gendered forces of American colonialism undermined the collective efforts of the chiefs and monarchs to secure Hawaiian sovereignty and cultural integrity. Osorio argues that in fact it was the "conversion to Christianity and Western laws [that] enabled haole to become powerful authorities in Hawaiian society while managing the systematic destruction of [the] relationship between chiefs and people. It was the dismembering of that relationship that crippled the Natives' attempts to maintain their independence and their identity" (2002, 13). A number of scholars (Hasager and Kelly 2001; Kameʻeleihiwa 1992; Linnekin 1990) have identified the Māhele and the massive alienation of the commoners thereafter as the primary source of societal breakdown and later colonial marginalization; others have argued for a more nuanced reading of the legislation as having worked to empower Hawaiians (Perkins 2006; Sai 2005). Though a strong case for empowerment may be made, the real impacts on families and nation have been documented and must therefore be accounted for. As McGregor (2007, 39) explains, "From that point on foreigners, primarily Americans, continued to expand their interests, eventually controlling most of the land, sugar plantations, banks, shipping, and commerce of the islands." The Māhele also accelerated the ongoing dismemberment of the makaʻāinana–aliʻi relationship, as commoner men who formerly had conveyed labor to their chiefs in return for continued residence on their natal lands in large part became dispossessed tenants or, less frequently, private landowners with newfound status and independence (Osorio 2002; Kirch and Sahlins 1992).

The final acts of colonization at the end of the nineteenth century culminated years of both overt and covert imperialist attempts by the American government to possess the islands as its "Pacific outpost." The region had been identified early on as the key to Pacific domination if a large naval base could be built at Keawalau o Puʻuloa, now known as Pearl Harbor (Ferguson and Turnbull 1999; Kajihiro 2000, 30). These imperialist desires coincided with those of the American and other foreign businessmen living in the islands, most of whom were engaged in the growing sugar plantation economy that boomed after a treaty of reciprocity with the United States in 1876 removed barriers to trade. As the economic influence of the businessmen grew, so too did their political power and their desire to make the islands a part of the United States. By 1887, missionary descendants and other haole business elite were able to exert the threat of militia action and force King David Laʻamea Kalākaua to sign what was to be known as the Bayonet Constitution. This act rendered Kalākaua politically impotent and led to the signing of a new reciprocity treaty with the United States that same year. The treaty represented the first major threat to territorial sovereignty as Hawaiʻi granted the United States rights of exclusive use of the Pearl River estuary for the development of a naval base in exchange for the duty-free export of Hawaiian sugar to American markets (Kent 1993, 46–55; McGregor 2007, 40–42).

With the rise of "King Sugar," the makaʻāinana raised their voices in protest and petitioned Kalākaua's sister and successor, Queen Liliʻuokalani, to draft a new constitution that would return the power to the crown and thus to the people she served. Knowing full well what this would mean to their de facto colonial rule, the "missionary party" of white planters and businessmen, with the support of U.S. Marines landed the day before by the American minister to Hawaiʻi John Stevens, staged the illegal overthrow of the Hawaiian monarch on January 17, 1893 (Trask 1999, 15). President Grover Cleveland launched an investigation headed by Commissioner James Blount, the results of which led the president to declare that the role of the United States in the overthrow represented "an act of war" and recommended that Congress "should endeavor to repair" this "substantial wrong" (cited in Trask 1999, 15). Despite President Cleveland's admonishment, no actions were taken to reinstate the queen. As America was not quite ready to accept its stolen goods, the sugar barons succeeded their Provisional Government (1893–94) with an equally illegitimate Republic of Hawaiʻi (1894–98) that worked tirelessly toward annexation.

Throughout the nineteenth century, and indeed from the time Cook first threatened the life and authority of Kalaniʻōpuʻu, Kānaka Maoli resisted colonization through a variety of strategies. These ranged from the printing of politically charged moʻolelo in the Hawaiian language newspapers to two attempted armed rebellions (McGregor 1989, 34–45; McGregor 2007, 42; Silva 2004a, 127–28, 138–39).[3] Silva (2004a) details many of these acts of resistance in the latter half of the nineteenth century, the most concerted and organized of all being an anti-annexation petition drive conducted by men and women of the Hui Aloha ʻĀina (Hawaiian Patriotic League) that produced over twenty-one thousand signatures (out of forty thousand Hawaiians). With support and direction from the deposed queen, and in combination with the petition of another political organization, Hui Kālaiʻāina, containing approximately seventeen thousand names (some duplicates), the written protests helped to defeat the treaty of annexation that was debated in Congress in 1897–98 (Silva 2004a, 151). It was notable that both men and women were equally active in these political efforts, which itself represented a continuity of ʻŌiwi gender practices that contested American ones.

Despite the success of these efforts, the Spanish-American War and a blatantly imperialist President William McKinley brought about a new sentiment in the U.S. Congress, which violated the U.S. Constitution by passing a joint resolution (called the Newlands Resolution) to annex Hawaiʻi without a treaty on July 6, 1898 (Kent 1993, 63–68; Trask 1999, 20–21). After the Newlands Resolution passed, leaders of the political organizations sent a letter of protest, in Hawaiian and in English, to the U.S. minister that invoked the Kumulipo in its expression of "kūlipolipo," or "deep, dark, and intense pain" (Silva 2004a, 161). The term also asserts a much deeper claim to indigenous place, being, autonomy, and culture through the Kumulipo to the Pō, which Kanaka Maoli still returned to as a place of empowerment, strength, and connection with their past and their ancestors.

Panalāʻau: Occupations of Identity

In 1900, Hawaiʻi was organized as an incorporated territory of the United States, a status that lasted until the Admission Act of 1959 conferred statehood upon the islands.[4] Tellingly, the Hawaiian term "Panalāʻau," the word used for "Territory" in the Hawaiian version of the Organic Act of 1900, also means "colony, dependency, territory, province, colonist" (Pukui and Elbert 1986, 13), aptly indexing the status of Hawaiians as both subject and object of colonial power (Jolly 1997). Similarly, I invoke the term "occupation" in recognition of the Hawaiian experience of American military occupation and the new regimes of work and labor that shaped their subjectivities, particularly for men.

The pre–World War II years witnessed massive expansion of the sugar and pineapple plantation economy, fueled by the appropriation and planting of Hawaiian lands that were fed by waters diverted from taro fields and worked by hundreds of thousands of imported Asian immigrants. During this period, the United States made Hawai'i its "Pacific Gibraltar" through the establishment and fortification of naval and army bases throughout the islands, most notably (and consequentially) Pearl Harbor on the island of O'ahu. The Territorial elite also recognized the profits to be had from the arrival of American soldiers and other visitors, and by the 1930s tourism was poised to become the "new sugar" of the islands. The conjunctures of militarism (which secured American state power) and tourism (which worked to disguise it) are aptly described by Teresia Teaiwa's conceptualization of "militourism" (1999). Militourism also opened new pathways for Hawaiian travel and mobility as both the images and actual bodies of women and men circulated on naval ships, the cruise liners, magazines, and radio waves (Brown 2002; Imada 2004).

The educated and urban Kanaka 'Ōiwi experienced initial success in organizing their own Independent Home Rule party in the early Territorial years; however, this soon gave way to an alliance in the Republican Party between Native Hawaiian and white American elites (Silva 2004b). McGregor details the political and occupational patterns: "Thanks to political patronage, Hawaiians held a majority of the government jobs and dominated certain private-sector jobs such as cowboys on ranches, longshoremen on the docks, and in the electric and telephone companies. In 1927 Hawaiians held 46 percent of executive-appointed government positions, 55 percent of clerical and other government jobs, and over half of the judgeships and elective offices. Through 1935 Hawaiians held almost one-third of the public service jobs and dominated law enforcement, although they made up only 15 percent of the population of the islands" (2007, 44). Though Hawaiian men were now fulfilling their roles as providers in environments quite different from the traditional taro patches or fishing grounds, their occupational choices were often informed by 'Ōiwi cultural logics, such as a preference for group-oriented and ukupau (pay by the job rather than by time) work. Based in subsistence economy practices, ukupau involved long periods of strenuous, though well-paid work, often in teams, that afforded long intervals of rest and opportunities to fish, hunt, or otherwise subsist. In part, this accounted for the types of jobs that Hawaiians in the city (longshore-men, road workers, teamsters) and in the country (ranch hands and cow-boys) gravitated toward (Beaglehole 1937, 27; McGregor 1989, 108–09).

McGregor (2007, 44) notes that close to half the ʻŌiwi population re-mained outside of the cities, and "a major distinction internal to the Ha-waiian community evolved between the urban Hawaiians who assimilated and accommodated to the socioeconomic system and the rural Hawaiians or kuaʻāina who remained in the backcountry areas and maintained a traditional Hawaiian way of life." Moreover, despite the political patronage enjoyed by a fair number of Hawaiian men, most struggled to get by. Unemployment rates were at 40 percent in 1930 (in part owing to the Depression), and most men "were part of the laboring classes, occupying the lower fringe of the middle class" (McGregor 1989, 108). Many also "shipped out as sailors or merchant marines" (McGregor 1989, 190) in pursuit of opportunity or adventure elsewhere, again following a culturally and economically deter-mined path of mobility.

One should not discount the ability of Hawaiians to thrive in the Ter-ritory, for many did; however, the primary concern, at least in the early years, was survival. Hawaiian civic leaders and politicians undertook massive efforts to "rehabilitate" the "dying race" (which numbered only 41,750 in 1920), and in 1921 the U.S. Congress passed the Hawaiian Homes Commis-sion Act, which created a homesteading program to allow "native Hawai-ians," defined as 50 percent blood quantum or more, to return to the land. Though the law had numerous and profound effects, one important and unfortunate outcome was that a false distinction was made between the industrious, assimilated part-Hawaiians, on the one hand, and the needy, full-blooded Hawaiians, on the other, who were dying off because they were unable to compete with the other races in the Territorial economy (Hasager and Kelly 2001; Kauanui 1999b; McGregor 1990).

The problem that needed to be rooted out, in the minds of at least some of the bill's crafters, was Native laziness. McClintock (1995, 252–53) notes that the rhetoric on black/native sloth and indolence is one of the oldest and most pervasive discursive tactics used by settlers in the appropriation of land and labor; the Pacific was no exception (Teaiwa 2001, 28). The discourse of "childlike indolence and laziness" emerged in Hawaiʻi in the mid-1850s, when "haoles attempted to make Native Hawaiians into a plantation labor force" (Merry 2000, 128); they proposed landownership and the discipline of the capitalist work ethic as the solution to depopulation, which they linked to the "twin vices of idleness and indifference" (Hasager and Kelly 2001, 195). In the "Big Five Territory,"[5] these notions were a part of a larger discourse of paternalism that placed natives and immigrant workers in a hierarchy of race, class, and gender that maintained the privilege of the haole oligarchy (Glenn 2002; Pierce 2004).

The discourse of the "lazy kanaka" was also one of Hawaiian emasculation because Hawaiian men were seen as being unable to compete with either the haole elite or the "hard-working" Chinese and Japanese men, who left the plantations to set up successful businesses in the city. In 1937 the ethnologist Ernest Beaglehole observed, in the somewhat decontextualized form of field notes, "It is a common characterization of the Hawaiians made by both whites and part-Hawaiians that they are incurably lazy. A part-Hawaiian woman said seriously that all Hawaiians are lazy. She explained . . . an easy climate demanded an easy life. The only manly thing about the old culture was its warfare and its games, but centuries of selection have bred into the Hawaiians habits of indolence" (Beaglehole 1937, 25). The internalization of these views by Hawaiians themselves indicates their pervasiveness. Young women expressed the tensions of gender and their refusal to marry Hawaiian men, whom they saw as "handy with their fists," "very jealous and always stirring up trouble" (59–60). An older Hawaiian man expressed self-loathing and insisted that Hawaiians were "defective in intelligence" in that they were "dispossessed of everything they owned, women and land included" (125). By marking the absence of the "manly" qualities of discipline, competitiveness, and (proper) aggression associated with military and sport, these passages construct the modern Hawaiian male as stupid, lazy, violent, sexually unappealing to Native women and doomed to failure in the marketplace. Despite whatever gains and footholds Hawaiians had made in the racial hierarchies of the Territory, the political economy was firmly directed by the white male elite.

War and Warriorhood: Militarization of Land and Men

One of the few sites in which Hawaiians were able to make some progress toward the creation of a small though influential middle class was through the Kamehameha Schools for Hawaiian children. Seeing education as the only means of checking the rapid decline of the aboriginal population, Princess Bernice Pauahi Bishop, who had inherited the principal lands of the Kamehameha dynasty, provided in her will in 1883 for the creation of the two schools, one for boys (opened in 1887) and one for girls (1894). The mission was to provide an "education in the common English branches" and "make good and industrious men and women" (Bishop 1883). Though Kamehameha was considered a select school in the late Kingdom and early Territorial period, well into the 1960s its primary focus was manual and vocational training. Goodyear-Ka'ōpua notes that "the aim was to produce an assimilated and docile citizenry by individualizing students, drawing them away from their cultural roots and social networks, and teaching them the kind of self-discipline that would make them suitable laborers for a modern capitalist society" (2005, 98).[6] This particular model of industrial education was developed in a transnational circuit of nineteenth-century civilizing and educational reform projects which linked the Hampton Institute in Virginia, the Carlisle Indian School in Pennsylvania, and the missionary and government schools of the Hawaiian kingdom in their shared efforts to "uplift" African Americans, Native Americans, and Hawaiians (Baker 2006; Goodyear-Ka'ōpua 2005, 93–98). Hokowhitu describes a similar pattern in the state education of Māori boys in Aotearoa/New Zealand, which emphasized "manual, technical, and agricultural skills" to produce a workforce of "practical-minded" Natives (Hokowhitu 2004, 267; 2008).

If the "virtue of industry" was the aim of the Kamehameha education, militarization was the means for disciplining it and inculcating its honor. Teaiwa notes that throughout Oceania social institutions such as schools, sport, and religion draw on military modes of discipline to correct Native "laziness" (Teaiwa 2001, 28). At the Kamehameha School for Boys (KSB), the school's first principal implemented military drills and uniforms and organized the boys into companies with student officers. In 1908, the same year that dredging of Pearl Harbor began (McGregor 2007, 43), the War Department stationed an army officer to serve as commandant at KSB, and in 1916 a Junior Unit of Reserve Officer Training Corps (ROTC) was officially organized on campus. Because KSB was a boarding school, militarism literally regulated every aspect of the lives of the cadets, as they were all called, for nine months of the year. A military chain of command established rank in the battalion, and a demerit system regulated infractions of behavioral, dress, and hygienic codes (Goodyear-Ka'ōpua 2005, 123–24; King and Roth 2006,

36–37; McGregor 1989, 128; Rath 2006, 75–97). This American militarized notion of warriorhood articulated with Hawaiian ones: for example, the school's mascot was a warrior, and Kamehameha's war cry was remembered in the school's fight song, "I mua — Forward!" For a short period there was a Hawaiian boy's club called Hui 'Ōiwi (Society of Native Sons) that, in a way similar to the Hale Mua, sought to relearn Hawaiian traditions of warriorhood through sport and cultural arts (Zisk 2002).

Many of these young 'Ōiwi men would go on to serve in the U.S. military or otherwise be employed in its service (McGregor 2004). In one particularly stunning example, 54 KSB students and alumni were among 134 young Hawaiian males who served as colonists for the United States in an occupation of the deserted coral equatorial Line Islands, a project aimed at securing American commercial and military interests in the period leading up to World War II. Elsewhere I lay out the ways in which the young men's participation was motivated by a mix of work, family, culture, and identity (Tengan 2004; Tengan 2008). Importantly, these sorts of issues coalesced around a militarized "pedagogy of citizenship." Ferguson and Turnbull (1999, 158) write that in the national security state of the United States and Hawai'i, the granting of citizenship and individual rights to young men has historically required a militarization of their masculinity. As Kann (1991, 292) writes, "The martial ethic in America was an enduring challenge to youth to prove their manhood, practice self-denial, demonstrate obedience, and exhibit the civic virtue that informally qualified them to assume manhood and citizenship in a society that treated masculinity, fatherhood, fraternity, and military service as necessary prerequisites to individualism" (cited in Ferguson and Turnbull 1999, 159). Ferguson and Turnbull (1999, 173) note that this pedagogy of citizenship is reproduced throughout the larger society of Hawai'i in such "capillaries" as the Boy Scouts, the Honolulu Chamber of Commerce, and the Junior Reserve Officers' Training Corps (JROTC).

Of course the ultimate calling was service in war, and many Hawaiian men from Kamehameha and elsewhere answered. Pukui et al. (1972, 2:305) note, "Though men were frozen in jobs, and draft was deferred in Hawai'i, the great proportion of Hawaiian and part-Hawaiian men of military age served in the armed forces. . . . If we judge by Hawaiian names, at least 56 Hawaiian and part-Hawaiian men who gave their lives in World War II had won such high military honors as the Distinguished Flying Cross with one, two, and three Oak-Leaf Clusters, Bronze and Silver Stars." One returning hero was Alexander Kahapea, Line Island colonist and 1936 KSB graduate. Kahapea served as a captain in the 83rd Infantry Division, Thunderbolt, in the European Theater and became the most highly decorated war veteran from Hawai'i (Kahapea 1990, 2:7). Other 'Ōiwi war heroes mentioned by Pukui et al. include Private First Class Herbert K. Pililā'au, the first Hawaiian to receive the Congressional Medal of Honor (Korean War), and Sergeant First Class Rodney Yano, recipient of the Medal of Honor in Vietnam. Both men lost their lives saving their fellow soldiers and were given their awards posthumously (Pukui et al. 1972, 2:305–6).

Despite the significant contributions of Kānaka in the U.S. military, their participation has been overshadowed by the accomplishments of the 100th Battalion 442nd Regimental Combat Team. This segregated unit of Japanese Americans came back as one of the most highly decorated units of the war, quelling any doubts of their loyalties. Yet for all the attention the Japanese Americans received, "Hawaiian and part-Hawaiian servicemen went almost unnoticed. . . . Today, Hawaiian heroism seems forgotten. In a group of Hawaiians and part-Hawaiians asked to list what they considered 'Hawaiian qualities,' not one mentioned courage" (Pukui et al. 1972, 2:305, 306). This erasure is, in many ways, consonant with the discourse of "disappearing Hawaiians" and missing Hawaiian men. This perceived lack of courage came to be one of the motivating forces in the establishment of Nā Koa (defined both as "the Warriors" and "the Courageous Ones"), as I trace out in the following chapter. It is also contrasted to the bravery of the Māori Battalion, who, as I note throughout this study, are frequently held up as points for comparison (Tengan 2002).

Comments by both Māori and Maoli men suggest that their ethnic/racial identities were salient markers of the types of masculinities they made claims to in the military (Erai 1995; Pukui et al. 1972, 2:306). By proving that their courage and fighting capabilities were equal, if not superior, to those of the white counterparts with whom they served, indigenous men may have repudiated the colonizer's superiority and validated their own masculinities. At the same time, though, rather than challenging the social practice of soldiery and the patriarchal structure of which it is a part, 'Ōiwi and Māori men become complicit in some ways with the maintenance of a Euro-American hegemonic institution that naturalizes colonial rule by mapping it onto a system of gendered, raced, and classed power relations.

Conversely, a strong argument can be made that 'Ōiwi and Māori men achieved specifically indigenous forms of masculinity through their involvement in the military. As some of Erai's male interviewees suggested (as did Gardiner [1992, 7–11]), a specifically Māori warrior masculinity may have been achieved. By entering the military in order to fulfill obligations to the community, increase the mana of one's family or tribe, improve one's socioeconomic status, or merely to put food on the table, Polynesian men were and are actively working to promote the survival and growth of their people. In a racist colonial society with very few employment options available to Pacific Islander men, this may have been one of the few ways that Māori and 'Ōiwi men could achieve a masculinity based on notions of family, leadership, providing, strength, and mana (Ihimaera 2002). Diaz (2002) notes that Native Hawaiians (one of whom was a Line Island colonist) who worked on Guam for the U.S. Navy in the 1970s created ties with other islanders through the formation of a youth football league. While using more recognizably masculine forms to contest the military's presence on the island (beating the navy's football teams), they also created surrogate familial relationships and performed a "masculinity in softness" when playing Hawaiian music and singing songs.

The connection between work and militarization is an important one, for it is not only ideology but also employment that serves as a draw for Hawaiians who may not otherwise have opportunities for advancement or mobility. McGregor is on point here: "Many Hawaiians left their rural enclaves to join the service or to work in high-paying military jobs in Honolulu. The military were also stationed in rural areas throughout the islands. The war experience broadened the social horizons and raised the expectations and aspirations of all Hawaii's people for a higher standard of living" (2007, 45)

World War II's effects on land and politics were dramatic. Martial law in the islands lasted for four years, during which time massive landgrabs led the military to control some six hundred thousand acres, including the island of Kahoʻolawe, which they used for target practice (Kajihiro 2007). That same military force destabilized the control of the haole oligarchy, and returning Japanese American veterans worked with leaders of the labor unions to orchestrate the so-called Democratic Revolution of 1954, which broke the grip of the Republican Party and the configuration of racial, class, and gendered hierarchy they had maintained. For Hawaiians allied with the Republicans, this represented a significant loss of what little power they had, and soon Japanese replaced them in government jobs. Statehood and the full economic transition to tourism came shortly after.

The Aloha State

If the overthrow and annexation were illegal acts, so too was Hawai'i's entrance into statehood, enabled by yet another breach of international law when the United States unilaterally removed Hawai'i from the United Nations (UN) list of non-self-governing territories slated for decolonization (Kauanui 2005a, 4). Additionally, the economic transformations that followed statehood in 1959 were rapid as agriculture was phased out and the infrastructure for tourism was put into place. "The number of hotel rooms more than tripled, and the number of tourists increased fivefold within the first ten years" (McGregor 2007, 46). Yet the seeds of Hawaii's "new kind of sugar" (Finney and Watson-Gegeo 1977) had been planted many years earlier, and in heavily gendered soils.

A number of scholars have argued that the rise of American hegemony was predicated upon the colonial feminization of Hawai'i and its people; the discourses of militarism and tourism figured Hawai'i as the "hula girl" waiting to be taken (Desmond 1999; Ferguson and Turnbull 1999; Halualani 2002; Imada 2004; Trask 1999). No clearer image of such feminization exists than that published in a cartoon on the front page of the *Honolulu Advertiser* on August 21, 1959, the day Hawai'i was admitted as a state: Uncle Sam, standing at the top of the gangplank on the "U.S. Ship of State," bends over to take the hand of a smiling hula maiden named "Hawaii" as she prepares to board.[7]

As Ferguson and Turnbull (1999, 40) write, "The ascension of white male power had not only spelled out safety for the sugar industry and the military, but it began to underwrite the sexual fantasies and social practices of tourism as well. Desire and anxiety worked together to create the exotic/erotic Other. Feminized Hawaiian males, desexed Asian menials, and exoticized Hawaiian 'hula-hula' girls constituted the sturdy labor base and the refigured subjects for this new order." The writers trace the ways in which the transformation of beaches for the tourist economy of the twentieth century resulted in the replacement of 'Ōiwi fishermen "by the domesticated gentle male Hawaiians," who "paddled canoes," "taught tourists to surf," "strung leis, sang, and strummed ukuleles" (38). Desmond describes the ways in which these "beachboys," who were always portrayed as "easygoing, playful, and happy-go-lucky" boys (not men), offered white women and men a bronzed, well-muscled promise of social, sexual, physical, and moral freedom and renewal in an Edenic paradise that was nonetheless modern, domesticated, familiar, and nonthreatening (1999, 127, 129). Such representations continue to underwrite today's tourist productions.

These images were furthered by the fame and notoriety of one of the original beachboys: the Olympic swimming gold medalist and "father of surfing" Duke Paoa Kahanamoku (Timmons 1989, 64–80). Kahanamoku was the first and most lasting mediator of the modern touristic understanding of Hawai'i and Hawaiian men: the embodiment of the Noble Savage, an ideal native whose "soft primitivism" was "childlike, libidinous, free, and natural" (Desmond 1999, 11). The desire and admiration for the Hawaiian male body were also linked to anxieties that were experienced by men who felt that civilization and modernity had softened them, thus creating a need to reconnect with the "primitive masculinity" embodied in colonial fictions like Tarzan (Bederman 1995). Tellingly, another Hawaiian Olympic swimmer, Buster Crabbe, literally embodied this vision when he starred in the *Tarzan* television series in 1933 (McGregor, personal communication, 1/31/07). Notions of race, citizenship, and masculinity, both primitive and yet American, were written on Hawaiian male bodies in ways that further facilitated the rise of Hawai'i as a tourist destination for both white female and male revitalization (Tengan 2008; Willard 2002).

To be sure, the reality of Hawaiian men's identities and practices was often at odds with the image. In 1962, the Lili'uokalani Trust (now Queen Lili'uokalani Children's Center), established by the queen for the welfare of Hawaiian children, issued a report that found Hawaiians "statistically overrepresented in virtually all categories of 'social problems' and underrepresented in socio-economic indicators of success" (Howard 1974, ix). Responding to the trust's request to the Bishop Museum to conduct more research on these issues, Alan Howard led a team of anthropologists, psychologists, educators, and graduate students conducting research in the Hawaiian homestead community of Nānākuli (leeward O'ahu) in 1965–68.

Half the families living there came from the outer islands or from rural Oʻahu, reflecting the war-related migration patterns, and half the men worked blue-collar jobs as heavy equipment operators, truck drivers, machine operators, policemen, firemen, and sailors (Boggs and Gallimore 1968, 17; Howard 1974, 15–16). Most of the men were not discontented with their statuses and did not draw comparisons to the American middle-class norm; "Rather, it is the *style* of life which is important. Being an adequate provider for one's family is considered the mark of a man" (Boggs and Gallimore 1974, 20). Yet while these men seemed to be satisfied with their lot in life, the familiar "ain't no big thing" stereotype of "easy-going, happy-go-lucky nature children" that tourists delighted in was actually a strategy for coping with lower socioeconomic status, and one most prevalent in men who were out of work (Howard 1974, 131, 134). Frequent drinking was a "secondary coping strategy," but one which represented a retreat from family to the peer group, indicating a failure as a husband-father provider (152). Howard noted that while the current economic boom had created a surplus of construction and other semiskilled work that most of the men had taken up, future shifts in the economy could dramatically affect their ability to find a job (221).

Indeed, the construction of the happy-go-lucky, safe Hawaiian male has always been an unstable one. In the mid-1970s, as professional surfing began to invade the spaces of the North Shore on Oʻahu, a group of Hawaiian men formed the surf club Hui ʻO Heʻe Nalu. The club members took an aggressive and at times violent posturing toward what was seen as a modern wave of neocolonialism, leading to a characterization of them as terrorists (Walker 2005). In part, this evidences what Connell (2005b, 113) calls a form of "protest masculinity," which often arises from an experience of powerlessness and leads to an exaggerated claim to the gendered position of masculine power. At the same time, it also reflected a longer-standing history in which surfers, including the beachboys of Waikīkī, subverted the colonial order of things in the ocean spaces they dominated (Ishiwata 2002; Walker 2008).[8] Perhaps most important for this discussion is that the embodied aggressiveness of the Hui ʻO Heʻe Nalu in the 1970s was a product of a new way of thinking about being Hawaiian in the face of massive economic and cultural change. In part, this shift in stance signaled the beginning of Hawaiian cultural nationalism.

Born in a period of economic transformations, political upheavals, civil disobedience, antiwar protest, assertions of minority rights in the United States, and decolonization movements internationally, the Hawaiian cultural nationalist movement began in the early 1970s with the parallel and related developments of the "Hawaiian renaissance" of the arts and culture and land protests over evictions and the U.S. Navy's bombing of Kahoʻolawe Island (Kanahele 1982; McGregor 2007; Trask 1999). My use of the term "cultural nationalism" is meant to suggest both the sentiment and process of nation building and the ways they are deeply informed by a sense of cultural morality: the revitalization of traditions, such as dance, customs, rituals, art forms, and religious beliefs, and their subsequent incorporation into the cultural foundation on which the political body of the modern nation is to be built (Hutchinson 1987). It is instructive to think of the Hawaiian movement as sharing many elements with what Anthony Wallace has described as a "revitalization movement," which he defines as "a deliberate, organized, conscious effort by members of a society to construct a more satisfying culture" (Wallace 1956, 265). The two primary pathways into the movement have been through universities, where young activist intellectuals are trained and new knowledge is developed, and in grassroots organizations, in which knowledgeable elders and community members take part in the struggle directly. These two arenas are by no means exclusive or discrete, and in the history of the movement both are detected throughout.

During the late 1960s and early 1970s, a renewed sense of identity and history as to what it meant to be a Hawaiian began to emerge. One of the first statements about this renewal made by a Hawaiian intellectual came in the form of John Dominis Holt's "On Being Hawaiian" (1964), a treatise ahead of its time in its affirmation of pride in an identity that had been debased in modern society. Most point to the writings of George Kanahele (1982) as both reflecting and shaping the renaissance as it began to take off in earnest in the mid-1970s. Writing in 1977, Kanahele noted that while the renaissance was a rebirth in the arts and revival of interest in the past, it was also a "'psychological renewal,' a purging of feelings of alienation and inferiority" and "a reassertion of self-dignity and self-importance" (1982, 1). Hawaiian music, ancient hula, literature, language, scholarship, and sports were flourishing along with a renewed political sense of community.

The development of the Hawaiian political consciousness came in early struggles to halt the tidal wave of change brought on by tourism and militarization. Already the activism of the period — civil rights, the anti–Vietnam War movement, black power, the ethnic minority (Asian American, Chicano) and American Indian movements — had brought a new air of protest to the islands. More locally situated political activism first came about with the protests in 1970 over evictions of farmers whose lands, owned by the Bishop Estate (which ran Kamehameha Schools) in Kalama Valley, Oʻahu, were slated for development as upper-income residential units (Trask 1999, 67); simultaneously, a broader, spontaneous protest arose over the naming of a Japanese businessman to the Bishop Estate Board of Trustees. Many Hawaiians and non-Hawaiian locals alike felt their lifeways and lands were being overrun by the new tourism state, and a series of other such protests followed. Most of these struggles were carried out through multiethnic, working-class alliances, and they were directly related to efforts to establish an ethnic studies program at the University of Hawaiʻi (Aoudé 1999). Yet the renewed sense of indigeneity — as distinct from a "local" working-class cultural identity shared by Hawaiians and immigrant descendants — began to articulate with the sorts of political strategies used in protest (Okamura 1998), especially with the Protect Kahoʻolawe ʻOhana (PKO).

In 1976, a group of Native Hawaiians occupied the island of Kahoʻolawe. As noted, Kahoʻolawe had been used as a military bombing target since 1941, and the goal of the occupiers was to draw "national attention to the desperate conditions of Native Hawaiians" (McGregor 2007, 252). On Kahoʻolawe, they found a spiritual connection that led them to seek out elders in the community to help them understand the meaning of their experience. The activists arrived at a new understanding of the island's sacred significance, which shifted the terms of the political struggle from one of anticolonialism to one of cultural nationalism informed by a "moral responsibility" of aloha ʻāina, which translates as both "love for the land" and "patriotism" (McGregor 2007, 265).

Simultaneously, the Polynesian Voyaging Society (PVS), formed in 1973, was undertaking efforts to construct and sail, by means of traditional navigational methods, a double-hulled Hawaiian voyaging canoe (Finney 1979a;

see figure 5 on page 31). This was partly an anthropological experiment carried out by Ben Finney, who sought to debunk scholarship that claimed Polynesians lacked the ability and technology to settle the Pacific Islands, and partly an outgrowth of the growing interest in the Hawaiian past. Calling upon the skills and abilities of the Micronesian navigator Mau Piailug, the PVS assembled a crew and successfully sailed the *Hōkūleʻa* to Tahiti in 1976. Conceived and funded, ironically, as part of a U.S. nationalist project, the Bicentennial of American Independence, the sail helped spark a revitalization of Polynesian voyaging and facilitated the reconnection of Kānaka Maoli with their Polynesian cousins and their own deeper histories and moʻolelo (Finney 1994; Finney 2003). The *Hōkūleʻa*'s voyage and the activism of the PKO thus became the primary cultural and political catalysts for the development of the cultural nationalist movement.

A wide range of political organizing on all islands marked this decade (McGregor-Alegado 1980). Claims to indigenous rights, lands, and reparations that emerged in this period led to the passage of the Hawaiian Affairs Package in the State Constitutional Convention of 1978, which included a reform of the Hawaiian Homes Commission, the recognition of Hawaiian gathering and access rights, the declaration of Hawaiian as an official language, and the establishment of a state agency called the Office of Hawaiian Affairs (OHA). The OHA was charged with managing the revenues derived from the "ceded lands" trust created in 1959, one of whose purposes was the betterment of the Native Hawaiian (McGregor-Alegado 1980, 49–50). Alternative sovereignty initiatives proliferated in the 1980s, among them Ka Pākaukau, which sought complete independence, and Ka Lāhui Hawaiʻi, which proposed a form of domestic dependent sovereignty (also referred to as nation-within-a-nation status) comparable to that enjoyed by federally recognized American Indian tribes (Kauanui 2005b). At the University of Hawaiʻi, a Hawaiian studies program was established in the 1980s, and ever since it has been a focal point for the production of cultural nationalist discourse. The efforts of the PKO resulted in an end to the bombing of Kahoʻolawe in 1990 and its return by the navy in 1994, to be held in trust by the state until such time as a sovereign Native Hawaiian nation is created (McGregor 2007, 275). The possibility of such a nation came in 1993 when President Bill Clinton signed into law the Apology Resolution (Public Law 103–150) acknowledging the U.S. role in the illegal overthrow of 1893 and the fact that "the indigenous Hawaiian people never directly relinquished their claims to their inherent sovereignty as a people or over their national lands to the United States, either through their monarchy or through a plebiscite or referendum" (Kauanui 2005a, 5). That same year, which was also the UN Year for the World's Indigenous People, occasioned the convening of Ka Hoʻokolokolonui Kanaka Maoli (the People's International Tribunal), which sought to bring global attention to the predicament of the Hawaiian people (Blaisdell 2005; Hasager and Friedman 1994).

Following what some considered to be the peak of nationalist activities in the mid-1990s, sovereignty initiatives were somewhat stymied by state efforts to contain and control sovereignty claims and by an anti-Hawaiian backlash, part of a larger national backlash against special interests, minority rights, and affirmative action, that resulted in the U.S. Supreme Court ruling of *Rice* v *Cayetano* (2000). This ruling found that the Hawaiian-only elections for the OHA violated the Fifteenth Amendment of the U.S. Constitution protecting against racial discrimination in voting; the larger question of whether Native Hawaiians constituted a race or a political group (defined by a history of unrelinquished sovereignty) was raised but not resolved (Kauanui 2002; McGregor 2002). This precedent fueled a number of other lawsuits aimed at dismantling Hawaiian programs, rights, and entitlements, which in turn led U.S. Senator Daniel Akaka and numerous Hawaiian organizations to redouble their efforts at achieving federal recognition of a Native Hawaiian nation through the much debated "Akaka Bill" (Kauanui 2005a; McGregor 2002).

At the same time, activity on the international front, begun in the early 1980s by activists such as Kawaipuna Prejean, increased as representatives from organizations like Ka Lāhui Hawaiʻi took part in the transnational indigenous rights movement, most prominently through participation in the International Working Group on Indigenous Affairs and the Permanent Forum for Indigenous Issues at the UN (Hasager and Friedman 1994; Kauanui 2005b; Niezen 2003). Adopting a different strategy for pressing sovereign claims, a group representing the Council of Regency of the Hawaiian Kingdom received a hearing in the Permanent Court of Arbitration, which in theory recognized the continuity of the Hawaiian nation-state (Osorio 2003; Sai 2004).

The progress made by the cultural and political movements has been impressive. Additional voyaging canoes have been built, Hawaiian language immersion programs have proliferated, Hawaiian studies and language centers at the University of Hawai'i have awarded undergraduate and graduate degrees, traditional dance and chant have been revived, and there has been an overall revaluing of things Hawaiian. Despite the fact that Hawaiian control over land, government, and resources has not materialized, there has been a paradigmatic shift in thinking since the 1960s on the reality of sovereignty and decolonization for Hawaiians.

The recuperation of old terms for native identity—such as Kanaka Maoli (Real People) and Kanaka 'Ōiwi (People of the Bone)—and an upsurge in usage of Hawaiian personal names index such redefinitions of self and society (Ayau and Tengan 2002; Blaisdell 2005; Burgess 1989). Given the high rates of intermarriage among Native Hawaiians—intermarriage had been occurring since the nineteenth century—people with Hawaiian ancestry do not always have Hawaiian names (Kana'iaupuni et al. 2005, 29–30; United States 2001).[9] This nonconcordance also stems from the colonial suppression of language and culture that led Hawaiians to take up English (or other) names and downplay their heritage as kanaka, a term which itself had been denigrated. By employing "Kanaka Maoli," "Kanaka 'Ōiwi" and inoa Hawai'i (Hawaiian names), Native Hawaiians reclaim pride in identity, affirm connections with other indigenous peoples in the Pacific and around the world, and rename their world and reality (Smith 1999, 157–58).

Such transformed visions of a new social order offer hope to 'Ōiwi, who experience marginalization under militourism and struggle against the high cost of living and lack of opportunity and land, factors that contribute to the growth of the Hawaiian diaspora. In the 2000 U.S. Census, Kānaka 'Ōiwi numbered 401,162, some 40 percent of whom live on the continent (Kana'iaupuni et al. 2005, 8). The 239,655 residing in Hawai'i made up about 20 percent of the 1.2 million residents of the state (Kana'iaupuni et al. 2005, 29–32). Hawaiians have the highest rates of unemployment, poverty, and incarceration of all major ethnic groups in Hawai'i (Kana'iaupuni et al. 2005, 80–87). They constituted the second least likely group, after Filipinos, "to work in a managerial or professional capacity" and the "most likely to be employed in construction, extraction, and maintenance positions and in production, transportation, and material-moving occupations" (Kana'iaupuni et al. 2005, 84–85). As far as health statistics go, Hawaiians have the highest rates of obesity, early morbidity, depressive symptoms, suicidal tendencies, and certain other "risky behaviors" (especially among young adults) (Kanaʻiaupuni et al. 2005, 94–98, 111–13, 197–203); they also had the second highest infant mortality rates (Kanaʻiaupuni et al. 2005, 157). Conversely, owing in part to increased self-identification, the Native Hawaiian population grew 90.1 percent since the 1990 census (Kanaʻiaupuni et al. 2005, 29). Though no longer considered a "dying race," Kanaka ʻŌiwi continue to struggle in a context in which identity matters in new and important ways.

As an organization born of the cultural nationalist movement, the Hale Mua takes as its goal the formation of a new Hawaiian male subjectivity defined through the past and looking to move both men and community forward. This "forward" is intentionally ambiguous; no political goals are set, and no positions on sovereignty are taken. Yet these discourses of nation, such as the prevailing use of "Kanaka Maoli" as both cultural and political identity, have an important influence on the group's goal of providing men with a space to learn, teach, practice, experience, and perform a Maoli, or Real, identity as Hawaiian men. Likewise, the men drawn to the Hale Mua often feel alienated from their Hawaiian-ness. Thus the men seek to develop community and cultural knowledge among peers who will accept them despite any status differentials based on education, occupation, or upbringing.

Restoring Balance: Men, Women, and Movement

Perhaps most significantly, the Hale Mua formed to address what has been seen as Hawaiian men's absence or lack of efficacy in projects of cultural revitalization and political decolonization, a correlate of the more broadly held notion that men were emasculated by colonialism and modernity. The cultural nationalist movement I described above was haunted by the imbalance between masculinity and femininity that had developed since Cook's time. The dramatic impact this imbalance had on the ʻŌiwi gender system was played out in the movement, as men and women struggled with and against each other.

Writing in 1984 about her participation in the PKO in 1978–80, Haunani-Kay Trask described the group as "a patriarchal institution pervaded by assumptions (and practices) of male domination and female subordination" (Trask 1984, 8) wherein young male activists made claims to spiritual authority through their rural roots (primarily to Molokai) and the guidance they received from elderly Hawaiian women. The men's positions were propped up by what she saw as a "bruddah culture" of misogyny and violence directed at their partners and children at home and at the young, educated, urban women such as herself in the group (ibid., 12–14).[10] Given the prominence of the Molokai women leaders Joyce Kainoa, Colette Machado, and Judy Napoleon, one may reasonably question the extent to which all women were silenced. Trask is correct, though, in critically examining the ways in which gender practices stymie efforts to achieve true decolonization.

In contrast to the losing "battle of double colonization" she fought in the PKO, by 1993 Trask was lauding the accomplishments of the female-led Ka Lāhui Hawai'i and the Center for Hawaiian Studies while pointing to the overwhelming tendency of men to collaborate with the state, as evidenced by their domination in the legislature and governor's office, and "sell out." Although there were some "male leaders in our movement," she argued "they are not the most visible, the most articulate, nor the most creative. By any standard—public, personal, political—our sovereignty movement is led by women" (Trask 1999, 94). Trask's analysis of men's privileged access to power in the world of Hawai'i's party politics is accurate, and the women she notes are indeed powerful leaders. Yet at the time she was writing, men like Kawaipuna Prejean, Soli Niheu, Keli'i Skippy Ioane, Kekuni Blaisdell, Bumpy Kanahele, Palikapu Dedman, Emmett Noa Aluli, Alapai Hanapī, Attwood Makanani, and Pōkā Laenui Hayden Burgess had all made substantial contributions to decolonization efforts. More important, Trask's polarities and dichotomies that describe men as collaborators and women as decolonizers contribute to an oppositional discourse on gender in the movement. Kaleikoa Ka'eo, an independence advocate and Hawaiian language teacher, argues that this dichotomy is flawed: "The movement is led by all genders; male, female, gay, lesbian, and transsexual," and "the diversity of voices that are more political and contentious to the haole system are the voices that the kanaka academic world must engage" (email to author 2/6/04).[11]

Despite the more nuanced reality of the Hawaiian cultural politics and decolonization efforts that Ka'eo outlines, "the haole system," which includes the news media complex, continues to perpetuate the image of the Hawaiian movement as a woman's movement (see, for instance, Apgar 2005).[12] In contemplating the real and perceived erasure of men from the political and cultural movements, Kyle Nākānelua, the leader of the Hale Mua, recalled discussions he had with Sam Kaʻai, the group's elder and advisor, and other men at the Puʻukoholā ceremonies in 1991:

The questions we always used to pose [to] each other was, "Where are the Hawaiian men, and why are they not interested, and why is it so difficult?" So looking at our fathers and grandfathers, we received a lot of the answers. There was just so much to do, and not enough time to do it. Their endeavors for their futures and their families' futures led them to doing things that we could probably perceive as "not Hawaiian," yet still a very Hawaiian, maybe even *human,* thing to do, which is putting food on the table, putting a roof ovah your head, putting clothes on your body, and giving your children an education. So, if that consumes your whole being, then you do your job. And that's what our kūpunas did, so that's no different from our kūpuna.

Nākānelua offers a historical understanding of Hawaiian modernity as a process that drew men more heavily into the realms of capitalist labor, electoral politics, and military service; the corollary is that women's intensified ties to home and family led them to also retain much of the cultural knowledge being discarded and supposedly forgotten by men. At the same time, Nākānelua recognizes the contributions of and continuities with previous generations.

Noting the patterns described by both Trask and Nākānelua, Dana Nāone Hall, a leading Hawaiian and environmental rights advocate and poet on Maui, observes that while women have been the more prominent activists, men have been dominant in the establishment organizations of government and the Hawaiian trusts. Thus their investment in "the system" precludes their participating too actively in the movement since they have more to lose. The same idea holds for men who do not enjoy political power but need to support their families through county, state, and federal jobs. Hall adds that this investment in the system leads these men, and many other Hawaiian men and women, to partition their lives into separate spheres such as "Hawaiian culture," "Western work," and "family" instead of truly integrating them all (Hall, personal communication, 11/3/02). In other words, people invested in and dependent on the capitalist system we live in can take the effort of Hawaiian decolonization only so far before risking not only their own livelihoods, but also those of their families.

The involvement with the state is an important one, for over half of the active members on Maui are government workers, some of them in law enforcement. The retired Maui police officer Carl Eldridge noted that he wanted to get involved in the movement in the 1970s but couldn't because of the illegality of some of the activities (e.g., occupations of Kahoʻolawe), and he felt "really torn" (personal communication, 11/6/02).[13] This is important, for many Hawaiians are in fact employed in law enforcement and in other para-defense and militarized institutions.

As I mentioned earlier, the impact of militarism requires special attention and discussion. Militarization of the land, which sparked the PKO resistance, also led to the martyrization of two of the movement's activists, George Helm and Kimo Mitchell, who disappeared in the waters surrounding Kahoʻolawe during an occupation (McGregor 2007, 265). More frequently though, it has been the militarization of men's bodies that has taken them out of the movement, as many have either been coopted or drafted into the service of empire. In the Vietnam War, more men from Hawaiʻi died, proportionally, than from any other state in the United States (McGregor 2004, 219), and most of those who came home struggled to put their lives back together.[14] For some, the ironies of serving in the colonizer's army abroad highlighted the injustices at home; the Vietnam veterans Skippy Ioane and Palikapu Dedman both became active in the PKO and in their own projects of decolonization on Hawaiʻi Island.[15] Hale Kealoha Makua (see figure 6 on page 63), another Vietnam veteran, became an important spiritual leader in the community and was one of the original advisors at the 1991 Hoʻokuʻikahi. Thus the military has both constrained and produced the subjects and objects of cultural nationalism.

Yet the omnipresence of state power remains, and while both men and women have been arrested in protest activities, the high-profile prosecutions have all targeted male leaders (e.g., Walter Ritte, Bumpy Kanahele, Keanu Sai). This follows a larger trend of criminalizing Hawaiian males generally, especially when they fail to "assimilate" properly. When I asked Kaʻai to describe the average Hawaiian man (see chapter 5 and the conclusion), he quickly pointed out that to say "average" was to oversimplify the complexity of Hawaiian men's experiences; what was generalizable (and generalizing) was the homogenizing tendencies of modernity and its enforcement by state power: "The 'average' Hawaiian man might be in a forceful area, where his conduct is alien to the occupying host, and therefore he occupies more places in jail. He lives in an environment where fish makes no difference, but beer is delivered regularly. . . . We feed the lowest in our society because it's 'good business' and internal revenue [services] would like to make higher and best use of business, including produce a group, which when it does not fit into society, drowns its pain with alcohol."

Decolonization and Masculinity

Set against the occupying power of the United States, Hawaiian men and women have responded in a variety of ways to maintain their culture and history. The central goal of this book is to describe the ways in which one group of Hawaiian men who are generally mixed race, middle aged, middle class, and mobile, have sought to form new identities based on culture and gender. While seeking to reclaim traditional histories and practices, they come to the group with their experiences of modernity shaped by work, education, and often the military. As such, many need to learn what it means to be a Hawaiian man, an endeavor which the Hale Mua has set itself up to pursue. Yet it has also worked to create a group of men who can relate to each other as men, despite status differentials created outside of the group.

Such an effort is far from easy, and a cautionary tale comes from one of the only documented and analyzed occasions when Hawaiian men have engaged in the cultural nationalist movement: the first voyage of the *Hōkūleʻa* to Tahiti in 1976. During the trip, a small group of Hawaiian men rebelled against the haole authority and elder male leadership; the day before they landed and "loosened" up with champagne offered by the Tahitians, an exchange of words quickly led to exploding tempers and a fight (Finney 1979, 240–48). In his ruminations about "the gang," Finney notes they were akin to other Hawaiian peer groups, "prominent in Hawaiian neighborhoods in and around Honolulu," groups that spent much time "drinking, fishing, surfing, and engaging in other male pursuits" (190). Analyzing the situation, Finney writes, "This may be partially a carry-over from ancient patterns of sexual segregation and male solidarity. But it probably has more to do with the collapse of the rigidly hierarchical ancient society wherein a man's status was largely determined by birth and regulated by custom. That collapse, plus the other shocks experienced by Hawaiians in the last two centuries, has been particularly hard on men, so many of whom now find themselves adrift in society in which status is determined by formal educa-

FIGURE 6. *Left to right:* Kyle Nākānelua, Keli'i Makua, Sam Ka'ai, Hale Makua, and Kāwika Davidson prepare to mix and serve 'awa at 'Onipa'a at the 'Iolani Palace, O'ahu, 1993. PHOTO BY MASAKO CORDRAY.

tion, business success and other alien criteria" (190). This, he argued, is what led to the development of peer groups, for "it is within the tight circle of his fellows that the Hawaiian deemed unsuccessful by the outside world can shut that world out and gain the mutual support, sense of belonging and measure of self-esteem he needs" (ibid.). His observations point to a reading of behavior as a historical consequence of social transformations. Here personal ambivalences and tensions around reclaiming a "real" Hawaiian male identity are embodied ones that are linked to larger macrosocial processes of change and played out through microsocial interactions.

Though not a crew member, Ka'ai was an important figure in this story. He carved the images for the canoe and led ceremonies before they departed and when they arrived at Tahiti (Finney 1979, 95–97, 278–86). Ka'ai would later travel on the *Hōkūle'a* on its subsequent Pacific journeys. Indeed, it has been the series of cultural exchanges and inspirations derived from the renewed Oceanic intercourse, including challenges issued by Māori to the Hawaiians, that played an important role in the rededication of Pu'ukoholā Heiau, Kawaihae, Hawai'i, in 1991 as a gathering place for men and women to practice and *live* their culture (see chapters 2 and 3). Organizers saw the event, entitled Hoʻokuʻikahi: To Unify as One, as an opportunity to revitalize cultural and spiritual traditions that were both *authentic* (i.e., not performed for tourists or as a pageant) and *masculine* (i.e., aggressive, strong, and disciplined). Nā Koa embodied this gendered reclamation of cultural identity, and they inspired an important segment of the Hawaiian male population that had previously been uninvolved in the cultural politics of sovereignty and revitalization.

The groups of Nā Papa Kanaka o Puʻukoholā (the organizational body of the Puʻukoholā ceremonies), Nā Koa, and Nā Waʻa Lālani Kahuna (ritual specialists) that were "born" at Puʻukoholā participated in the later commemorative events such as the 1993 ʻOnipaʻa march and commemoration of the illegal overthrow of the Hawaiian Kingdom (see figure 6). ʻOnipaʻa represented the single largest and most influential gathering of Hawaiians in the twentieth century as over fifteen thousand people marched through downtown Honolulu and rallied at the ʻIolani Palace (Trask 1999, 82). A march organized in 1995 by Nā Papa Kanaka o Puʻukoholā in observance of Kamehameha's conquest of Oʻahu drew a modest but dedicated crowd of about three hundred. In 1998, the men of the Hale Mua joined over five thousand people to participate in the Hawaiʻi Loa Kū Like Kākou (All Hawaiʻi Stand Together) Annexation Centennial Commemoration march and gathering in Honolulu. At each of these events, Nā Koa was a visible force whose presence signaled the new strength, aggression, and resolve with which cultural nationalists were engaging in their struggles for self-determination and sovereignty. In response to a colonial discourse of death and disappearance, Kānaka Maoli have asserted a counterdiscourse of life and have engaged in projects of revitalization, revival, and healing. With Marshall (1999; 2006), I argue that healing the historic pains and memories of colonization on all levels represents the most fundamental principle of ʻŌiwi decolonization and recovery of nation, for after the healing comes the rebuilding. This is one of the central aims of the ceremonies at Puʻukoholā and the practices carried out by the Hale Mua. As I detail in later chapters, these processes are inescapably gendered, and as such they present numerous challenges for those who seek to heal wounds that are understood differently by men and women.

RE-MEMBERING NATIONHOOD AND KOA AT THE TEMPLE OF STATE

....

One of the primary (in some narratives originary) sites of re-membering masculinities is Puʻukoholā Heiau, which is at once a U.S. National Historic Site, a memorial site, and a Hawaiian temple of state associated with Kamehameha's conquest and unification of the islands. On this site in 1791, Kamehameha sacrificed his primary rival and first cousin Keōuakūʻahuʻula (Keōua) in fulfillment of a prophecy that foretold the end of war when one was laid on the altar. The bicentennial commemoration of 1991 entitled Hoʻokuʻikahi (Unify as One, or Reconcile) attracted some twenty-five hundred attendees and ushered in a new chapter in the already deep history of the site. Each year since, between two hundred and three hundred cultural practitioners have returned to Kawaihae on Hawaiʻi Island to conduct rituals involving the offering of prayer, chant, dance, martial arts exhibitions, food, gifts, labor, and personal mana (spiritual power and essence) to make the heiau (temple) and the nation that was established there live again.

At Puʻukoholā the men of the Hale Mua join the ranks of Nā Koa (the Courageous Ones/Warriors), one of the core organizing groups of the event. In the next two chapters I describe and analyze the ways in which the Mua's ritual performances of masculinity and koa (warriorhood) become strategies of political, cultural, and psychological self-determination by (re)claiming and asserting Kanaka ʻŌiwi Maoli identity and community. The embodying of koa and nationhood actively shapes subjectivities that are both felt and culturally constituted. These subjectivities enable new sorts of political and social identifications that contest the feminized, domesticated, and commodified notions of Hawaiian culture, land, and bodies that circulate globally.

The identity work of re-membering koa operates through a coordination of personal and national narrative, individual and social memory, and emotive and embodied action. However, each act of re-membering is also one of forgetting, and the claiming of a warrior model for masculinity as well as other gendered tropes of strength simultaneously produces new tensions and exclusions even as it works to contest older ones associated with American neocolonial hegemony in the islands. In chapter 3, I present an ethnographic account of the Hale Mua's discursive and embodied performances of re-membering masculinities at the ceremonies in the early 2000s. First, I develop in this chapter a framework for understanding the ways the moʻolelo (narratives, histories, stories) of koa at Puʻukoholā create the context for such remembrances, with a special focus on the defining event of Hoʻokuʻikahi 1991.

Moʻolelo: History, Memory, and Identity Practice

As anthropologists and historians have noted for some time now, discourses of history and the past are used within local frameworks of meaning and action as models to think with (Borofsky 2000). As Geoffrey White explains, "Histories told and remembered by those who inherit them are discourses of identity; just as identity is inevitably a discourse of history. . . . Whether we call them 'social history,' 'life history,' or 'personal stories,' retrospective narratives create the present through idioms of remembrance" (1991, 3, 5). Studies of subjectivity and identity formation at the juncture of history and memory have flourished in recent years (Birth 2006), elucidating the multiple ways in which the self interfaces with society. In narrative practice, individual subjectivities are culturally organized and shaped by and feed back into larger discourses on identity (White 2000).

Narrations of self in and through a society defined by a shared history and collective memory become especially prominent in contexts of nation making (Kelly 1995; Ochs and Capps 1996; White 2004). In the Hawaiian cultural nationalist movement, moʻolelo — narratives of the past and present both written and remembered — become potent and affect-rich "cultural tools" (Wertsch 2002). The Hawaiian nationalist and historian Jonathan Osorio notes, "Any history that we tell . . . is not merely informational, but carries an activist content. The stories are meant to persuade and motivate, but they are also meant to explain our lives" (2001, 360). Osorio's comments are particularly relevant here, for as he argues elsewhere (Osorio 2002), the expansion of American empire in the Pacific undermined the historical modes of relating between chiefs and commoners in the nineteenth-century Hawaiian kingdom and set the stage for the cultural and political dismemberment of the lāhui (nation, people, race).

For Kanaka ʻŌiwi Maoli, struggles for self-determination, sovereignty, and decolonization involve a critical remembering of the past, a project that Fujitani et al. (2001) characterize as both denaturalizing dominant historical narratives and recuperating the distorted memories of the marginalized. As Wende Marshall (2006) details in her study of Hawaiians on the Waiʻanae coast of Oʻahu, local decolonization efforts proceed in community health centers, where workers and clients focus on both the internal and social processes of healing traumatized memories and experiences of shame that are the products of colonization. Such strategies focus on "(re)membering and (re)creating the ways of . . . ka poʻe kahiko (the people of old)" (187). Not only are these efforts at decolonizing the mind, but they are also acts of self-determination as community members seek to assert control over the destiny of the lāhui while defining the self (through group membership) as Hawaiians struggling with the burdens of history. Importantly, Kanaka ʻŌiwi Maoli have always made and remade their identities through the re-membering and retelling of their moʻolelo, especially in times of rapid change that threaten their continued existence as a people.

What makes the current moment of remembrance doubly critical is that ʻŌiwi Maoli are recuperating not only alternative stories about self but also the very language with which to narrate them. The almost successful linguicide that was implemented by the banning of Hawaiian language in the American school system "created a language barrier that ruptured Hawaiian families and created the conditions of 'forgetting'" (Marshall 2006, 192). Given this history, acts of relearning, remembering, and renarrating indigenous moʻolelo work to address the intergenerational rupture that both precluded cultural transmission and produced a legacy of "shame and self-loathing" (Marshall 2006, 187). Here Barbara Myerhoff's theorization of re-membering as a "special type of recollection" that calls attention "to the reaggregation of members" (1982, 111) provides useful insight. Memory work is important at all levels of Hawaiian society precisely because it works toward the integration of present Hawaiian selves and collectivities with earlier states of being and disparately situated members (ibid., 110). Moreover, the ritual process carried out in the Hawaiian ceremonies at the heiau creates an especially powerful context for the embodied re-membering of historical and personal mo'olelo (see below).

Mo'olelo of Pu'ukoholā: Koa, Nation, and Memory

Pu'ukoholā (Mound of the Whale) is located in Kawaihae (Water of Wrath) in South Kohala, on the island of Hawai'i. The large natural (and later modified) harbor has always distinguished Kawaihae as one of the most important anchorages on the island. Pu'ukoholā measures approximately 224 feet by 100 feet and stands directly above a smaller heiau known as Mailekini (Many Maile Vines); both overlook the nearby shoreline, where a now-submerged shark heiau called Haleokapuni (House of Kapuni [a priest]) rests.[1] Though commonly associated with Kamehameha, the three heiau have a longer history, one that extends as far back as the mid- to late 1500s to the chief Lonoikamakahiki (Fornander 1996, 103–22; Kamakau 1992, 55–61). While Kamehameha ruled the Hawaiian archipelago as its first sovereign (a status secured by his rededication of the site), he resided for part of the year at Kawaihae on the beach below the heiau in an area now called Pelekane (Britain or British) and variously referred to as the King's Residence and Royal Courtyard (Greene 1993, chap.7 F1 online; Kelly 1974, 18–26).[2] John Young (also known as Olohana), one of two British advisors (the other being Isaac Davis) of Kamehameha, acted as governor of Hawai'i island (1802–12) and took up a more permanent residence with his family in a nearby upland area. Foreign captains would stop over at Kawaihae to procure supplies, make repairs, pay respects, and gain blessings from Kamehameha.

Capitalist ventures and transformations in government and land tenure during the nineteenth century and the twentieth brought radical changes to this small fishing village that previously thrived on the productivity of its fishponds, saltpans, and other marine resources. Sandalwood and pulu (tree fern fibers used for pillow stuffing) trade, whaling, potato farming, cattle ranching, sugarcane growing, and military training contributed to the denuding of nearby forests, degradation of the environment, and transformation of the harbor until finally Kawaihae became the dry and arid shipping town that it is today (Greene 1993; Kelly 1974). As described on its Website, Puʻukoholā has been managed by the National Park Service since being named a National Historic Site in 1972 for its significance as "the one structure in the Hawaiian islands" that is directly associated with the "founding of the Hawaiian kingdom" (www.nps.gov/puhe).

In 1991, the relevance of Puʻukoholā lay as much in its future as it did in its past; or, rather, its past was seen as a source of the future for Hawaiian cultural nationalists. Two hundred years prior, Kamehameha, a Kohala chief, was at war with his cousin Keōua, chief of Kaʻū, for control of the island of Hawaiʻi. As the most widely accepted version of the story (that by Samuel Kamakau) goes, a prophecy (itself a moʻolelo) given to Kamehameha by a powerful seer from Kauaʻi named Kapoukahi foretold that all of Hawaiʻi would be his "without harm to his skin" if he rebuilt and reconsecrated Puʻukoholā, which was situated above the older Mailekini heiau at Kawaihae.[3] This he did between 1790 and 1791, and upon its completion Kamehameha invited Keōua to meet at Kawaihae (South Kohala) to end the nine-year war. Despite warnings and objections from his advisors, Keōua accepted the offer and sailed with his retainers, fully aware that the outcome would be his death. Along the way, he stopped at a site called Luahinewai to prepare to die by bathing, ritually cutting off the end of his penis, and selecting those of his party who would accompany him in death. When they arrived at Kawaihae, all but two of the men on Keōua's canoe were slaughtered, and the Kaʻū chief's body was placed on the altar. Puʻukoholā became the house of Kamehameha's family god Kūkāʻilimoku, the island snatcher, and by 1810 all of the islands were united under him. It was there, then, that the Hawaiian nation was born; perhaps it might also be reborn there.

Following the occupation of Hawaiʻi by the United States in 1898, the moʻolelo of Kamehameha's warriorhood and campaign to unite the islands became a battleground of history and memory as Hawaiians struggled to define their own destiny as a lāhui. Between 1905 and 1906, Joseph Poepoe, a newspaper editor, lawyer, and Territorial legislator and a member of the Home Rule Party that ran a "Hawaiʻi for Hawaiians" campaign, wrote a biographical serial on Kamehameha that was intended to recruit the memory of the conqueror of the kingdom to inspire Hawaiians of the time to "struggle not with the spears" of Kamehameha's warriors but with the ballots that Hawaiian men had been enfranchised with (Poepoe, 11/28/1905).[4] The episode at Puʻukoholā, however, had been a source of much disagreement among historians. Was this act of seeming treachery and deceit by Kamehameha what the Swedish-born folklorist and Hawaiian Kingdom judge Abraham Fornander would later call "the darkest blot upon his otherwise fair name" (Fornander 1996, 331)? Reviewing the available literature and drawing upon unpublished manuscripts and interviews with knowledgeable elders, Poepoe instead constructed a scenario of a Kohala chief whose deep and sincere love for his cousin could not outweigh the political demands and spiritual influence of his advisors and ritual experts. Thus Poepoe could not "hookuikahi aku i kona manao me ko kekahi poe kakau moolelo e ae (reconcile his thinking with those of other historians)" (Poepoe, 7/8/1906).[5] Tellingly, the word he uses for "reconcile" is "hoʻokuʻikahi," the same term that would be employed in 1991 to bring together the families (and a few historians) who were still divided by this memory.

Another discursive engagement came in 1920–24 with the writings of Reverend Stephen L. Desha, another newspaperman who was also a pastor, legislator, and member of the Royal Order of Kamehameha. Based largely on Poepoe's narrative, Desha's moʻolelo of Kamehameha and his mentor Kekūhaupiʻo[6] frequently commented on the social and political status of contemporary Hawaiians through allusions and comparisons to the battles Kamehameha fought. The Home Rule Party by this time was defunct, as the Hawaiian elite had entered into an alliance with the business-backed Republican Party. The Republican delegate to Washington, D.C., Prince Jonah Kūhiō Kalaniʻanaʻole, a close friend of Desha, had played a pivotal role in creating the Hawaiian Homes Commission Act (1920–21) in the U.S. Congress that aimed to "rehabilitate" the Hawaiian people (long thought to be a dying race) by returning them to the land (see chapter 1). Desha spoke directly to this development during one of his discussions of the famous prophecies of old, noting that "the life will return again to this Race, just like the famous saying of Hewahewa high Priest of Kamehameha . . . at the time that Puʻukohola was restored, 'Lift up until high is the station, and turn the face to the sea, and then, from the sea indeed shall come the blessings'" (Desha, *Hoku o Hawaii*, 7/13/22).

The discourse of Hawaiian extinction was the principal topic of the day, and it had made its way (though with a different valence) into the recently published *The Napoleon of the Pacific: Kamehameha the Great* (1919) by Herbert Gowen, a professor of Oriental Languages and Literature at the University of Washington. Bemoaning what he saw as the great chief's "degenerate off-spring of to-day" (316), Gowen wrote that "no Hawaiian has arisen with a hundredth part of the manhood possessed and used, mainly for good, by this heroic savage" (11). The qualification of "good" was a reference to what he would later describe as the one "ugly episode" of Puʻukoholā, which he explained to his American and international audiences was a product of "a people steeped to the lips in barbarism" whose wars would be best compared not to those of the historically coincident Napoleonic, but rather to the "Greek or Trojan" (202).

Contesting Gowen's narrative of emasculation, degeneration, and temporal othering (Fabian 1983; Said 1978; Sinha 1995),[7] Desha explicitly frames his own moʻolelo as a project of re-membering koa:

O ka manao nui . . . oia no ka hoonaauao ana aku i ka hanauna hou i kekahi mau mea pili i na Moolelo kaulana o na Alii me ko lakou mau kanaka koa o kela au kahiko, ai mea hoi e hiki ai ia lakou e hoomaopopo i keia oiaio ano nui. He mau Alii koa kaulana loa no ka ko Hawaiʻi nei, a he mau kanaka koa loa no hoi e hilahila ole ai ka Oiwi Hawaii ma kona ano Hawaii i kona Lahui aloha, ae loaa ai hoi iaia na manao e keha ai oia.

The main idea . . . is the education of this new generation about certain things pertaining to the famous Moʻolelo of the Chiefs and their courageous people/warriors of that ancient time, and so they will remember/recognize this important truth. This land, Hawaiʻi, has indeed had very renowned Chiefs of courage, and extremely brave individuals because of whom the Indigenous Hawaiian as a Hawaiian should feel no embarrassment in his/her beloved Lāhui, and from whom he/she should gain insight that will make him/her proud.[8]

In numerous passages like this one, Desha frequently wrote about the need for the newer generations to remember the acts of bravery and honor of Kamehameha and the other aliʻi of old and to preserve the places, songs, and legends that told of their stories.

Such a vision was promoted by the Royal Order, which was revived in 1903 by Kūhiō as a fraternal political support network, mutual benefit society, and cultural and historical association. Desha mourned the unkempt state of Puʻukoholā and chastised the legislators and young folks who were neglectful of the indigenous traditions of Hawaiʻi. In true Royal Order fashion, Desha mused, "Mea paha o hoala hou ia mai keia manao malama i na Mea kaulana kahiko o Hawaii nei" (Perhaps there should be a reawakening of the idea to care for the ancient famous Things of this Hawaiʻi).[9]

Some six years later, the Royal Order did in fact place a commemorative bronze plaque at Puʻukoholā heiau, an act noted in the park's official history as "the first formal commemoration of its importance in Hawaiian history in modern times" (Greene 1993, chap. 7 K.1 online). Though this was an important beginning, it would be a number of years before the moʻolelo of Puʻukoholā emerged once again. The Hawaiian language continued on its precipitous decline, and in 1948 the Hilo-based *Hoku o Hawaii,* which had been experiencing financial difficulties even as Desha was writing his moʻolelo of Kekūhaupiʻo, became the last secular Hawaiian-language newspaper to shut down (Mookini 1974, xiv). Desha's and Poepoe's moʻolelo, like the vast majority of cultural texts of the ʻŌiwi archive, disappeared from circulation and resided primarily on the shelves of libraries or in museums, where they were forgotten by all but a few (Stillman 2001).

Commemorating, Re-membering and Unifying Lāhui

Puʻukoholā gained recognition once again when it was designated a national historic landmark on June 10, 1966, almost seven years after Hawaiian statehood, and a pageant was held there to honor the site (Clark 1991, E7). The heiau and the lands around it received even more prominent status when on August 17, 1972, Public Law 92–388 (86 Stat. 562) authorized the establishment of Puʻukoholā Heiau National Historic Site to "restore and preserve in public ownership the historically significant temple associated with Kamehameha the Great . . . and the property of John Young" (Greene 1993, chap. 7 K.1, N.2(a) online). Beginning in the mid-1970s, the National Park Service (NPS) and the Waimea Hawaiian Civic Club sponsored an Establishment Day cultural festival on the weekend closest to August 17 to celebrate the establishment of the park (rather than of the lāhui). The festival included a pageant with a "royal court" that proceeded down from the heiau to the flats below to accept hoʻokupu (ceremonial gifts) that were presented in the form of dances and the fruits of the land. Following the ceremonies, a fair held at Pelekane featured crafts, food, games, demonstrations, and hands-on workshops (Kaʻai 2003).

As was the case with most "Hawaiian" things in the twentieth century, the Puʻukoholā festival became a type of commodity spectacle for both touristic and local consumption. This speaks to the nature of festivals, pageants, parades, and other performances of culture and history in the tourism-based and military-dominated cultural and political economy of Hawaiʻi. Within this context, such performances operate within a pervasive "discourse of aloha" (Pierce 2004) that works on multiple levels to domesticate difference, obscure racial and ethnic tensions and hierarchies, erase claims of indigeneity, feminize the landscape and its people, and sell Hawaiʻi as an open, generous, hospitable, safe, attractive, multicultural paradise (Desmond 1999, 2–9; Imada 2004; Okamura 1998; Trask 1999). Since the early 1900s, celebrations of May Day (later Lei Day) and the Mid-Pacific Carnival often featured nostalgic representations of Hawaiʻi's past and its multiethnic and harmonious present as a part of the United States (Friesen 1996; Pierce 2004). Parades and pageants were also events where Kanaka Maoli celebrated their history and their connections to place, especially through the Kamehameha Day celebrations and parades (Stillman 1994).

Yet as Pierce (2004:138–46) argues, by commemorating and memorializing Kamehameha through festive parades and floral pageants, the discourse of aloha assimilates and domesticates his image, thereby neutralizing any potential he might hold as a model for antihegemonic practice. Such a dynamic is epitomized in the yearly Aloha Festivals (aka Aloha Week), a series of events that invests so-called royal courts on each island to ride in parades, attend royal balls, preside over ceremonies, and make appearances at concerts, celebrations, and block parties; it has even served as a model for other culture-tourism projects in Pacific nations (Bossen 2000). During its peak week in 2001, it brought in over eight thousand visitors and eleven million dollars to Oʻahu alone (Lynch 2001). Thus even a site such as Puʻukoholā, so heavily steeped in traditions of political battles, war, and struggle, became a victim of colonial sacrifice, and on its own altar no less.

As I discussed in the previous chapter, the Hawaiian cultural nationalist movement that began in the 1970s brought about transformations in the ways that Kanaka ʻŌiwi imagined their history, culture, and sacred sites. During the late 1980s, acts of commemoration started to take on new meaning as a number of events marking the rise and fall of the Hawaiian Kingdom loomed on the horizon. Focus shifted from remembering a culture and history of the past to re-membering a lāhui today, one that would follow in the footsteps of the ancestors.

Thus in 1989, the organizers of the 1991 bicentennial observation of Kamehameha's consecration of Puʻukoholā planned an event that would be unlike any other activity before it. They asked Sam Kahaʻi Kaʻai, a master carver, storyteller, and cultural practitioner from Kaupō, Maui, if he would chair the bicentennial committee. Kaʻai had been involved in the Puʻukoholā cultural festival since 1979 as a pū (conch shell trumpet) blower and as an artisan. He agreed but warned them that "he's not gonna make you one bettah Aloha Week, he goin *change* you" (Kaʻai 1999a). The organizing committee was comprised of NPS staff, Hawaiian Civic Club members, elders from the Hawaiian community, and individuals that Kaʻai brought in, such as the kumu hula, chanter, and educator John Keolamakaʻāinana Lake. Lake recalled that the original intention was to plan a "commemoration of Puʻukoholā, and of course all the goals and the virtues and values of Kamehameha" (Lake 2003). Eventually the committee decided that the event would be "not only a commemoration of a place, but there had to be a . . . recapturing, revitalizing, and literally that is why we called it Hoʻokuʻikahi (unify) . . . challenging again, slamming together as one" (Lake 2003).

The word hoʻokuʻikahi, which means to unify, reconcile, and literally "pound" or "slam" together as one, perfectly encapsulates an important dimension of commemorations and other types of "memory work." As Gillis points out, "Commemorative activity is by definition social and political, for it involves the coordination of individual and group memories, whose results may appear consensual when they are in fact the product of processes of intense contest, struggle, and, in some instances, annihilation" (Gillis 1994, 5). Concerned with the (re)production of community through the collective cotelling of (life) historical stories—in her case among Holocaust survivors in a care home—Myerhoff eloquently describes re-membering as a "special type of recollection" that calls attention "to the reaggregation of members" (Myerhoff 1982, 111). She writes, "The focused unification provided by Re-membering is requisite to sense and ordering. A life is given a shape that extends back into the past and forward into the future. It becomes a tidy edited tale. Completeness is sacrificed for moral and aesthetic purposes. Here history may approach art and ritual. The same impulse for order informs them all. Perhaps this is why Mnemosyne, the goddess of Memory among the Greeks, is the mother of the muses. Without Re-membering we lose our histories and our selves. Time is erosion, then, rather than accumulation" (ibid., 110). Re-membering creates an "integration with earlier states of being" and provides a "sense of continuity and completeness" (ibid., 110). Emile Durkheim's theory of religious practice as generative of collective representations of society is also relevant here, for it is the larger social re-membering and integrating through ritual practice that links the self with society.

For Kaʻai and the other committee members, Hoʻokuʻikahi represented this type of memory work through collective enactment: a unification of Hawaiians today and an integration of their modern selves with their ancient ones. Re-membering the moʻolelo of Puʻukoholā would involve the reunification of elements of Hawaiian culture and society that had been dismembered. This involved healing the divisions and animosities between the descendants of Kamehameha and those of Keōua, unifying Kanaka Maoli in search of cultural identity, spiritual guidance, and political sovereignty, and reconnecting with other Polynesian and indigenous peoples whose histories we shared.

The event was to "commemorate in an authentic Hawaiian manner" the event of 1791, but also to "unite in harmony . . . all Hawaiians" and to "heal . . . the bitterness, grievance, and enmity of the past 200 years" (Ceremony 1991; Clark 1991; Kaʻai 1991).[10] Representatives from the Keōua-kūʻahuʻula lineage would travel on the *Hōkūleʻa* to retrace the Kaʻū chief's voyage and end at Puʻukoholā, where the descendants of Kamehameha and his chiefs would greet their cousins with aloha, conduct a special ʻawa ceremony, and then end in the afternoon with a public event that would include the presentation of offerings brought in by the various organizations (see figure 8 on page 82 and figure 23 on page 201). The organizers made a special effort to dissociate the heiau and its akua with its common characterizations as "Kamehameha's war temple" and "god of war." They argued that such a reading is wrong because it examines only one element in what is a larger project of governance, industry, and uprightness, which Kū represents in his multiple facets. Instead, Puʻukoholā was to be a temple of state for those seeking a new Hawaiian nation, and by petitioning the heavens where unification was accomplished, Hawaiians would once again unite and erect the lāhui.

This would require "authentic" cultural practices and rituals, which meant that they were *not* doing it as a pageant or tourist-oriented (read *in*authentic) performance, which had become the norm. Much of the impetus for this remembering of an authentic identity came from a very profound sense that most Hawaiians had indeed forgotten what it meant to be Hawaiian, especially people in Kaʻai's generation, who had grown up during the Territorial and early statehood period of forced cultural amnesia.

This sense of a lost cultural identity was further reinforced by comparisons with other Oceanic peoples whose culture seemed to be more "intact." Lake recalled in 2003 that when the Festival of Pacific Arts (then called the South Pacific Arts Festival) was first held in 1972, the organizers did not invite the Hawaiian people because "they were already known as 'they had lost their culture,' that the Hawaiians didn't exist" (Lake 2003). Yet as the cultural revitalization flourished, especially with the construction and successful sailing of the double-hulled voyaging canoe *Hōkūleʻa,* organizers of the next festival in Aotearoa/New Zealand (1976) extended the invitation to Hawaiʻi. Lake, who at the time was on the State Foundation on Culture and the Arts, chaired the committee that selected and sent the first contingent. Because the Hawaiian contingent was composed primarily of women (who Lake said were the main practitioners of the arts at that time), certain Māori groups became offended since only men were allowed to speak on their marae (ceremonial meeting places).[11] At another festival that Kaʻai attended, the inability of most Hawaiians to speak their language coupled with their "hotel-style" aloha shirts, slacks, and ʻukulele proved to be a source of chagrin as the extent of their Westernization was brought into high relief when contrasted with the other Pacific Islander participants.

These cultural insecurities became outright shame when the Hawaiians were taken to task by Māori who visited Hawaiʻi. Lake recalled that when their delegations came from Aotearoa, they often asked, "Where are your meeting places? What do you do with them? Where are your men?" (Lake 2003). Kaʻai remembered that when the Tūhoe leader John Rangihau asked, "What do your Hawaiian men do on their maraes? What do Hawaiian women do? . . . I see you grow a lot of . . . weeds. But if you do not know, *I,* your Māori brother, will show you, if you are that empty. But if you are challenged, then invite me, I want to see" (Kaʻai 2002).

Thus, in addition to the renewed focus on revitalizing traditional practices, this commemoration was also meant to respond to the questions of the

Māori cousins, to reclaim a place for Kānaka Maoli to congregate, to come together, and to hoʻokuʻikahi. Lake explained that "in the 19th century, the churches took the place of the heiau; they became the meeting place" (Lake 2003). For the organizers of the Hoʻokuʻikahi, though, the ceremonies were meant to reclaim the heiau as the meeting place for the people, a site where authentic rituals and cultural practices would ground and support political and social endeavors. By rededicating Puʻukoholā, the committee intended to bring new life to the heiau, which in turn would bring new life to the people.

Re-membering Koa: Warriorhood, Courage, and Masculinity

Hoʻokuʻikahi, especially for Kaʻai, was also meant to answer the question, "Where are your men?" In seeking to emulate the values of Kamehameha, Kaʻai decided that the first and foremost value was koa — a culturally and spiritually grounded bravery, courage, and warriorhood that had been lost, especially among Hawaiian men. As I mentioned in the introduction and chapter 1, it was Kamehameha's unification of the islands and centralization of government that put an end to actual warfare and warriorhood (Paglinawan et al. 2006, 62). Thus the work of re-membering koa truly was one of recapturing a practice and philosophy that had become a memory.

Thus Kaʻai decided to gather a group of forty men to stand as Nā Koa, (the Courageous Ones/Warriors). He explained that Nā Koa was "not about being *warlike,*" but "being courageous enough to look at your *spirit.* . . . It's about spending yourself, and in the *spending* you know more about yourself, things you already *are*" (Meyer 1998). He later noted that when he put Nā Koa together, "the primer to all of this was ʻA ʻoe maoli? Are you real?' What have you *done* to *prove* you're real? Will you be disciplined?" (Kaʻai 1999a). It was also important that Nā Koa come from Hawaiʻi Island and have some genealogical connection to the place.

Kaʻai went on a speaking tour throughout the islands and called all Hawaiians (especially the men) to gather at Puʻukoholā at Kawaihae in 1991 to remember who they were as a people. To an audience of students at the University of Hawaiʻi at Mānoa, Kaʻai said,

It is really important that we *renew* ourself at the seventh generation because the Lord *Makani* is *waiting* to blow away your memories. The Lord of the *Wind* is going to *erase* everything you hold *dear* at the *eighth* generation. And *who* are *you?*

You're the eighth generation. You can choose to be anything you want. You can *let* your legacy be blown away. You can *forget* things that are Hawaiian. You have been *eating* from the *buffet* of the world and *neglect* the plate of your *'ohana* [family], and lost the taste for such . . .

History is either a *living* thing, or it's already been blown away. How important is this metaphor? In the *canoe*, the navigator holds a story, a song, that's *all* he has. And exactly three hundred yards behind the canoe, his road is being erased. He pushes into the unknown and has only a *small* glimpse of the past; except that he remembers the song, and sings it again. So *you* will *live* if you remember the song. (Ka'ai 1991)

The themes of renewal, remembering, and living history recurred frequently throughout his talk, as did his usage of compelling metaphors. The example of the navigator's song reveals also the sort of Oceanic triangulation of knowledge and self that Diaz and Kauanui (2001, 316) suggest as a mode for Native Pacific cultural studies analyses and politics (introduction; see also Diaz 2006). This is as well a mode of intergenerational reckoning and encompassing of collectivities.

After first displaying the use of a Hawaiian spear he had carved and brought with him, Ka'ai called upon a younger Hawaiian man named Keone Nunes to don a large brown ti-leaf cape and take hold of the weapon; this was the paraphernalia of Nā Koa and the type of embodied transformation Ka'ai sought for the young Hawaiian men who would literally take up the spears of Kamehameha. He ended by telling the audience that "it is not an *ask* to come togethah . . . if you wish — it is a command. It's a masculine call. If you *are,* be; and if you are *not,* you need not be there, but remember what you are *not*" (Ka'ai 1991). One person in the audience — Kamana'opono Crabbe — did in fact answer, and in a life changing way (see the introduction). The activist filmmaking duo of Nā Maka o ka 'Āina was on hand to record his presentation of history — a new version of an old mo'olelo that would enter into the succession of tellings by Desha, Poepoe, and Kamakau.

The Work and Tension of Re-membering

Besides these stories and their tellers, a number of others collaborated in the production of Ho'oku'ikahi 1991. The historian Fred Kalani Meinecke combed the archives and historical accounts and discovered nine different versions of what happened on that day in 1791. Lake organized Nā Waʻa Lālani Kahuna (chanters and ceremonial attendants) and researched the protocols and ritual practices appropriate to the event. Parley Kanakaʻole, a descendant of the kahuna from that heiau, took on the role of Kahuna Nui. The Vietnam veteran and respected spiritualist Hale Kealoha Makua became an advisor for Keōua Gora and Kaliʻi Gora, the descendants of the Kaʻū chief that would represent their families. William ʻĀkau, a descendant of Kamehameha, was one of a number of individuals whose lineage qualified him to form an Alo Aliʻi (chiefly entourage) that would meet the Alo Aliʻi of Keōua. The Kahaialiʻi family of Maui (Manu and his sisters Thelma and Ulu), whose ancestors were keepers of the original heiau in the fifteenth century, were actively involved in the production of the feather standards, helmets, and cloaks. Representatives from the Park Service and the civic clubs such as Rose Fujimori, Daniel Kawaiʻaeʻa, Lorna Akima, Jerry Shimoda, Elaine Flores, and others helped to organize logistics and gather support from the Hawaiʻi Island communities. Countless individuals from the community volunteered their time and energies for nearly two years to help with the manufacture of the garb, weapons, and implements that would be utilized at the event. A select crew trained in the practices of ceremonially preparing and serving ʻawa, a soporific Pacific root that is brewed and consumed on ritual and social occasions; for Hoʻokuʻikahi, the ʻawa ceremony would bind the participants together as they shared the sacred drink. Over 750 special invitations went out to Hawaiian organizations and various Polynesian and indigenous nations.

Yet, despite these efforts at authentic reproduction, tensions developed as older forms of remembrance and commemoration, which associated the past with the dead, conflicted with the newer forms of practice and ritual that sought to bring new life and energy to the culture. The strivings for "authenticity" created disjuncture when rehearsals were called. As Lake related, "In our discussions . . . we had this conflict . . . was it meant to be a pageant or not? And it was never meant to be a pageant, but we had to rehearse things, because people didn't know how to hold a damn spear in the first place" (Lake 2003). At the same time, others chastised the committee for possibly being *too* real. A number of Hawaiian elders told them they did not know what they were doing or what they were dealing with, and they should not be going to such places (Kaʻai 1999a; Lake 2003). Many Christian

FIGURE 7. Nā Koa o Puʻukoholā stand below Puʻukoholā heiau (in background) at Hoʻokuʻikahi, Puʻukoholā, Hawaiʻi, 1991. PHOTO BY FRANCO SALMOIRAGHI.

Hawaiians were quite resistant to what they saw as the revival of heathen, dark, and primitive customs; for them the old religion was dead and should be left in the past (Friesen 1992).

Another obstacle emanated from the very problem that Kaʻai especially sought to correct, namely, the absence of Hawaiian men. Women were quick to lend their efforts to the production of ti-leaf capes, cloaks, and other pieces to be used during the ceremonies. Men, on the other hand, were hard to come by, especially those who would work with Kaʻai to carve the weapons. Owing to a lack of carvers as well as institutional barriers to procuring wood in a timely manner Kaʻai enlisted the work of inmates at Kūlani Correctional Facility to help with the carving of spears.

More pressing was the need for men to stand as Nā Koa, the regiment of forty courageous ones and spiritual warriors that would be garbed in malo, ti-leaf cape, and rope sandals and armed with sixteen-foot battle pikes (see figure 7). Since Puʻukoholā was a sacrificial temple, women were traditionally prohibited from stepping onto such a structure. Thus a gathering on such a site might have appealed to Hawaiian men who felt they no longer have a place of their own *as* Hawaiian men. However, many Hawaiian men were too embarrassed to put on a malo and display themselves so openly, a testament to the efficacy with which colonization inscribed new regimes of propriety, decorum, and domestication on the body (Stoler 1995). Ka'ai recalled, "I had this kid come up to me — he dives with levis on — *big* kanaka. He says, 'I like one spear, but the *heck* if I goin get naked fo' you guys.' We had *two years* of resistance about the malo" (Ka'ai 1999a). So difficult was it for men to overcome their embodied inhibitions that up until the morning of the ceremonies Ka'ai only had thirty-nine men. The place of the body in the rituals is an important one (a subject I will take up shortly). For the most part, wearing a Hawaiian loincloth was (and still is) a very foreign and unusual thing for most modern Hawaiian men. This, for many, was *the* challenge.

Ho'oku'ikahi: Reconciling Living Histories

Despite the problems and difficulties, the organizers managed to push through and on Saturday, August 17, 1991, Ho'oku'ikahi was held. At about 9:30 a.m., Keōua and Keali'i Gora arrived at Kawaihae on the *Hōkūle'a* after completing a five-day journey. By the time the ceremonies had started, a full ka'au (forty count) of Nā Koa had been achieved; the forty men descended from atop the hill and assembled on the beach to greet the Ka'ū delegation. Nā Wa'a Lālani Kahuna chanted various songs of praise as the descendants of the rival chiefs greeted each other in aloha. An 'awa ceremony honored the ali'i, invited guests, Hawaiian societies, state dignitaries, and representatives from Tahiti, Sāmoa, Marquesas, Rapa Nui (Easter Island), and a number of contingents from Aotearoa/New Zealand (see figure 8). Through the sharing of the 'awa, participants pledged their commitment to unite in peace and to maintain traditions for the next seven generations as individuals chanted, sang, and gave speeches in their native languages.

Following a break in the activities, the public ceremonies commenced at about 3:30 in the afternoon. Approximately twenty-five hundred people had gathered for the official ceremonies. Programs were handed out, and an announcer narrated some of the historical occurrences the event was meant to commemorate. The representatives of Kamehameha's lineage "returned" (a reproduction of) the cloak of Keōua to his descendants in a symbolic gesture of reunification. Thereafter followed the presentation of ceremonial offerings and tributes, which included dances, chants, taro, sweet potatoes, bananas, sugarcane, fish, 'awa, and other foods. International delegations

FIGURE 8. John Keola Lake (foreground) chants at an ʻawa ceremony at Hoʻokuʻikahi, Puʻukoholā, Hawaiʻi, 1991. Keōua Gora and William ʻĀkau (to the left and rear of Lake) stand before the Alo Aliʻi (chiefly entourages) and Nā Koa. PHOTO BY FRANCO SALMOIRAGHI.

also presented gifts and gave speeches. A noted Māori tohunga (ritual expert) named Tahuparae, who came as a supporter of Kaʻai, presented the heiau with a taonga (treasure) in the form of a carved stone named Māuiroto (see the conclusion). The ceremonies ended at about 7:00 p.m. with chanting and the sound of Kaʻai's pū. By all accounts, the event was a success and marked an important new beginning in the spiritual growth of the Hawaiian people.

Steve Friesen, a professor of religious studies at the University of Missouri, Columbia, who attended the event, describes a number of the parameters of change and contexts for negotiation that framed the event (1992). He notes that Hoʻokuʻikahi "included overt attempts to change contemporary understandings of the narratives about 1791," the most prominent of which was the role of Keōua (Friesen 1992, 12). As Kaʻai later related to me, Kalani Meinecke, who is from Kaʻū, reviewed nine different accounts of the event; in order to truly unify the people, the discrepant and painful histories needed to also be reconciled in a way that held both aliʻi in esteem. Thus in retelling the moʻolelo at Hoʻokuʻikahi, organizers spoke of Keōuakūʻahuʻula's act as one of self-sacrifice in order to spare the lives of his people and ensure the survival of his region (Friesen 1992, 13).

Another site for reinterpretation was Keōua's act of cutting off the head of his penis, of which Kamakau writes, "'O ka make ia a Uli" (It is the death of Uli).[12] A footnote by the editors of the English translation says that this referred to the practice of a sorcerer using the body part to pray to death the victim's killers (Kamakau 1992, 156, fn*). There is also, perhaps, a play on words, for the term "Uli," the name of the female deity invoked in the use of such magic, bears a phonetic resemblance to the word "ule," which means penis.[13] This has been read as a final act of defiance that made him an imperfect sacrifice (Meyer 1998). Friesen writes that Ka'ai offered him a different reading: "By submitting to the will of the akua (god) through great pain and humiliation, Keōua bound himself eternally to Kamehameha as his messenger to heaven . . . who would make petitions on his behalf"; thus, Friesen argues, Keōua becomes "a cultural model for self-sacrifice" (Friesen 1992, 13). Such historical reinterpretations provide a model of increased cooperation among descendants, who actively form their identities through understandings and interactions with their past.

Such an exercise is always constrained by the larger social, political, and economic conditions that frame the activities. As Friesen notes, the heiau's designation as a National Park precluded organizers from officially billing the activity as religious or spiritual lest they be charged with "illegally establishing a religion"; thus Ho'oku'ikahi was billed as a cultural festival. As I explained earlier, the harshest criticisms came from the devoutly Christian sectors of the Hawaiian community, those who accepted only presentations of the old ways in pageants, parades, and shows that were qualitatively *not* real. One must also remember the longer history of pageants and festivals that preceded Ho'oku'ikahi, celebrations that reified the definition of the site as a memorial, not as a site of living culture or history. Thus it should come as no surprise that efforts to conduct "real," "authentic" ceremonies and rituals were constantly frustrated by others' interpretations and perceptions of what *was* and what *should have* been taking place there. This speaks to the nature of any site of public culture, for, as White explains, "conflicts over public memory . . . reflect ambiguities in the means and modes of historical representation in public spaces, especially national institutions marked as sites of official culture" (White 1997, 8). Thus at the end of the event, a Hawaiian man who had nervously come to what he thought would be a religious ceremony, went up to Ka'ai with a smile and said, "Why didn't you *say* it was a pageant?" Ka'ai almost replied, "If that was a pageant, we should have sacrificed *you!!*" Yet he realized that "they grew up with that, an antiseptic separation from their spiritual beliefs" (Ka'ai 2003).

In light of the foregoing discussion of antiseptic separations and sliced-off penis heads, I would like to restate one of the central questions of this book: How does one re-member a sense of Hawaiian manhood that was quite violently dis-membered? In Friesen's discussions with the organizers, gender issues surfaced often. He notes, "In general, there was agreement that male aspects of Hawaiian culture had not been maintained as they should have been," and that this neglect was one of the motivating factors leading to the formation of Nā Koa (Friesen 1992, 23). He also heard the various statements that ranged from "women have done a good job of transmitting the culture and the men now need to do their part" to "in the absence of male leadership, Hawaiian women have become too assertive" and "men now need to take their rightful place" (ibid., 23–24). In the preparations for the ceremonies, women played an important and enthusiastic role in producing the capes and cloaks to be used; in contrast, men were hard to come by when carvers and Nā Koa were needed (24). During the actual ceremonies, though, women generally played a secondary role. In his opinion, "there was a subtle suggestion in the official discourse that was critical of public activities by women"; this was evidenced by what he saw as a negative evaluation of Ka'ahumanu, the daughter of Ke'eaumoku who is credited with killing Keōua, and the wife of Kamehameha, who played an important role in dismantling the 'aikapu religiopolitical system of separate eating after Kamehameha died (25).

Many observers noted the prominence of men and masculinity on the heiau, especially as displayed by Nā Koa. Newspapers commented on "the impressive sight of Nā Koa, a company of warriors, in ti-leaf capes and bearing pololu" who "stood at attention during the ceremony and at times chanted praises to the two chiefs" (Ward 1991). One reporter noted the performance of "warrior hula" and posited that "the observance sparked renewed interest in traditional Hawaiian male activities and games" (Conrow 1991b). Many of the men who participated as Nā Koa give testimony to their own personal transformations. John Roberts related, "As a Nā Koa, every one of the members has committed to preserve it for seven generations. And I'm very strong into the culture now, and I'm very proud that I'm

Hawaiian" (Meyer 1998). Arthur Kepoʻo, further asserted, "It is not like any pageantry . . . [or] Aloha Week. It signifies that whatever took place 100 years ago, 200 years ago, we are sort of saying that this is us" (Meyer 1998).

The correlations between personal testimonies and newspaper coverage points to the ways in which public and discursively produced subjectivities (the image and ideal of warriorhood and masculinity) become felt and experienced subjectively (men feeling proud to be warriors and identifying with actors and events of the past). One of the primary ways this operates is through the very context that the heiau was created for—the ritual process.

Ritual, Body and History in Hoʻokuʻikahi

> After the ceremonies finished, within *two weeks* we had guys walking into banks with malo and T-shirt! You understand that transformation? Nā Koa literally means "courageous." Yeah it means soldier too, but it means courageous. That's why we laugh when these guys come up to us and say, "My malo stayed on!" 'Cause for most of these guys, they always wonder, "Will this damn thing stay on? Will I embarrass myself?"
>
> —Sam Kaʻai

Kaʻai's words represent one of the more memorable and telling recollections of Nā Koa's transformations. Rituals create a context to hoʻokuʻikahi—to unite in body, mind, and spirit—in multiple ways. Victor Turner's work *The Ritual Process* (1969) directs our attention to this dynamic. Starting with Arnold van Gennep's seminal thoughts in *The Rites of Passage* (1960[1908]), Turner notes that van Gennep defines "rites of passage" as "rites which accompany every change of place, state, social position and age" and are comprised of three phases: separation, margin, and aggregation (Turner 1969, 94). Focusing primarily on the "liminal" stage, that of margin, a transition from one state to another, Turner develops the concepts of liminality and communitas. When individuals or groups of individuals enter the liminal stage of the ritual process, there is a dissolution of identity preliminary to transformation. Turner describes this condition as "neither here nor there . . . betwixt and between . . . a 'moment in and out of time,' and in and out of secular social structure" (95, 96).

Turner juxtaposes "two major 'models' for human interrelatedness," one "of society as a structured, differentiated, and often hierarchical system of politico-legal-economic positions" and the other "of society as an unstructured or rudimentarily structured and relatively undifferentiated *comitatus,* community, or even communion of equal individuals who submit together to the general authority of the ritual elders" (96). Turner labels the second model of antistructure, which emerges in periods of liminality, as "communitas"; this, he argues, is a "modality of social relationship" through which individuals relate to one another as "total beings," as opposed to status positions (96). Communitas comes to possess an existential, affect-filled quality that is highly generative of cultural forms, for example, symbols, metaphors, myths, art, and philosophies, that provide subjects with templates for reclassifying their relationship to society and incite them to action and thought (127–29).

Situations of liminality and communitas frequently occur during times of historical and societal change, and they give groups of people, particularly those that are marginalized, oppressed, and structurally inferior, an experience of renewal, regeneration, revitalization, and even status elevation and reversal; this in turn enables them to return to society more fully capable of participating in its structure (128–33). The close connection between structure and property, which is frequently the source of status-related inequalities that lead to yearnings for communitas, precludes the possibility of maintaining communitas when the material and organizational needs of humans are to be met; thus communitas (antistructure) must by definition give way to structure if society is to proceed (129).

Hoʻokuʻikahi 1991 at Puʻukoholā provided a symbolically rich and historically deep site for the ritual production of liminality and communitas. The event produced an oppositional vision that works to displace dominant structures of the American, neocolonial, late-capitalist society of Hawaiʻi. By reinstituting an indigenous religiopolitical order that was controlled by the ritual experts and elders, participants who became Nā Koa, Nā Waʻa Lālani Kahuna (chanters, priests), and Nā Alo Aliʻi (members of the chiefly entourages) took on new identities, statuses, and roles. The fact that roles were indeed created and a new structure implemented suggests that the situations of liminality and communitas created there were inherently partial, that is, contained elements of structure *and* antistructure), which Turner himself acknowledges is often the case (1969, 127).

The production of the ritual space crucially counterpoises the dominant

American structure with a Hawaiian one and in doing so allows participants to be renewed, revitalized, and reunited upon their return to their regular lives. The ceremonies at Puʻukoholā functioned along many of the fundamental lines laid out by Turner. A deep communion was forged among the groups that participated, a mode of social relation made possible by seeing others not according to their jobs or status outside of the ceremonies but as fellow Hawaiians coming together (cf. Schwalbe 1996; 1998). These dynamics will become more clear in discussions on the Hale Mua below, but these processes are operative in the rituals that were enacted at Puʻukoholā.

Within these rituals, bodily experience, action, and movement also played a fundamental role in the creation of new subjectivities of culture and gender. This speaks to the "body-reflexive" nature of gender and identity practices that I described in the introduction; in this construct, bodies are "both objects and agents of practice, and the practice itself forming the structures within which bodies are appropriated and defined" (Connell 2005b, 61). In addition to inculcating the specific values, norms, attitudes, sentiments, and beliefs of the community, the "pedagogics of liminality" also works to condemn two kinds of separation from the generic bond of communitas: those derived from "rights" conferred by one's office in the social structure, and those based on psychobiological urges at the expense of others (Turner 1969, 105).

There is also at work here a pedagogy of the body, for, as Farnell reminds us, "dynamically embodied signifying acts," such as those found in rituals, ceremonies, sports, military, dance, martial arts, and fighting, "generate an enormous variety of forms of embodied knowledge" that are "constitutive of human subjectivity and intersubjective domains" (1999, 343). On the level of epistemology, theories of Hawaiian knowledge and self locate the processes of empirical validation in bodily experience. As the Hawaiian educator Manulani Meyer (2001, 142) explains, "Knowing something is *feeling* something, and it is at the core of our embodied knowledge system. Knowing something, however, is metaphorically housed in our stomach region because that is also the site of our emotions, our wisdom, as if knowledge also shapes how we emote. Perhaps then, feelings precede emotions, then wisdom develops." At Hoʻokuʻikahi, the pedagogies of liminality and the body challenged Nā Koa to overcome bodily inhibitions and don malo, stand in formation for hours, wield sixteen-foot wooden battle pikes, and take on the collective identity of the "brown cloud," a unit whose individual members were indiscernible but who all embodied and performed an aggressive posturing of cultural strength (Friesen 1992, 26).

The bodily experience became even more important in light of the fact that most of the individuals on the heiau did not speak Hawaiian, the language in which the rituals were conducted. Linguistic discourse became a barrier for many to overcome, and it highlighted the novices' ignorance of cultural practices and their liminal situation. Participants who did not understand the verbal articulations had to rely on their feelings and other sensory perceptions in order to fully understand the rituals. Here the emotive quality of the chant played a key role in the creation of meaning. Though many people had been accustomed to chant in hula performances, this was the first time they had seen and heard them performed in actual ceremonies. The chants moved the participants at a very deep level; even if the thoughts were not understood, the sentiments were.

Representation of the event documented the emotional nature of remembering nation and identity at Puʻukoholā. In the documentary *Hoʻokuʻi-kahi: To Unify as One,* written by Meleanna Meyer and John Lake (see chapter 3; Meyer 1998), Hauʻoli Akaka narrated, "As participants and invited guests assemble, they are greeted with chants in our ancestral tongue, ka ʻōlelo kupuna, which speaks to our entwined emotions, to our naʻau, our shared feelings." Newspaper coverage, such as an article written by Enomoto (1991), also highlighted the affect-filled testimonies of those present. Katherine Domingo, a former park ranger and volunteer maker of Nā Koa's ti-leaf capes, expressed "ʻOluʻolu, I feel happy inside." Hale Kealoha Makua, an elder and a spiritual advisor for the event, stated, "I feel more than healed — more truth. You can't explain, you just know." Finally, William ʻĀkau, the representative of Kamehameha's lineage, revealed, "I cried because, during the chant as the Hokuleʻa approached, it was a special moment. It comes from inside, a feeling of love and appreciation in doing this. Peace and understanding are with Nā Koa [the warriors] and aloaliʻi [chief's entourage]" (Enomoto 1991).

Attention to the role of chant as a form of embodied action and mediator of bodily experiences, especially those of emotion, helps one understand the ways in which "dynamically embodied signifying acts (including spoken language) in symbolically rich spaces are the dialogical, intersubjective means by which persons, social institutions, and cultural knowledge are socially constructed, historically transmitted, and revised and so are constitutive of culture and self" (Farnell 1999, 344).

Upon their return to society, the participants were renewed and imbued with a new sense of Hawaiian identity. As Ka'ai related, two weeks after the event men were walking into banks in T-shirts *and* malo. On one level, this may be read as an individual's effort to live and represent their Hawaiian identity in their daily life and enact resistance to colonial American society by disturbing normative rules of dress and decorum in the most highly regulated and formalized institutions of capitalist activity. As Merry (2000, 221–31) argues, colonization in Hawai'i, as elsewhere, has historically operated in very intimate ways through the control, management, and refashioning of the Hawaiian body and sexuality (see also Stoler 2002). To flout these rules is to directly challenge the raced, classed, and gendered colonial order of things.

Yet the "in-betweenness" and hybridity of the T-shirt / malo combination may also mark an unwillingness to give up the deep and pleasurable experiences of liminality and communitas and thus a corollary attempt to recreate them in bodily rituals of dress and action. This highlights the ambiguities and contradictions of a ritual process that returns one to a still-colonized social order. In the Hale Mua, men describe people who have a difficult time getting back into their regular routine after Pu'ukoholā as "burning up on reentry." This astronomic metaphor is also applied more generally to those who had lived a predominantly Euro-American lifestyle, often on the U.S. continent for some duration of time, and later returned to the culture and land of Hawai'i only to be overwhelmed emotionally and spiritually by the experience of reconnection and subsequently incapacitated as they questioned their whole way of life. Like a shuttle returning to earth from its voyage to other realms and the darkness of the unknown (in Hawaiian, the Pō), the drastic spatial and temporal transition from one realm to another poses a threat to the very constitution of one's being. Men may experience "structural damage" and an inability to cope with their normal lives, instead constantly longing for a return to Pu'ukoholā and the old ways and the fellowship they experienced there. Yet, as Turner argues, liminality and communitas must give way to structure and must not be prolonged lest they subvert the very purposes they were created for, namely, to renew, regenerate, and revitalize individuals who will be more fully capable of participation in societal structures. The processual structure theorized by Turner parallels work on social movements, beginning with Max Weber, that have analyzed the temporal structure of movements that originate in the vision of charismatic leaders, followed by routinization or institutionalization; if successful, these visions displace the dominant structures they challenge.

The ritual process also worked to reclaim a sense of authenticity for Hawaiians and the Hawaiian body. Following Terence Turner (1994), Farnell (1999, 347) urges us to recognize "the appropriation of all aspects of bodiliness in the production of personal and social identity within the culture of contemporary late-capitalism." In Hawai'i, the apparatus of global tourism has most visibly appropriated the Hawaiian body as a commodity. Desmond argues that a "physical foundationalism" operates in touristic discourse and posits the body as "that which is really 'real,' a repository of truth" through bodily performances (1999, xiv). She notes that "bodies function as the material signs for categories of social difference, including divisions of gender, race, cultural identity and species" (xiv). Bodily performances serve as the final authenticator of the commodity of difference, and thus the industry highlights the "centrality of the performing body, binding notions of 'facticity,' presence, naturalism, and authenticity together under the sign of spectator corporeality" (xv).

As I mentioned in chapter 1, the sexualized hula maiden and the feminized, subservient native boy are the dominant images through which Hawai'i is marketed internationally. Many Kānaka 'Ōiwi view these images as gross misrepresentations of real Hawaiians; yet at the same time, many others have internalized these images and seek to embody these representations in their quests to achieve beauty. Hawaiians do not control the images of almost naked Hawaiian bodies shown in advertisements. The embodied liminality performed on Pu'ukoholā heiau can thus also be seen as a concerted effort on the part of Hawaiians to control their own images and bodies and thus reclaim authentic ones by separating from and contesting the dominant touristic images. Ho'oku'ikahi created a ritualized liminal space betwixt and between that of the neocolonial modern Hawai'i and that of the precolonial past, and it was there in the interstices of structure that new identities were forged. It was also a site in which Hawaiians could embody traditions and practices that had once been foreign to them and that they (usually) would not enact outside of the contexts created by such rituals, practices such as wearing a malo or carrying a spear.

Yet, as I mentioned earlier, the romanticized images have become so normalized and domesticated through Aloha Week pageants and other putatively local productions of the past that efforts to contest the dominant are quickly understood within those very frames. This dynamic became apparent when one observer, as noted, told Ka'ai "Why didn't you tell me it was a pageant?" The speaker's confusion comes from the fact that visible bodily performance is the hallmark of touristic productions, historical pageants, and indigenous cultural practices all at once. This reiterates a point I raised in the introduction and chapter 1: the need to recognize and engage in the situatedness and hybridity that is a fundamental condition of any activity, whether it be hegemonic or counterhegemonic.

Conclusions

I have argued that identity formation through historical discourse depends not only upon which histories are re-membered, but also on how and in what contexts these processes take place. I argue that a number of oppositions are made by the men when differentiating between older forms of pageantry and newer forms of practice. Generally speaking, the pageants are seen as being inauthentic, fake, Western, performed for tourists or for money, and feminine. Participants describe the rituals and practices of Nā Koa as authentic, strong, real, Hawaiian, done for oneself/family and culture, and masculine. I will explore this dynamic in the next chapter as I describe the ceremonies I attended between 1999 and 2006. There I trace out ways that re-membering masculinities as Nā Koa and as a Hale Mua at Pu'ukoholā speak to the larger interconnections between culture and gender in the Hawaiian movements today, dynamics that have important implications for the possibilities and impossibilities of true ho'oku'ikahi.

PUʻUKOHOLĀ

....

At the Mound of the Whale

On March 29, 2002, the Celebration of Arts in the Ritz-Carlton, Kapalua, screened *Hoʻokuʻikahi: To Unify as One* (Meyer 1998), a documentary film by Meleanna Meyer (cowritten with John Lake) that detailed the history of Puʻukoholā heiau, the preparations for and conducting of the commemoration in 1991, and the continuation of gatherings in later years (see figure 9). The proliferation of representations of Puʻukoholā on Websites (see below) and in film testifies to its importance as a site for the production of (mass-)mediated (national) imagination. Following the viewing, a panel entitled "Puʻukoholā . . . Beyond the Pageantry" featured seven of the younger Puʻukoholā leaders (between their thirties and fifties) speaking about their experiences and addressing the as-yet-unresolved tensions of "not being a pageant" (cf. White 2001). The majority of the panelists affirmed the reality of the ceremonies by expressing deeply felt emotion and juxtaposing it as a site of history and tradition to other venues of tourism.

Dan Kaniho, a member of the Nā Papa Kanaka organizational board and the Alo Aliʻi of Papa ʻĀkau, described growing up in Waimea, Hawaiʻi, and not knowing anything about the nearby heiau. His professional life took him away from Hawaiʻi, and now it brought tears to his eyes to know that he had "lost" his "Hawaiian identity." His ancestors nevertheless continued to bring him back to Puʻukoholā so that he could have the experience and "reclaim" his Kanaka ancestry.

The next speaker was Daniel Kawaiʻaeʻa Jr., the superintendent at Puʻukoholā Heiau National Historic Site and son of the aliʻi Papa Kawaiʻaeʻa. He

FIGURE 9. The Hale Mua (holding spears) and Nā Koa Kau i ka Meheu o nā Kūpuna join together to perform the haʻa (ritual dance) Mahaʻū on the flats below the heiau, Puʻukoholā, Hawaiʻi, 2002. PHOTO BY TOM WHITNEY.

placed his dual obligations to the park and to the Hawaiian community in the context of National Park Service (NPS) initiatives to increase partnerships with Native peoples. He proclaimed that Puʻukoholā was the only place where Kānaka Maoli conducted ceremonies in Hawaiian for the benefit of Hawaiian people first and haole (white, implied as visitor) people second. This, in essence, was an offer of antistructure to the group—ironically coming from the lone panelist representing the federal government. Everyone got "a traditional Hawaiian experience," and thus Puʻukoholā had "excelled to a level of realism far beyond pageantry."

An emotional Kaponoʻai Molitau, the Kahuna Pule (ritual specialist, see the introduction) of the ceremonies, stated that he returned because he continued to strive to be a Hawaiian male who had to balance between his professional and his cultural lives. Although they coincided in his work as a performer in the theatrical presentation "ʻUlalena," located in the heavily touristic town of Lāhainā, Maui, he still felt he struggled to balance the two worlds. Going to Puʻukoholā was "an identity" and "an honor." Sam Gon, an ecologist and (like Molitau) a chanter of John Lake's Nā Waʻa Lālani Kahuna, opened with a greeting chant and expressed his profound love and respect for the sanctity of the place. At that site, he saw the lāhui (people, nation) living through the language, chants, arts, skills, and actions that confirmed their continued persistence and growth.

The third of Lake's three students present, Kēhau Kruse, was also the sole woman of the group; she quipped, "I thought I was gonna get 'attack' by all these *men*." When the audience stopped laughing, she explained that she represented the women of Puʻukoholā and that Mailekini was their heiau. She adamantly denied the idea that Puʻukoholā was a pageant and contrasted it with working as a cultural educator at the Outrigger Hotel. There, she found it difficult to "walk the line" because there were certain things she was not willing to share with tourists; at Puʻukoholā, she rejuvenated her spirit and practiced her culture as a "real Hawaiian." Defying the idea that culture was to be found "only in books and museums," she stated, "This is who we *are*. We're still here; we will continue to be here." In voicing her felt alienation of being museumized, Kruse points to the dialectic between the realness of Puʻukoholā and the ever-present discourses of the touristic Hawaiʻi, the same dialectic found in the Hale Mua.

Keʻeaumoku Kapu, the founder of Nā Koa Kau i ka Meheu o Nā Kūpuna (the Warriors Who Walk in the Footsteps of Our Ancestors) on Oʻahu and in Lāhainā, stated that his job was to find diligent young men and women, "infect them with my disease," and lead them "like the pied piper" to the Puʻukoholā. He stated that as a construction worker, he built freeways that destroyed the history and lands he should have been protecting; now he was working in Lāhainā to restore cultural sites and to repatriate bones that were unearthed in developments. As a kaukau aliʻi (junior chief) of Puʻukoholā, he stated, "My duties are to prepare the men for battle with my protégé right next to me" (pointing at Kyle Nākānelua). He explained that the two of them always guessed what the other would do at Puʻukoholā each year and tried to be prepared. "It's a constant thing of hoʻopāpā [contest in wit and strength]."

After making a quick retort to Kapu's comment about his being a protégé, Kyle Nākānelua gave his genealogy, which placed him in a succession of individuals who had rights and responsibilities to stand on the heiau. As a Hale Mua (Men's House), his group looked at Hawaiian things "with a *masculine* point of view" and conducted activities "in a *traditional* Hawaiian way." When he was growing up, pageantry was the reservoir of what Hawaiians had as a people to maintain contact with the ancestors and to know who the modern Kānaka were. If one went to Puʻukoholā just as a spectator, he would see the event as a pageant; however, if one were a participant, he would have the choice to look outside at the spectators or to look inside at what he was doing and who he was. The only risk was that some individuals look so deeply inside that when they go back to their daily lives, they "burn up on reentry."

As the panel members attested through their personal moʻolelo, the ritual process and embodied experiences of Puʻukoholā were deeply transformative (cf. Cain 1991; Swora 2001). Their yearly rededication at the Mound of the Whale was a testament both to the existence of cultural politics in ritual and the potency of ritual in the larger realm of cultural nationalism and decolonization. Yet as the title of the panel implied, older conceptions of pageantry and inauthenticity remained, a commentary on the entrenchment of neocolonial ways of seeing that were produced by discourses of tourism and domestication. Moreover, once the participants left the sacred space of the ritual, they returned to face the same colonial system they had left. Thus many of them felt they had to "walk the line" and live in two worlds that did not fit together nicely. Significantly, these worlds were not the same for men and women. Kruse's wariness of being attacked by men was a joking yet serious commentary on the type of masculinities being produced on the heiau, especially by Nā Koa. In channeling and ritually performing violence, did men truly escape the older practices that harmed women, children, and other men? And what of the women who wanted to be recognized as Nā Koa? Though women certainly had a place at the heiau, was it one premised on the recognition of male authority? The ratio of men to women on the panel was not a radical overexaggeration of the approximate three to one representation of participants; it was, however, a clear indication of women's representation in the leadership ranks.

These sorts of tensions of identity and gender are characteristic of what I have already noted are situations of liminality. Others have also drawn on the framework of the ritual process to describe the dynamics of tourism, especially in its close linkages with pilgrimages (Graburn 2001). Edward Bruner has characterized the in-between site of tourism as a "borderzone, a point of conjuncture, a behavioral field that I think of in spatial terms usually as a distinct meeting place" and also as "a localized event, limited in space and time, as an encounter between foreign visitors and locals" who perform in the "touristic drama" (2005, 17–18). Bruner reflects that the borderzone is "a site of new subjectivities and consciousness where new culture and relationships emerge" (18). These new cultural forms, of both tourist and native, are emergent in and constituted by performance and thus all are "authentic — that is, authentic tourist productions" (5). He also draws attention to the ways in which narrative structure experienced through a pre-tour narrative is shaped and reshaped in the lived experience and then retold as posttour narratives (22).

I find these ideas to be useful for thinking through some of the issues that characterize Puʻukoholā, which as a site and as an event is held in tension with tourism and pageantry, attended by Kanaka Maoli who are looking for an "authentic experience," most of whom do so by leaving home to attend the event. While we are the "natives" and "performers," we are also the "tourists," but in this case we tour and consume ourselves (see Linnekin 1997). The fact that five of the seven panelists were not from the Big Island (as Hawaiʻi Island is commonly referred to) was also reflective of the number of off-island attendees at the annual event at Kawaihae. Furthermore, the very context of the panel presentation, namely, a cultural arts celebration that brought cultural practitioners to a luxury resort in West Maui, evidenced the interpolation of the touristic with the cultural as well as the operation of personal, collective, and metanarratives in the re-membering of subjectivities.

In the previous chapter I discussed the ways in which the larger historical moʻolelo of place served as the foundation for Hoʻokuʻikahi 1991 and provided a template for new personal narrations of self and nationhood. Against the colonial discourses of erasure, death, and emasculation, Kānaka Maoli strove to deploy new discourses of spiritual health, vibrancy, and strength. Importantly, the ceremonies represented not only a rededication of the temple of state and the histories and traditions inscribed there, but also a ritual refiguring and re-membering of the bodies that were present. The heiau became a ceremonial ground for the installation of what many men saw as a new model for a positive masculine cultural identity, Nā Koa. In the ritual context, the men experienced and practiced alternatively situated modes of being and acting that were also inherently hybrid. The "brown cloud," as they were referred to because of their brown ti-leaf capes and their coalescence into a single mass, presented a tough, aggressive, and proud image of "regular guys" exhibiting bravery by overcoming personal fears and standing up, ready to defend their culture (see figure 7 on page 80). Their embodied liminality worked on multiple levels to reform their subjectivities and enable them to be more visibly active men in a changing Hawaiian society.

When contrasted with older forms of commemoration and pageantry at the site, the newer ways of re-membering identity and koa at Puʻukoholā produced binary oppositions of authentic/inauthentic, strong/weak, serious/playful, Hawaiian/Western, for tourists/for community, for monetary profit/for spiritual growth, and, especially for the men of the Hale Mua, feminine/masculine. Reworking history and memory also entailed a remaking of the body. As Farnell reminds us, the past remains with us "not only in words but also in our neuromuscular patterning and kinaesthetic memories —the way in which specific experiences and concepts of time/space are built into our bodily modus operandi" (1999, 353). Combining the (corpo)reality of embodied experience with the multiple significations inscribed on the marked bodies, ritual practices created a distinctly different way of knowing and living a historically contextualized cultural identity.

In this chapter I show how attention to the role of rituals and bodies helps one understand the transformations of self and society that are at least partially accomplished at Puʻukoholā. I describe the Hale Mua's participation as Nā Koa at the Puʻukoholā, with a focus on the 2002 event. I also point to the tensions that emerge at Puʻukoholā when the multiple projects of cultural reclamation, nationalist imagining, touristic appropriation, and gender empowerment converge on site.

Puʻukoholā: Re-membering and Performing Nationhood

Though the size of subsequent events never matched the 1991 ceremonies, a dedicated core of approximately 100–150 returned to Puʻukoholā each August to conduct ceremonies over a four-day weekend that involved rituals, workshops, feasts, dance and martial arts performances, and reconnection with community and place. These ceremonies were oriented toward the larger goals of revitalization and education, though still through the modes of re-membering identity in ritual performance. In addition to these activities, the long-standing culture and arts festival sponsored by the Waimea Hawaiian Civic Club continued to be held at Pelekane Bay. Over the years, the numbers continued to grow, and between 1999 and 2006, when I attended, there were on average 200–300 participants each year. Taken together, the weekend events have alternately been referred to as Hoʻokuʻikahi (following the 1991 theme) and Establishment Day Festival, which, as I mentioned in chapter 2, marks the establishment of the National Historic

Site on August 17, 1972; this connection with former modes of celebration persisted in that the events of and following 1991 coincided with the weekend closest to the seventeenth. Most participants, however, refer to the weekend's events by the name of the site — Pu'ukoholā.

The mo'olelo of Pu'ukoholā traveled in a number of ways beyond the shores of Kawaihae. The images of the ceremonies and new histories written appeared on constantly updated versions of the park's Website (nps.gov/puhe). Meyer's film *Ho'oku'ikahi: To Unify as One* found audiences in film festivals and college seminars. A multivocal narrative of the contemporary ceremonies as well as a historical, cultural, and geographic survey of the Kawaihae area appeared on the Pacific Worlds indigenous geography Website that serves Hawai'i-Pacific Schools (pacificworlds.com). Ceremony participants such as Franklin Pao, a member of Nā Wa'a Lālani Kahuna, gave detailed and intimate accounts on personal Websites (Pao 2006). This same availability for public narration also left the ceremonies vulnerable to the ever-present danger of folklorizing and subsuming in tourist discourse, and Internet travel sites and tourist brochures were quick to add the "cultural festival" to their events calendars and the list of "Fun things to do on the Big Island" (Big Island News 2007; "Fun Things" n.d.; see figure 10).

Announcements for the event appeared frequently in the local Hawai'i Island newspaper *West Hawaii Today* and the statewide monthly paper of the Office of Hawaiian Affairs *Ka Wai Ola o Oha;* the state's two largest dailies, the *Honolulu Advertiser* and the *Honolulu Star-Bulletin,* occasionally printed announcements and articles on the event (Cultural festival 2001; It's festival 1998; Tsutsumi 2001). More often, local newspapers and periodicals featured stories on individuals associated with the ceremonies, including John Lake, Sam Ka'ai, Kyle Nākānelua, and Ke'eaumoku Kapu (Barnhart 2006a; Barnhart 2006b; Hale 2004; Wood 2006). Such discursive productions point to the ways in which leaders with vision, charisma, and articulate language produce narratives that also work powerfully in the service of (personal) transformation (Lindholm 2002).

An instructive contrast emerged in the *Honolulu Star-Bulletin* edition of August 12, 2001. The first article, appearing in the travel section and aimed primarily at *local* tourists, was entitled "King's spirit lives at Big Island festival" and gave a short history, with testimonies from park rangers, of the modern ceremonies held at Pu'ukoholā (Tsutsumi 2001). In the business

FIGURE 10. The Hale Mua performs the Mahaʻū with the ihu aʻu (marlin-bill dagger), Puʻukoholā, Hawaiʻi, 2006. The audience includes other participants situated at the edges of the ceremonial space, including tourists (far left in background, seated under umbrella). A few members of Nā Koa Kau i ka Meheu o nā Kūpuna (foreground, left) spontaneously joined in. PHOTO BY SHANE TEGARDEN.

section, a lengthy article entitled "The Economics of Aloha" presented the economic contributions of the Aloha Week Festivals, which were to start the same month (Lynch 2001). The juxtaposition is telling: just as Puʻukoholā tries to distance itself from the Aloha Week Festivals, it is inevitably the comparative frame against which Hoʻokuʻikahi is held. Moreover, the temple of state itself is constructed as a destination, in this case for both locals and off-island tourists. An especially clear example of this came in the edition of *West Hawaiʻi Today* for August 13, 2006, which featured a story and photos of the previous day's ceremonies with the title and byline reading, "Recapturing a culture: Festival gives visitors a chance to see the glory of old Hawaii" (Lucas 2006b).

At Puʻukoholā, the partial and situational dissolution of status and identity allows for an interface of self and other in a borderzone between Hawaiian and non-Hawaiian, past and present, tradition and capitalism, lāhui and state, and men and women. Acts of remembrance produce new subjectivities that are felt emotionally and bodily but that also produce anxieties about what is "real." This arises precisely because the "real" of being "Maoli" is defined in opposition to the touristic, yet the tourists are ever-present.

The tensions of culture, history, gender, and discourse are thus productive of what I call ritual slippage. On the one hand, participants are conscious of their ability to slip out of their modern identities and into their maoli ones, embodied in the very act of donning traditional garb, the malo for the men. On the other hand, that very process makes such identities difficult if not impossible to secure, especially in a site where the modern and touristic are physically present. This worry is expressed bodily by men, who are worried that their malo will slip off during the ceremony. Recall Kaʻai's comments cited in the last chapter: "For most of these guys, they always wonder, 'Will this damn thing stay on? Will I embarrass myself?'" (1999a). This is more than just a matter of exposing one's physical nakedness; it is also a deeply felt anxiety about one's knowledge of and security in self, one that is in process of being defined culturally as maoli and real, yet is carried out by slipping in and out of identity and of the malo. While this anxiety is most acutely felt upon the return to work and economic life, leading some, as noted, to wear malo *and* T-shirts in banks, it is also ever present in the ceremonies precisely because the space is a borderzone occupied and traveled by multiple parties and agencies. It is thus even more notable that men and women are still able to find transformation through the ritual process.

The ritual slippage of identities, at times shot through with ambivalence, thus both motivates and animates the travel to Kawaihae. For many, the annual journey is seen as a pilgrimage; for some, it is a vacation. Those who have been to numerous ceremonies look forward to renewing fellowship with participants they see only once a year. Usually all of these motives are present, a dynamic which has been noted in analyses of more explicitly touristic modes of travel (see Graburn 2001) but which might be less expected in practices that are avowedly antitouristic. My autoethnographic account of one such journey attends equally to the ritual processes of travel and dwelling (Clifford 1997) in the borderzone of Puʻukoholā.

Puʻukoholā 2002: At the Mound of the Whale

ARRIVALS

After a forty-five-minute flight from Honolulu International Airport, my three companions and I, who were traveling from Oʻahu, arrived at Kona International Airport on Hawaiʻi Island. We met the rest of the Maui members of the Hale Mua, greeted them with the honi (a pressing of noses to exchange breath), and then loaded our personal belongings, sleeping bags, ceremonial implements, including carved spears and padded sticks, ritual foods and offerings, and fresh ʻawa roots onto the large flatbed trucks provided by the NPS and driven by a park ranger. After splitting up into four or five rental vans, we purchased groceries and supplies at the Costco warehouse in Kona, picked up Hawaiian sweet potatoes from a farmer at Kainaliu, and drove the twenty-eight miles from Kona to Kawaihae.

At the National Park gate we turned off the main highway and drove down the access road that took us past the heiau and below to Spencer Beach Park, our home for the next four days. Local people were enjoying the beach and sporting facilities while the new throng of visitors was busily setting up tents and campsites. After unloading our belongings and setting up our cots (provided by the army)[1] in the pavilion, most of us slipped out of our collared shirts and pants and put on shorts or pāʻū, a wraparound waist garment worn by both men and women. We began setting up, cooking dinner, swimming in the ocean water, and preparing ʻawa that would be used for ceremonial and social drinking. A fair amount of social chewing also accompanied the process of cutting, debarking, and pounding of the roots, and thus we prepared to offer up the food of the gods.

ORIENTATIONS OF PEOPLE AND PLACE

At about 6:00 p.m. all of the participants in the weekend's events gathered in the pavilion for an orientation meeting. Kahuna Nui John Lake, the spiritual leader for the weekend, began the meeting by leading chants, which all were expected to know from previous years or to learn by the end of the weekend. Shortly thereafter Lake's students distributed sheets that contained the words to these chants, a schedule of events, and a mission statement that included the following statements:

Nā ʻElemākua (Advisors), Nā Alo Aliʻi, Nā Waʻa Lālani Kahuna and Nā Aliʻi koa of Puʻu Koholā shall provide a unique and fitting opportunity of the new generations of Hawaiians to learn, understand, appreciate, preserve and advocate their cultural heritage, therefore unifying their rich past with the present and future generations. As the spiritual seventh generation, these components shall endeavor:

   •to develop the ways and means of insuring the integrity and dignity of our kūpuna and to establish a priority of long range objectives

- to establish Pu'u Koholā heiau as the center for the revitalization, perpetuation and promotion of traditional native Hawaiian culture
- to recognize that Pu'u Koholā heiau at Kawaihae, South Kohala, Hawai'i stands as a historical symbol of rich cultural heritage and of a civilization that was on the threshold of nationhood. It is a heiau established by Kamehameha I as a temple of State. (Nā Papa Kanaka 1999)

Lake spoke at length about the history and purpose of the weekend's events, reiterating the goal of the 1991 commemoration: to ho'oku'ikahi and unite the people at the temple where the prayer for unification was answered once before. Lake introduced the various parties that made up the organizational body called Nā Papa Kanaka o Pu'ukoholā (Order of People of the Whale Mound): Nā 'Elemākua (the advisors) Sam Ka'ai and Thelma Kahaiali'i Ka'awaloa; Nā Alo Ali'i (the chiefly entourages) of William 'Ākau, Daniel Kawai'ae'a, and Mel Kalahiki; Nā Koa (the warriors) of Kyle Nākānelua and Ke'eaumoku Kapu; Lake's own Nā Wa'a Lālani Kahuna (ritual and prayer specialists); and Nā Wāhine (the women's contingent), composed primarily of the Maui women who accompanied Aunty Thelma.

Lake noted that each year had seen new growth, as did this year, when some 100–150 men and 30–50 women were in attendance. The increased attendance indexed the fact that Pu'ukoholā is a site for collective expression of a vision of a social movement that was gaining force throughout this historical period. In welcoming newcomers, Lake recognized the presence of the regular participants Kanu o Ka 'Āina, a New Century Public Charter School that provided an alternative culture-based education for primarily Hawaiian but also non-Hawaiian students at nearby Waimea town (see kanu.kalo.org). They were also a part of the Hawaiian education movement, one that articulated with the larger transnational indigenous education movement. Kanu o Ka 'Āina faculty introduced two groups of guests they had brought with them: a cohort of Native American educators and students who had come to Hawai'i to work with Kanu on indigenous education programs; and a Humboldt State University summer field school class led by the anthropologist Brett Blosser. Lake then recognized another visiting contingent: a small group of Māori, four women and one man, who had come at the invitation of Ke'eaumoku Kapu. Finally, he welcomed the doctors and staff of the Native Hawaiian Health Care Systems (NHHCS), who would be giving free health screenings over the weekend.[2]

Lake then proclaimed a kapu aloha, an injunction to extend kindness, empathy, and love to one another. Part of this regulation of behavior entailed a prohibition of alcohol, tobacco, and drugs during the ceremonial period that began at the initial meeting and ended on Saturday night. This practice enacted a separation from ordinary social life and began the ritual process collectively. Though purity is never completely attainable, such rituals are nevertheless important enactments of purification that mark the activities as sacred and a departure from the secular.

Lake briefly outlined the schedule for the weekend: Friday included the Hāʻule Lani ceremony at 4:00 a.m., workshops from 8:30 a.m. to 12:30 p.m., and an afternoon ʻawa ceremony for first-timers at 4:00 p.m. Saturday occasioned the Hoʻolaʻa Aliʻi ceremony from 7:00 a.m. to 9:00 a.m., the Puʻukoholā Festival at Pelekane immediately thereafter, an evening International ʻAwa ceremony beginning at 4:00 p.m., and an ʻAha ʻAina (feast) starting at 6:30 p.m. Finally, he would give a Catholic prayer service at Pelekane on Sunday morning for anyone interested. Kaʻai also talked at length, defining the event as a gathering of people who were Maoli, or Real. His was a self-conscious statement of realness set in opposition to the alienating shallowness of touristic representations, which are oppressive for those who must contend with them in the omnipresent, suffocating machinery of mass tourism. Others spoke too, but since everyone was eager to get to sleep early, the speeches were cut short.

Once the other groups left, Nākānelua proclaimed his own kapu on the space — that of the Hale Mua. As we were to be the sole occupants of the pavilion, the kapu prohibited women from entering the site, which was then sanctified for the men and our specific forms of worship, specifically our ʻaikapu on Saturday. It was also a mechanism to prevent the men from being distracted by the sight of any young women who might seek access to the ocean from the staircase at the back of the pavilion that led to the water's edge. Likewise, men would frequently change into their malo in the pavilion, and thus it was important that the space be all-male as men exposed themselves physically and culturally.

Indeed, the delimitation of the quite heterogeneous space was a tricky process at Puʻukoholā, one which would only become more complex as the weekend progressed and visitors other than ourselves came to the festival. Even within our group alone, the introductions above give some indication of the diverse backgrounds and motivations of the participants. And on top of it all, there was more than one (professional) anthropologist in our midst! Upon hearing the "anthropology" in Blosser's introduction, one of the men in the Mua turned to me and said, "Hey, isn't that what you do?" Although I should not have been the least bit surprised, it was quite a surreal and disconcerting moment for me, something akin to the meta-anthropological encounter of Edward Bruner and Hildred Geertz in the Balinese border-zone where ethnographers, tourists, natives, and artists met in "a site of in-betweenness, of seepage along the borders" (Bruner 2005, 198). Bruner's concept of the touristic borderzone has both relevance and limitations in its application to the site of Puʻukoholā, for while the site is on the itineraries of things to do on the Big Island, the ceremonies and cultural productions enacted there are done for Hawaiians first and are intended to be nontouris-tic. Yet my predicament of being a visiting indigenous anthropologist who would be gazed upon by other anthropologists, natives, and tourists alike signals the inherent difficulties of finding or creating purity in such a space.

Nonetheless, the men of the Hale Mua looked to the sea precisely for such purification. After dinner, we went down to the beach, stripped naked, and conducted a hiʻuwai, a ritual bathing and purifying in the warm ocean waters of Kawaihae. We formed a circle in the shallow water to meditate, pray, and idly talk story. After about fifteen minutes, I joined a few others who were getting out of the water and showering in the public bathrooms. Upon re-turning to the pavilion, I followed the lead of one of my elders by making a ritual call home on my cell phone. Twenty minutes later I was sleeping in my cot.

HĀʻULE LANI AND HEAVENS FALLING

At 4:00 a.m. we assembled with the other groups on the flats below the heiau. Wearing our malo, kīhei (over-the-shoulder garment), and rope san-dals (some made by hand, other purchased from Birkenstock), we gazed up at the strikingly clear night sky and counted the shooting stars (see figure 1 on page 4). Kaʻai blew the conch shell that signaled the beginning of the ceremony, and John Lake chanted from atop the walls of Puʻukoholā, which was ringed with burning torches. The men proceeded up top to Puʻukoholā, while the women entered the Mailekini heiau below it. (During the ʻaikapu of the precolonial period, women were not allowed on the sacrificial temples of Puʻukoholā or Mailekini. The practice has held at Puʻukoholā in the context of current ceremonies, but in 1996 Nā Papa Kanaka designated Mailekini a women's heiau in order to provide the women with a place for their own ceremonies.)

Once we were seated on the hard, uneven stones of Puʻukoholā heiau, Nā Waʻa Lālani Kahuna began chanting prayers, calling out the names of deceased individuals associated with the heiau, and burning ceremonial bundles of leaves in remembrance of those who had gone before us to literally and metaphorically lay the foundation we sat on. After Nā Waʻa Lālani had finished their list of names, representatives from Nā Alo Aliʻi and Nā Koa took turns calling out the names of people they sought to commemorate. With each name called, a new bundle was burned and all the men chanted "Eia kou mano, hele ʻoe, ke hele nei ʻoe, hele loa (Here are your descendants, you go, you are leaving, gone forever)." The women's voices from below sang out through the darkness as they chanted and called out their own names. This process of collective remembrance lasted for some time until the last of the bundles had turned to ash.

Lake gave a speech, first in Hawaiian and then in English, on the meaning of the ceremony as one of remembering of the ancestors and thus remembering who we were. As the majority of the men sitting there did not speak Hawaiian, Lake's explanation had the force of a double translation, one of language and one of experience. Other leaders voiced their own concerns and feelings. The Aliʻi Papa Ākau and Kawaiʻaeʻa spoke of the joy they felt in being with the men again on the heiau, while Kalāhiki urged further unification in the political battles taking place in the Hawaiian community. Kapu spoke in frustrated yet dogged tones of his fights to protect his family lands and burial sites in Kauaʻula from the threats of developers seeking to create luxury homes there; for him, Puʻukoholā was his time to "plug back in," to be reenergized for his return to his "miserable existence" in the world "out there."[3] Nākānelua, on the other hand, expressed his pleasure at seeing the new numbers of young boys and adolescents in attendance, for it was they who would carry on the work in the next generation. Lake noted that therein lay the balance, between the good that Nākānelua spoke of and the pain that Kapu felt. As pō (night) became ao (day), the early morning gray colored each of the men's faces. Most were between thirty and sixty, though this year there was a small but significant number of youthful visages.

When sunrise came, we all stood up and chanted "E Ala E," a song to wake the sun in the east.

WORKSHOPPING IDENTITY

With the Hāʻule Lani (Fallen Heavens/Chiefs) ceremonies completed, we returned to the pavilion to eat, change clothes (most of us into our pāʻū), and talk story while we got ready for the workshops. When we arrived at the grassy lawn outside of the NPS visitors' center located above and behind the heiau, Nākānelua was leading morning stretches and exercises for about fifty people wanting further physical exertion. Tents were set up for workshops on lua, language, chant, dance, ethnobotany, therapeutic massage, crafts, weaving, and cultural protocol. The educational project of learning to be Hawaiian was engaged in by all the parties present for the ceremonies, with the addition of a handful of mainland and Japanese tourists who had also come for the Establishment Day Festival advertised in the newspaper and on the park's Website.

One year, the health care workers of NHHCS set up tables where participants could sign up for free cholesterol screenings and health consultations.[4] One of the female doctors was conducting a survey among the men to get their responses to a new pamphlet put out by the Native Hawaiian Cancer Committee of the American Cancer Society. Entitled "Nā Koa: Cancer Facts," the pamphlet featured on its cover "Warrior drawings courtesy of Bishop Museum" (recognizable as belonging to the corpus of images produced by eighteenth-century expedition artists) and the phrase "ʻO ka ha o ke koa—Ke eaʻo ka lahui (The breath of a warrior—the life of the Nation)." On the inside, images of modern Hawaiian men, warnings of "greater risk for many cancers," and the translation of the above phrase all presented a clear message that cancer, and Hawaiian men's health generally, was an urgent site of nationalist struggle and regeneration (see also Marshall 1999, 2006). So, to the list of anthropological, touristic, and indigenous (Hawaiian, Māori, and American Indian) gazes, one must add the medical gaze upon the Hawaiian male body.

FIRST CUP

After our workshops finished, we returned to the pavilion, ate, and rested for a few hours. At four oʻclock, we assembled back at the visitor center lawn for an 'awa ceremony held to welcome and initiate the first-timers, both men and women, into the Pu'ukoholā community and ritual space. This was the first large group ceremony of the weekend not to be segregated by sex. The novices to the heiau ceremonies were now to be inducted into the Pu'uko-holā community by drinking their first cup of 'awa before those gathered there, both living and deceased. The 'awa ceremony represented a communion between the people and the gods, and it was meant to represent a commitment of the people to each other and to the heiau.

While the 'awa was being served, many of the same leaders who had spoken in the morning on the heiau shared their reasons for coming to Pu'ukoholā and the commitments they made when they had their first cup of 'awa there. Most of the discussion was in Hawaiian, this time with little translation into English. Ritual leaders thus were able to convey an important metamessage, even to the nonspeakers: we are Maoli and we are recovering our 'ōlelo.

The audience for such performances of identity included both male and female participants seated in a ritual space, which was cordoned off by a sennit rope barrier, and spectators watching from outside. Most onlookers were returning participants who had gone through the ceremony before, though there were also a couple of tourists and a fair number of local families who had come to support their children from Kanu o ka 'Āina. After the last cup of 'awa was served and the kapu was lifted, approximately fifty students between the ages five and eighteen entered the space and performed chants and dances that told the stories of the gods, chiefs, and the first taro. Proud parents and appreciative visitors alike applauded the performance with great enthusiasm, and as it came to a close the Hale Mua quickly exited and returned to the pavilion to prepare for their own, private ceremony.

'AIKAPU

An exchange of chants occasioned the gathering of the men of Nā Koa and the Hale Mua in our 'aikapu, a sacred eating of the ritual foods that represented a bodily manifestation of the male deities. The event prepared us for the next day's activities and offered the men of Pu'ukoholā an opportunity to meet, pray, and share food in the context of a mua. Once gathered inside, the sixty men began chanting, and their unified voices, amplified by the acoustics of the pavilion, literally shook the walls. This had the dramatic effect of instantly transforming the space into a powerfully felt sacred space, altering the men's consciousness.

Nākānelua organized a group of men to serve the fish, breadfruit, taro, squid, banana, pork, and sweet potato that had been prepared by the Hale Mua. He explained that by eating these foods, the men assimilated the bodies of the gods and the spiritual essences associated with them: the erectness and aggression of Kū, the knowledge and life of Kāne, the fluidity and depth of Kanaloa, and the fertility, growth, and peace of Lono. Nākānelua added that most of the dishes, including the taro he grew (see figure 21 on page 179), had been prepared by hand rather than purchased at the store, where fresh ahi, or yellow-fin tuna, was considered a delicacy and was priced as such. He also constructed an explicit metaframe of re-membering by stating that what we were doing that night was what our ancestors had done two hundred years ago, and we were doing it again that day as modern Hawaiians on an ancient place.

Nākānelua then invoked a Christian metaphor and described our meal as the symbolic "last supper" for those who would metaphorically die on the fields of Pu'ukoholā in tomorrow's sham battle, which we had been training for over the last six months (see chapter 4). Unlike most other previous sham battles that involved the throwing and dodging of spears, this year's battle would be a spear and club fencing contest. Our men, armed with padded spears between seven and eight feet, were to face off against Kapu's guys, who would be wielding pairs of two- to three-foot-long clubs, also covered in padding (see figure 12 on page 113). The goal would be to strike the designated targets on the opponent's torso, arms, and legs, with a "kill" occurring when a vital organ such as the heart, kidney, liver, or stomach was hit. Because we would be using padded weapons, there would be no serious risk of death or major injury; however, given the history of the site as one consecrated in the death of warriors, and in light of the recognition that harm could be done in ways that were not merely physical, dangers did exist. Minor injuries like cuts, scrapes, bruises, sprains, and pulled muscles were entirely possible, even expected, especially given the likelihood of wayward strikes landing outside the strike zone on the face, head, and groin areas and the potential for mock battles becoming real ones if tempers flared. Yet it was precisely that tension that made it a real offering of courage, discipline, self-sacrifice, and strength that Nā Koa were meant to embody. This unity, the goal of Hoʻokuʻikahi, would be reflected in a haʻa (ritual dance) we would perform as a group after the battles had finished (see figure 9 on page 94). Thus tonight's ʻaikapu was also aimed at fostering good will, recognition, and identity as men and as koa. We ate, engaged in subdued, friendly conversation, and cleaned up so that we could each spend the rest of the night preparing.

ʻAHA HOʻOLAʻA ALIʻI, SANCTIFYING CHIEFS

Dressed in our malo and carrying our real, padded ihe, we joined the other groups gathered on the ceremonial grounds below Puʻukoholā heiau at about 6:00 a.m. (see figure 11). To our right stood Keʻeaumoku Kapu and his koa, men and women, as well as the Māori guests who joined them. To our left, sitting on mats, were the women of Maui, a hālau hula from Hawaiʻi Island, and Kanu o ka ʻĀina with their guests from the Indian reservations and Humboldt State. In front of the assembly and directly below the path leading up to the heiau stood a lele, a three-tiered wooden altar that would receive the physical offerings given by each respective organization. On a flat clearing to the side of the lele sat the female contingent of Nā Waʻa Lālani Kahuna, their male counterparts standing atop the heiau with John Lake and at the top of the pathway waiting to descend with the Alo Aliʻi. The purpose of the ceremony was to sanctify the chiefs, the human embodiments and connections to the gods, and thus their elevation both spatially and socially. Though both Nākānelua and Kapu were in fact given the titles of kaukau aliʻi (junior chiefs) and the capes and helmets that marked their status as such, the two chose to stay below on the flats. This was a statement of their desire to be seen as aliʻi who led by example and whose status was achieved (each had more members than any of the Alo Aliʻi) rather than aliʻi whose rank came through descent. This tension between the junior and senior chiefs reproduced some of the strains that came with performance as pageantry versus action and practice.

The small but growing crowd of spectators added to the tension. By about 7:00 a.m., between fifty and seventy-five onlookers had gathered around the outside of the sennit rope boundaries of the ceremonial space. This outside audience included locals from the Big Island, tourists from outside Hawaiʻi, and members of the participant groups who chose not to take part in the ceremonies. There was also a small group of photographers and filmmakers

FIGURE 11. The women of Nā Waʻa Lālani Kahuna (right) chant on the flats of Puʻukoholā, Hawaiʻi, 2002. Directly behind them stands the Hale Mua (holding spears), and to the left in the foreground is Nā Koa Kau i ka Meheu o nā Kūpuna. On the perimeter of the ceremonial space (background, from left to right, ascending) are onlookers, female participants from Nā Wāhine Kauhi a Kama and Nā Koa (under the makeshift shelter), teachers and students from the Kanu o ka ʻĀina Charter School, and members of a hālau hula. PHOTO BY TOM WHITNEY.

who had been following the activities throughout the weekend and who were situated on a small knoll off to the side. Some belonged to one or another of the constituent groups of Nā Papa Kanaka and were documenting the event for their own purposes; at my request, one was taping the event with a digital camera I had borrowed from my anthropology department. The well-known activist-documentary filmmaking duo Nā Maka o ka ʻĀina (Kauanui 1999a), whose footage of the 1991 ceremonies and the events leading up to it (including Kaʻai's talk at the University of Hawaiʻi) was featured in *Hoʻokuʻikahi: To Unify as One* (Meyer 1998), had been recording the events of the weekend and had their cameras set up.

The health workers from the NHHCS had set up a first aid tent outside the perimeter and were prepared to supply water over the next few hours as the ceremony took place. Indeed, one of the major disincentives for tourists and a challenge for participants was the heat of the Kawaihae sun during the event, which in some years caused the warriors, who might be standing for two to three hours with no shade and very little clothing, to become dehydrated and faint. The physical ordeal thus also served as a validation of the event for those who took part, especially given some of the charges of pageantry and specters of staged authenticity associated with performances of culture in public, nationalist, and touristic spaces, all of which were present in this site (Bruner 2005; Jolly 1992; MacCannell 1999). Self-inflicted discomfort and pain, with no monetary compensation, proved to be an important authenticator of experience. There was also, of course, the possibility of injury from other sources, at least for Nā Koa in the battle, and thus the presence of physicians was comforting.[5]

The ceremonies began around 7:15 a.m. with the sounding of the temple drums and the conch shell trumpet. The various groups gave offerings of chants, dances, and gifts that would make the mana of the gods, chiefs, land, and people grow. Ours was received with bated anticipation. It was not every year that Nā Koa battled, though such performances were always hoped for; in some years we performed haʻa incorporating the weapons we had carved, and in other years we engaged in wrestling contests. This year Nā Koa was to deliver, and the orators Kamanaʻopono Crabbe and Mele Pang presented chants to the gods and chiefs and speeches to the masses (in Hawaiian) that explained our offering of body, spirit, and courage through the sham battle.

Once all the warriors were in position, the battle began with the call from Crabbe: "Lele a hākākā (Fly into the fray)!" After a brief moment during which each combatant sized the other up, the men rushed at one another in a crash of bodies, wood, and duct-tape padding. The loose dirt that covered the ground exploded into the air and became the literal "brown cloud" of Nā Koa (see figure 12). The action was fast and intense, and an inordinate number of "supermen" kept fighting even after they were struck by a "death blow"; thus the preassigned referees, of which I was one, were kept quite busy breaking up and restarting individual duals. A second round featuring contests between the adolescents of our groups followed. When one of our boys took a blow that brought him to tears, our men circled around him and gave him support and encouragement, as did the entire assembly with their applause when they witnessed the act. The third and final round showcased the top eight fighters from each side squaring off one at a time. A hoʻopāpā, or verbal contest of wit and exchange of challenges, preceded each match, highlighting the intellectual and spiritual components of battle and warriorhood (recall Kapu's and Nākānelua's exchange at the Ritz-Carlton that I opened this chapter with).

When the final round was over, Nā Koa o ka Hale Mua retrieved the

FIGURE 12. The men of the Hale Mua and Nā Koa Kau i ka Meheu o nā Kūpuna face off in a sham battle, Puʻukoholā, Hawaiʻi, 2002. Participants take care to embrace and affirm friendships at the end of individual matches, as the two men at the far left of the frame are doing. Men of Nā Waʻa Lālani Kahuna (in background, above to the right) stand at the base of the lele (three-tiered altar) and watch the sham; women from the group are seated (to right, barely visible through dust cloud). This image was featured in the *Hana Hou!* magazine of Hawaiian Airlines.
PHOTO BY TOM WHITNEY.

carved spears we had brought with us, and we joined Nā Koa Kau i ka Meheu o Nā Kūpuna in the center of the field for our presentation of the haʻa (ritual dance) called the Mahaʻū (see figure 9 on page 94 and the description in chapter 4). Three women from Kapu's group beat gourd drums while Keʻeaumoku Kapu chanted the verses telling the story of the pig-god Kamapuaʻa. The weapons we had carved, blessed, and trained with over the past seven months danced on the heiau as we twirled them through the air and moved with them as a unit. When we finally finished, the assembly of Nā Papa Kanaka and the spectators applauded wildly. The Hoʻolaʻa Aliʻi ceremony then ended with the procession of participants back to the visitors' center.

ʻAWA MIHI / MAIKAʻI:
CEREMONY OF RECOGNITION AND RESPECT

Nā Koa seated themselves on pandanus leaf mats to partake in a ceremony we variously called ʻawa mihi or ʻawa maikaʻi. The ʻawa shared honored the combatants and provided them (individually and collectively) with a forum to apologize (mihi) for any actions that may have caused another harm during the battle and to reaffirm (or reconstruct) good (maikaʻi) will and relations among each other as koa. Kaʻai reminded those gathered that the "mihi" in Māori is also the term for a greeting, and so the men in this ceremony would be greeting each other to renew friendships. The combatants took turns serving each other ʻawa and exchanging honi and words that were needed to restore pono, balanced and correct moral being (see figure 13). The level to which any given year's ceremony took on the mood of celebration (maikaʻi) versus repentance (mihi) depended largely upon the nature of the sham, if indeed there was a sham. One year a mass fight nearly erupted when the battlers began using their fists as well as their spears in a close-quarters skirmish, and the ʻawa mihi afterward was quite dramatically aimed at reconciliation (hoʻokuʻikahi). This year, in part owing to the unification in dance following the sham, the men were in high spirits and the cups given were in mutual honor, appreciation, and, most important, respect.

Indeed an important goal for the displays of courage and warriorhood at Puʻukoholā each year was the earning and recognition of respect in the eyes of fellow koa and of all gathered at the ceremonies. In his study of inner-city Puerto Rican crack dealers in "El Barrio" ghettos of East Harlem in New York, Phillipe Bourgois (2003) argues that participation in the underground economy and performances of gendered violence need to be understood (though not justified) as strategies for survival and for earning respect as men living under American apartheid. Though most of the men of Nā Koa did not face nearly the same degree of radical economic and social marginalization described in Bourgois's account, the need to regain respect, including self-respect, as a people has been an important component of the remembering process. I would argue that while this certainly plays out quite differently across class lines, the need for respect, as Bourgois notes, is felt more by men. Having suffered American political occupation and subsequent racial, political-economic, and cultural transformations that characterize the colonized, displays of bravery and courage in the sham battle brought respect, honor, and mana to the lands, communities, and culture Nā Koa represented. For the warriors it was also a search for respect from others in the Hawaiian community who would recognize their status as real (Maoli) men and as leaders in the community. For both nationalist and personal

FIGURE 13. Kyle Nākānelua (left) and Keʻeaumoku Kapu (right) exchange breath in the honi after a sham battle, Puʻukoholā, Hawaiʻi, 2005. PHOTO BY SHANE TEGARDEN.

aims, Puʻukoholā became the proving grounds of cultural masculinities of Nā Koa representing Maui.

Women, too, demanded respect, and in many ways their struggles were more challenging in the context of increasingly masculinized spaces such as Nā Koa. Following the exchange of ʻawa between combatants, a bowl was given to one of the women who had played the gourd drums. She took it and spoke of how she had seen her children grow up at Puʻukoholā and how she hoped one day the women would have a chance to prove themselves on the battlefield since they also trained and wanted a chance. There was a noticeable effort on her part to suppress some deeply felt emotions in her voice and her face. No response was given and none was required, but it was an important and courageous statement, and it was recognized as such. It raised the question of how women's contributions were to be recognized in the now-masculinized spaces of warriorhood, one which in earlier times made some space for women (Desha 2000, 418; Kamakau 1992, 228; Poepoe 8/20/1906), even if it was perhaps more important for the men (Paglinawan et al. 2006, 62). Indeed, this was a memorable moment, for it gave voice to the tensions I argue are inherent in the project of re-membering and remaking masculinities, namely, that the project is a selective one that, in its selectivity, affords space to certain memories and little room for others. If our goal was to bring back balance and pono, we would do well not to lose sight of the other women, besides the wives we left at home, who provide it in such ritual spaces.

Apart from the individual and group projects Nā Koa pursued, their exhibitions of koa on the heiau aimed at recuperating respect for the Hawaiian people and nation in the eyes of the state, federal, and international communities. Thus the presence of photographers and camera crews was quite important and central to this process. Despite the fact that these technologies of representation invoked the crass commodification and cultural prostitution of the hula girl image in the selling of Hawai'i, these same gazes would provide an avenue for Nā Koa, and indeed for everyone gathered at Pu'ukoholā, to re-present their identities in the larger fields of discursive production. The presence of Nā Maka o ka 'Āina suggested that we might have roles in their upcoming documentary of resistance. At the same time, these optics were just as likely to reproduce warriorhood in the service of corporate global tourism. Case in point: the May/June 2003 edition of *Hana Hou,* the magazine of the Hawaiian Airlines carrier that flies both interisland and Hawai'i–U.S. routes, featured a cover story on the revival of lua entitled "Way of the Warrior" (Sodetani 2003). The article contained pictures of Nā Koa from the 1991 Ho'oku'ikahi and images from the sham battle that we, sitting there drinking our 'awa, had no idea would make for in-flight entertainment (see figure 12 on page 113). Then again, perhaps that was one of the prayers lifted up on the heiau; maybe there were multiple, even competing prayers.

PU'UKOHOLĀ CULTURAL FESTIVAL

After the 'awa, we all got into the vans and drove down to Pelekane, the site of a former residence of King Kamehameha and of the modern day Pu'ukoholā Cultural Festival put on by the park and the Waimea Hawaiian Civic Club. Though held in conjunction with the ceremonies, the festival was a separate event. Indeed, the initial tensions I laid out in the last chapter over *not* wanting to be a pageant continued to arise as the older event sponsored by the civic club and the park proceeded as it always had. The organizers of the cultural festival wanted our ceremony to start later in the morning so that more visitors would come, but Nā Papa Kanaka resisted and thus started it early; this decision was based on both a conscious desire to distance our activities from touristic modes of performance and a more practical concern with the heat of the midmorning sun.

Yet the connection between the two activities persisted, especially since many of the organizers were involved in the planning of both the heiau ceremonies and the festival. We walked around and visited the free workshops in carving wooden drums, playing gourd instruments, and sailing on a double-hulled canoe. Some vendors sold books, T-shirts, and jewelry. Other groups offered samples of Hawaiian foods and 'awa. Not surprisingly, we ended up in the two lines of people waiting to try the samples. The civic club prepared a free lunch of stew and rice, and we all had a plate. Some of the men stayed and took part in the workshops and waited to go sailing on the canoe. I was quite drained at that point and so walked back to the pavilion with some of the others who were ready to go.

CLOSING

All parties reassembled at the visitors' center lawn at 4:00 p.m, for the International 'Awa Ceremony, which would honor guests and bring the weekend to an end. John Lake began chanting and entered with Nā Wa'a Lālani Kahuna. They were followed by the other contingents of Nā Koa, the Alo Ali'i, Nā Wāhine, Kanu o ka 'Āina, and the special guests. In previous years, members of the Royal Order of Kamehameha, representatives of the park, officials from the army, and others also joined us at night.

The Hale Mua was in charge of the ceremony, and Crabbe offered chants for the drinking of 'awa and the health of all the people gathered there. With that we proceeded to serve those present, acknowledging the lesser chiefs, the malihini, the 'Elemākua, the Kāhuna, and finally Papa 'Ākau, who was esteemed above all others. When he finished, he placed his cup on the ground and signaled the end of the kapu.

When the ceremony was completed, people began lining up for the feast of roasted pig, fried and raw fish, sweet potatoes, poi, and other delicacies prepared for us by the park staff, local families, and the civic club. Having been freed of kapu and restriction, the 'awa was served in a social manner to anyone who requested a cup with a clap of their hands. Nākānelua asked Puka Ho for his neʻe (pointed fighting staff) and proceeded to perform a dance that honored the weapon; in the process, he stripped off his pāʻū so that he was only in malo, and the women of the assembly showed their appreciation with enthusiastic applause and cheering. Kapu's men and women stood up next to present their haʻa about Paiʻea, the hard-shelled crab that was also the nickname of Kamehameha. Afterward, Lake's dancers and singers, perhaps encouraged by all the clapping already taking place, stood up and gave lively performances. One dance was a mele maʻi, a song praising the genitals, for the men who had been seen and admired by Lake's women (from what I gathered from the words of the song, I assumed it was in reference to the year [1996 or 1997] when all the men did a hiʻuwai in broad daylight and, as Nākānelua described it to me with a bouncing index finger, "was all ding-dings comin" as the women watched from Mailekini). The night went on for awhile in that fashion, and eventually all made their way back to the camps.

<h2>PĀʻINA</h2>

Back at the pavilion, people were buzzing with excitement as the final kapu on alcohol had been lifted and we could now purchase the modern-day ʻawa, beer. The reentry into normal social life had begun. The beer runners took up collections and went to the local convenience store in Kawaihae. Some mixed the ʻawa that we had saved for the late-night activities. We relocated two tables outside (the kapu on women inside the pavilion still held), and Rick Bissen had a ʻukulele in hand and began singing some Hawaiian and classic rock. People who were partying at other campsites soon arrived at ours. I made my way to a site where a young woman was dancing a hula; she was a worker from the NHHCS who was also the niece of one of our Mua men. I eventually made my way back to another table where a few of us passed the hours contemplating the memories we had of our time at the heiau. Ten o'clock eventually became four, and soon I was falling asleep to the sound of the last few singers left.

<h2>DEPARTURES</h2>

After we finished cleaning up the pavilion on Sunday morning, just a few hours after some of us had fallen asleep, Nākānelua called us all together for one last meeting before we went our separate ways; he asked if anyone wanted to share their thoughts with the group.[6] One of the first-timers expressed his realization that now he had a responsibility to share his experience with his children, family, and friends in order to "water the seed" that had been planted. Martin Martinson, an old-timer, regretted that he had not brought anyone new into the group this year, though he was always recruiting. He said the camaraderie he felt at Puʻukoholā was something he had experienced only in the military, and he wished everyone the best of speed in their journeys. Glenn "Puhi" Gibson, a Māori man who had just joined our group (which, in part, led Nākānelua to revise the Hawaiians-only rule for membership), thanked everyone for allowing him "to be a part of this ʻohana [family]." He vowed to take it back to his own ʻohana and teach his young boy who had just entered the Hawaiian language immersion program. Greg Nee, who along with Roger Marble had come from Oregon, said that despite his earlier apprehensions about staying with a group of men he didn't know, the hospitality and welcome he felt convinced him to take our "water" back to Oregon. He noted that as he spoke, he got "chicken-skin" and revealed that he had felt like this only when he stood with his ʻohana, and although he had been coming back to Hawaiʻi for twenty-five years, this was the first time he felt like he came home. Following Nee, Marble expressed his admiration for what we were doing and promised that the two of them would "do *everything*, and then some, to not only spread the word, but make it back here." Kamika Nākānelua, Kyle's cousin, asked that we remember those in the group who could not make it this year.

Kyle Nākānelua ended by recalling his experiences in the military and in the fire department where he was part of a team that relied on one another in life and death situations. Bringing it back to the Hale Mua, he had this to say:

As far as teams go, I've nevah *been* on a better team befoah. As far as cohesiveness, discipline, strength; I've nevah been wit' a more *diversified* team, or *powerful* team than this. This is the *Hale,* the *Hale Mua.* The Hale Mua is not just a building; it is a concept, an ideal. The Hale Mua is *here* [extending his arms out to point to all of us]. The Hale Mua is *here* [touching his head with two hands]. The Hale Mua is *here* [touching his stomach with two hands]. So, you can all remembah dat no matter where you *go,* no matter *when* you can come back, and *when* we can all be togedah again, just remembah: you always have a place in da Hale Mua.

FIGURE 14. Hale Mua at the Kona International Airport, Hawai'i, 1999. Most men are wearing the Hale Mua shirt, emblazoned with group's logo of the Hoaka (crescent moon) on the right breast. AUTHOR'S PHOTO.

I include the above section at length because it exemplifies the major themes I will return to in chapter 5, namely, the ways in which the Mua, by providing a safe environment, creates a context for the verbalization of emotions and thoughts and telling of life stories. It also shows something of the social demography of the men who arrive in the Hale Mua, often routed through the military and/or the diaspora. It also lays out the emotional interpretation of what the Hale Mua is, at least for its leader, and where it can be located.

With that said we all exchanged honi one last time and said our goodbyes and departed for Kona town. Before returning the vans, we refueled at a local gas station. Upon entering the convenience store to pay the cashier and pick up snacks, we spotted on the front page of the *West Hawai'i Today* a picture of our own Walter Kanamu battling one of Kapu's men. The title above it read "Reliving history at the heiau." Animated by a tangible confirmation of historical and discursive agency, or perhaps emotionally manipulated by commodity images, the men bought almost every last paper on the newsstand. We then made it back to the airport, caught our afternoon flights home, and returned to slip back into our "regular" lives to burn up on reentry (see figure 14).

Postscript: Puʻukoholā as a Contact Zone

I have argued that Puʻukoholā, as a borderzone, enables a ritual slippage of identities and a proving grounds for cultural warriorhood, even as it is susceptible to the processes of touristic appropriation against which it defines "realness." The renewal and remaking of a Maoli subjectivity is the most significant aspect that has fed into the formation of the Hale Mua, which I trace in the next chapter.

Puʻukoholā may also be seen as a type of "contact zone," which Pratt defines as a "space of colonial encounters, the space in which peoples geographically and historically separated come into contact with each other and establish ongoing relations, usually involving conditions of coercion, radical inequality, and intractable conflict" (Pratt 1992, 6–7). Clifford usefully applies this framework to understand Native peoples' struggles over representation in museums, where they find themselves "caught up in shifting power relations and competing articulations of local and global meanings" (1997, 144).

Competing visions of how to represent, maintain, and redefine the site have recently led to some controversy. In 2001, the park announced plans to build a new visitors' center below and to the side of the heiau; in 2006, construction was complete, much to the dismay of Nā Koa leaders, who saw it as a further "museumification" of the site. A much more contentious issue arose in 2003, when one of the senior aliʻi suggested that neighboring lands owned by the Queen Emma Foundation be used to create a sort of cultural and educational center that would house cultural artifacts. In particular, he sought to store a set of objects taken from a burial cave (aka Forbes Cave) in Kawaihae and sold to the Bishop Museum in Honolulu in 1905; following the passage of the Native American Graves Protection and Repatriation Act (NAGPRA) in 1990, the objects had become subject to return to Hawaiian claimants. This particular case had become extremely divisive within the ʻŌiwi community, in large part because of the history of dispossession and loss that fueled an objectification and salvage mentality with regard to all things Hawaiian.[7] By 2006, the discussion had morphed into one of establishing a "cultural village" where visitors could come year-round to engage in dialogue and commerce with Hawaiian artisans and cultural experts. More important, it was also suggested that many of the activities currently being carried out around the heiau, including the camping, workshops, 'awa ceremonies, and closing dinner, could be relocated to the site. Again, Nākānelua and Kapu opposed the move, which was seen as further alienating the participants from the heiau. Such dynamics highlight the contradictions that arise when a historic memorial site seeks to avoid becoming a theme park, yet must also attract visitors to maintain its economic viability; such issues emerged prominently at Pearl Harbor, also a National Historic Site (White 2001).

On October 15, 2006, two massive earthquakes of magnitudes 6.7 and 6.0 off the Kohala coast of Hawai'i rocked the islands, causing no deaths but leaving many without electric power that night and into the next day. As Kawaihae was the town closest to the epicenters, Pu'ukoholā and Mailekini heiau sustained massive structural damage. This inevitably led Hawaiians to seek out the spiritual causes of the catastrophe. Some thought it was a sign that the religious ceremonies needed to stop, as they were waking malevolent gods (see Web comment on Lucas 2006a). Others have told me that it was a result of the removal of the Forbes Cave burial objects, while still others saw it as a sign of disapproval of the recently opened visitors' center. Perhaps it was nothing more than bad luck.

As of this writing (January 2007), discussions on whether and how to rebuild the fallen walls were under way. The heiau had been partially restored once already in the 1970s, though to a lesser extent than would be required for the upcoming task. Already talk has been contentious as different parties have expressed different ideas about how best to proceed. These tensions are likely to intensify as aid from the federal government will bring in a whole new set of dynamics. There has been no word yet as to how or if future ceremonies will be conducted there; if the walls are not stabilized, the park will not allow people on it. Uncertainty marks the present moment.

Sam Ka'ai interprets this as a wake-up call and a new test of leadership. Those who could gather the men to do the work would display the mana of true ali'i. This in fact was one function of monumental heiau structures in the precolonial era; they symbolized not only the ritual authority of the chief, but also his ability to organize the labor and resources to construct them. Measuring 224 feet by 100 feet with 16- to 20-foot-high walls, Pu'ukoholā was one of the most labor-intensive undertakings by any chief of any time; thousands of men formed a human chain some twenty miles long to pass stones from the far-off Pololū Valley (Lucas 2006a; www.nps.gov/puhe/faqs.htm). It should be recalled that Kamehameha's was also a project of rebuilding and reconsecrating the heiau on its old foundation (see chapter 2). Perhaps there would be an opportunity for a new era of chiefs and people to step forward and literally pick up the stones of industry and nation and rebuild the temple of state. It will require many hands, though, including those of women and children. This may be the time we find out just how "real" the prospect of hoʻokuʻikahi — to unify as one — actually is.

KĀ I MUA—CAST INTO
THE MEN'S HOUSE

....

When Nā Koa becomes Hale Mua, warriorhood is transformed into a project for creating a space for men to explore what it means to be a Hawaiian man today. Material culture production, ritual space making, and physical training become modes of remaking masculinity and identity that are
framed by a metapragmatics of "learning/doing the things that Hawaiian
men should be learning/doing" (Boggs 1985; Briggs 1986). In this chapter I
provide an overview of the development of the Hale Mua and its use of the
discursive practices of carving, ritual, and training to address the ambivalences men bring with them to the group, ambivalences about cultural identity, status differentials, violence, and gender politics. The chapter also incor-
porates life stories and moʻolelo to highlight the ways in which the self
interfaces with the social in the context of "pushing men forward." In that
vein, I end with a dialogue on Kū and Hina that seeks to critically examine
our gender practice and that of the lāhui.

Warriorhood Reborn: The Courageous Ones and Fighting Arts

The assembly of Nā Koa at Puʻukoholā in 1991 signaled the beginning of
what today might be called a warrior movement that came out of two related
though separate developments: Puʻukoholā and the revival of the Hawaiian
fighting art lua in 1993. Though separate, these two strands of cultural revitalization frequently overlapped, so that many of the members of Nā Koa
were also involved in the pā lua (fighting arts schools).

While Nā Koa began as the original group of forty Hawaiʻi Island warriors, Sam Kaʻai had intended that each island would develop its own group

and that each would attend the ceremonies annually. Eventually Nā Koa groups were established on Oʻahu (by Keʻeaumoku Kapu) and Maui (by Kyle Nākānelua). Nākānelua first attended the ceremonies in 1991 as one of Kaʻai's helpers, primarily to assist with the ʻawa ceremony. He was inspired by the courage exhibited by the men, who overcame their bodily and cultural inhibitions and wore a malo, "because at dat time, Hawaiian men nevah *wear* malo" (Nākānelua 1999). He also recalled, "It was the first time that I knew of that Hawaiian males got togedda, othah than hula, at a cultural level. If there was one, I was unaware of it" (Nākānelua 2002b). His awareness of "masculine forms" of Hawaiian culture, including the concept of the hale mua, grew as he spoke with the prominent Hawaiian men present at the event, including Sam Kaʻai, John Lake, Hale Makua, Parley Kanakaʻole, and Keone Nunes. Upon his return to Maui, he continued meeting with Kaʻai and the others who assisted him, and they returned to Puʻukoholā in 1992 and conducted the ʻawa ceremony at the 1993 ʻOnipaʻa event (see figure 6 on page 63).

Nākānelua, a charismatic leader, soon attracted a number of followers, who were drawn to him because he embodied someone with great mana (prestige, spiritual power), personality, and vision of a more fulfilling way of being Hawaiian. A number of men from the aging Royal Order of Kamehameha, looking to recruit younger members and renew the organization, also filled the ranks of Nā Koa. Public awareness of their activities grew as they came to participate in Hawaiian cultural events on Maui (frequently aired on the local cable access channel) such as the Celebration of the Arts at the Ritz-Carlton Kapalua and the East Maui Taro festival, and the greeting of the *Hōkūleʻa* in Kahului Harbor (see figure 15, figure 17 on page 137, and figure 18 on page 148).

The main activity of Nā Koa continued to be attendance at Puʻukoholā, and in 1997 Nākānelua took a group of nearly twenty members, including two women, to stand as Nā Koa of Maui. That year Nā Papa Kanaka, the governing body of Puʻukoholā, bestowed on him the title of junior chief (kaukau aliʻi); Keʻeaumoku Kapu, who had also drawn a sizeable following of men and some women on Oʻahu, received his title at the same time. Nā Papa Kanaka also assigned to each an orator, or talking chief; Kamanaʻopono Crabbe (see the introduction) went with Nākānelua, and Mele Pang went with Kapu. The rise of these two leaders and their Nā Koa groups filled the

FIGURE 15. Nā Koa o Maui carrying feather standards and spears as they prepare to welcome the *Hōkūleʻa* in Kahului Harbor, Maui, 1997. PHOTO BY MASAKO CORDRAY.

void left by the original Nā Koa o Puʻukoholā, who by 1995, after being censured for breaking protocols, had dissociated from the heiau.

One of the primary reasons Nākānelua and Kapu grew was their advancement as students in the pā lua. In 1993, The Native Hawaiian Culture and Arts Program (NHCAP), funded through the NPS and housed at the Bishop Museum, sponsored a series of workshops and seminars on lua that were given by four of the few living experts in the art form (Paglinawan et al. 2006). This first school was called Pākuʻialua, and it offered classes to both men and women. Like Nā Koa, the pā lua appealed strongly to men, though a number of women, including Nākānelua's sister Debbie, a former Miss Hawaiʻi, also joined. Billy Richards, Debbie's husband and a former Marine and Vietnam veteran, recalled that when he took up lua in 1994, it presented "that missing piece of the puzzle" he felt when the Māori ritually challenged him and his crew on the *Hōkūleʻa*. He remembered, "In New Zealand, 300 came out and did *haka*. . . . But we couldn't respond as warriors because we didn't know how, so we would send hula dancers out instead. And they would always ask, 'Where are your men?'" (Sodetani 2003). As I noted in chapter 2, a similar challenge from the Māori played a role in prompting Kaʻai and Lake to fashion the Puʻukoholā ceremonies in the way they did.

In 1996, two of the original four lua masters formed a new school called Pāku'iaholo, and both Nākānelua and Kapu followed them. While most of the members of both Nā Koa groups were also in the pā lua, the organizations were separate and distinct. Most people outside of the groups could not tell the difference though and would refer to Nā Koa as "the lua guys." By 1997, this slippage created tensions that eventually erupted into conflict, and both Kapu and Nākānelua left the pā lua. Generally speaking, the blurring of boundaries between pā lua and Nā Koa led to disputes over the appropriate and inappropriate use and dissemination of the knowledge being shared in the pā lua.[1] The result was that Nākānelua and Kapu were, from that point, on their own.

From Nā Koa to Hale Mua: (Re)creating a House for Men

At the time of the split, Nākānelua had one woman member in his group.[2] When forced to chose between the pā lua and Nā Koa, she, unlike the men on Maui, did not follow Nākānelua. This is the point at which the group became all male, and it is frequently narrated as "it just happened like that." The story usually goes, "We started out as a few guys who got together, we went to Pu'ukoholā, we got involved with the pā lua, and after the split we became the Hale Mua." Rarely is the woman's departure, which created an all-male space, raised as a significant, or at least enabling, factor contributing to the shift. This partial erasure suggests that the intent of the group was always to create a space for men. Indeed, Crabbe and Nākānelua had already been talking about making a Hale Mua at the time. It is likely that the woman sensed the direction that Nā Koa was going, and perhaps her alienation as the lone woman was what prompted her to not follow Nākānelua. This is not to say that there was an unspoken disdain for her presence; all of the men who knew her spoke very highly and affectionately of her and acknowledged her presence in and contributions to Nā Koa while she was a member.

Nākānelua did admit that after the group became all-male, things just "took off." Physically, they were able to train harder, as most of them would not go full speed when they were practicing lua, wrestling, or spear dodging with the woman. This partly reflects a belief that men are physically more powerful than women, a common though not always accurate assumption. The men measured their prowess in performance against other men; to beat a woman meant little, and to lose to a woman was a mark of shame. Nākā-nelua also explained that in one sham battle at Puʻukoholā, a man threw a spear straight in her face and the whole crowd gasped. That reaction made him feel like they were being villainized for hurting her, which raised the specter of gender violence so frequently attributed to Hawaiian men. Thus it was understood as a lose-lose situation when a man was forced to go up against a woman, and this was one reason that they would later refuse to fight the women from Kapu's group in the sham battles (see chapter 3). Thus Nākānelua explained that when the group came to be all men after the split, the "real" training could take place. Despite the fact that women could theoretically occupy a warrior identity in Nā Koa, in practice hegemonic gender assumptions of masculine warriorhood prevailed.

Kā i Mua: Cast Forward/Into the Men's House

At this point, Nākānelua and the other men regrouped to figure out their next step. Kaʻai recalls that when they conferred with him, he told them, "Be Maoli. . . . The Hawaiians had a house, the hale mua. Basically the word means 'to go forward.' You suffah da pain, and now we mad. . . . Let's pound each addah until we meld togethah like poi. . . . That means, whatever you are, you must transform by being meld into one. And what it's done fo'? To go *forward*" (Kaʻai 1999a). In part, the notion of developing an institution for unifying and moving forward came out of Kaʻai's experiences in Aotearoa / New Zealand, where he witnessed the power of the marae (ceremonial gathering space) in creating belonging and identity (see chapter 5 and the conclusion). Though this influence was present, it was not primary. Rather, the restoration of a Hale Mua was the means for addressing not only the immediate displacement created by the split, but also the historic loss of men's status associated with the end of the ʻaikapu.

As I discussed in chapter 1, the hale mua of the ʻaikapu period functioned as the men's eating house, the domestic temple where the ancestors were worshiped and fed. Young boys were initiated in a ceremony called kā i mua, which means "cast into the men's house" or "thrust forward," and given their first malo. The hale mua then became a space in which boys were socialized and learned the skills and stories of fishing, farming, cooking, canoe and house building, fighting, sailing, lovemaking, fathering, and providing for the family. Those taking a functionalist approach to culture and society argue

FIGURE 16. Hale Mua o Maui on lawn of the visitors' center of the park at Puʻukoholā, Hawaiʻi, 1999. AUTHOR'S PHOTO.

that when the kapu system and the hale mua ended, men lost their way and have remained adrift in society ever since (Nunes and Whitney 1994; Paglinawan et al. 2006, 62–63; Pukui et al. 1972, 2:230). As mentioned before, this notion is problematic and works to perpetuate a colonial discourse of emasculation — ineffectual or absent men. I do see the loss of the hale mua as contributing to the social decay that has been visited upon Hawaiian men, but I do not see it as the sole source, nor do I feel all Hawaiian men were equally affected. With that said, the hale mua can metaphorically serve as a useful model for action and transformation by providing an idealized space for the performance of embodied and discursive practices associated with feeding, praying, and rearing.

Crabbe was one of the few people who had both researched and implemented the hale mua model in a modern setting. As I noted above, he had been talking to Nākānelua about the idea even before the split with the pā lua had occurred. As a part of his doctoral degree coursework in psychology, Crabbe developed a hale mua "as an alternative form of treatment for adult Hawaiian males suffering substance abuse and family violence problems" who were clients at a mental health clinic in Waiʻanae, Oʻahu (Crabbe 1997, 2). Reflecting on the characteristics he observed, Crabbe noted that the men he worked with "were very displaced in society. They were searching for . . .

their responsibility. I dunno if searching, but just not knowing" (Crabbe 1999). Crabbe associated what he saw as a lack of self-knowledge with the loss of traditional cultural practices and institutions (see Kaholokula 2007). He developed a program that focused on Hawaiian concepts of healing and understanding that ended in a retreat to the island of Kahoʻolawe where a kā i mua ceremony was held. He found that many of the men expressed feelings of newfound pride in their Hawaiian ancestry and emotional communion, especially through their participation in cultural activities, large group discussions, and connection with sacred places and spaces.

Although each man had a powerfully moving experience on Kahoʻolawe, the return to Waiʻanae proved challenging for some, who, back in their old environs, returned to drinking and violence. Though one may question the framework of certain mental health approaches to therapy, which assumes a problem to be treated, the salience of what Crabbe identified as anxiety due to "personal transition and life adjustment" (1997, 12) speaks to the fraught subjectivity of the men whose experiences of marginalization were products of the larger structural transformations of modernity and occupation (see chapter 1). These tensions remain as challenges for the pragmatic implementation of the hale mua model, but the recognition of such issues, as well as the comparatively privileged positions of most of the men in the Maui group, motivated Nākānelua, Crabbe, and Kaʻai to "go forward" with their own transition from Nā Koa to the Hale Mua.

The basic aim of the Hale Mua was to establish a cultural foundation for Hawaiian men by creating a space for learning and practicing culture, engaging in the ritual process of self-transformation, and establishing networks among the men. The general premise of the group was that colonization and modernity had led to a loss of Hawaiian life and culture, especially for the men. By reestablishing a Hale Mua, men would gain a deeper understanding of their history and acquire the skills, knowledge, and courage to be more effective as members and leaders in their families and communities.

The Architecture of the Hale Mua

As the men's eating and feeding house, the group would provide physical, psychological, and spiritual nourishment for those who were cast into it. Nākānelua developed a physical regime that relied largely on the practices developed as Nā Koa — exercise, dance, and martial arts. Kaʻai led workshops in which he trained men in the techniques and philosophies, modern and ancient, associated with the production of material culture. Crabbe took charge of training men in chants, prayers, and ʻŌiwi philosophies of spirituality. Under Nākānelua, the more senior and experienced members led subgroups called lima (literally "five" or "hand"); the first such leaders included Cliff Alakai, Kyle "Elama" Farm, Keoki Kiʻili, and Kealiʻi Solomon.

Yet even this structure was quite loose, and in practice most relations were very egalitarian and tended to avoid hierarchy. In fact, one of the ways in which the Hale Mua defined itself was in opposition to the more rigidly structured and hierarchical organizations of the hālau hula (dance academies) and the university classroom. Both Nākānelua and Kaʻai rejected the label of "kumu" (source) or "teacher," and instead saw their roles as facilitators of knowledge production who created contexts in which "innate" and "intuitive" knowledge could emerge through ritual, woodcarving, exercise, sparring, dance, and chant. Their other goal was to facilitate networks among the men, who would then be able to help one another in their various endeavors. This was just one of many ways, as I will discuss below, that the Mua has developed an identity in contradistinction to the hālau — not the least of which was also along the lines of masculine versus feminine.

The yearly activities of the Hale Mua were to correspond with the Hawaiian ritual calendar. The first eight months of the year (approximately February–September) were devoted to the activities of Kū, god of work, industry, farming, fishing, temple worship, and political maneuvering, including war. The remaining four months (approximately October–January) celebrated Lono, god of fertility and peace, through the Makahiki harvest festivals; all work ceased, and the people engaged in sport, games, hula, relaxation, and the giving of offerings.[3]

Following this pattern, the Hale Mua's activities on Maui coincide with the season of Kū. The majority of the discussion that follows covers the season of 2002, during which I was systematically recording on digital video and audio and in a journal the group's activities, which included a weapons crafting workshop in February, the Wehe Kū ceremony in March, once-a-week training between April and August, Puʻukoholā in August (see chapter 3), and the Pani (closing ceremony) in September. That year members of the Mua also participated in the Celebration of the Arts at the Ritz-Carlton, worked with the graduating boys from the Hawaiian language immersion program at King Kekaulike High School, and held an 'awa ceremony for a visiting martial arts master from Japan, who gave the group a sword.

The active membership that year fluctuated between twenty-five and thirty-five in any given week, the numbers increasing at the special ceremonies and events. Most of the men were middle class, though there were a few working- and lower-middle-class men as well; most came from a working-class family and were thus upwardly mobile. The median age was in the midforties, though there was fair representation of different age groups between thirty and sixty. All were heterosexual, or at least claimed to be when I asked (I did not ask everyone). Though the men held a wide range of occupations, just over half were government salaried workers. This percentage is quite a bit higher than that reported in the 2000 Census for Hawaiians statewide (21.7 percent) and in Maui County (17.9 percent), though it strongly resembled the pattern of Hawaiian male employment during the Territorial years (McGregor 2007, 44; OHA 2006, 145, 149). Government jobs included county work in wastewater plants, horticulture division, and public pools; state employment in the fire department, police force, and prosecutor's office; and federal jobs in the military and air traffic control. Private sector workers included professionals in the fields of medicine and business and blue-collar workers in construction and utilities. Most were married or divorced and had children (a very few had grandchildren); at the time, three younger boys (ages eight, nine, and thirteen) were participating with their fathers or uncles. The majority of the men in the group could claim at least one ethnicity in addition to Hawaiian; most could claim two or three.

Though the Mua was primarily a group for men of Kanaka Maoli ancestry, Nākānelua began to open it to men who had Hawaiian children, who were indigenous Polynesians of other island nations, or who had connections to an indigenous heritage from elsewhere. Though few in number, these individuals included a middle-aged Māori man and his young son, who was attending the Hawaiian language immersion elementary school, and a man in his early thirties who was seeking to reconnect with his Mayan heritage, indicating that pancultural innovations are also possible. Most of the men felt a dual sense of alienation, from Hawaiian culture because of their Americanization and class status and from American culture because of their Hawaiian ethnic background and upbringing. A desire to find one's place was a common theme running through the discussions, as many of them had experiences of travel and mobility.

The Hale Mua provided and continues to provide its members with a ritual space that allows them to embody and perform those ʻŌiwi traditions and practices that give them a deeper sense of identity as Hawaiian men who must live and work in the Western world—even if it is one they seek to transform—outside of the sanctuary of the Hale Mua. Beyond its function as a house of cultural learning and transformation, the Hale Mua creates a space for socializing, bonding, hanging out, and "talking story," a communicative event that involves the sharing of stories, feelings, and experience in a relaxed manner (see chapter 5). Friendships established in the Hale Mua extend beyond the weekly meetings, workshops, and rituals as men drink ʻawa or beer at each others' homes or at the bar, go surfing, fishing, or canoe paddling together, or otherwise follow more familiar (that is, modern Hawaiian) cultural patterns of relating as Hawaiian men. The occurrence of these other sorts of relationships and activities help to normalize and affirm the realness of the less familiar cultural projects like wearing malo and dancing with a spear, which are aimed at reforming an ʻŌiwi subjectivity. Anxieties of status, education, and violence underlay men's motives for transformation and were worked out through bodily practices. To illustrate this ethnographically, I will describe and analyze the three major areas of discursive and embodied action in Hale Mua: production of material culture, ritual invocations of Kū, and training of the body, mind, and spirit.

Hana Kālai: Shaping Identity, Making Your World

Nākānelua and Kaʻai often framed the activities of the Mua within a meta-pragmatics of enacting Hawaiian identity and masculinity. In the case of carving, they constantly reiterated that we were not only making a weapon but also perpetuating Hawaiian culture and carrying on the knowledge of our kūpuna. Thus the importance lay not in what shape the wood ended up taking but rather in the fact that we went through the process and in so doing made our own mana. Another important lesson constantly reiterated in these workshops and in the process was that being real or Maoli was about understanding the function as well as the symbolism of the objects created and distinguishing these products of cultural learning and teaching from the more readily available, familiar commodity forms of Hawaiian art that circulate locally and globally.

In February 2002, the Hale Mua held weekend workshops in which the men crafted twenty ihe, spears eight to nine feet in length, and six neʻe,[4] pointed fighting staffs five to six feet in length, out of ʻōhiʻa wood purchased from a Hilo lumber company. The workshops began at 8:00 a.m. in Pukalani at the houses of Cliff Alakai and Sam Kaʻai, both of whom had fully equipped workspaces complete with power and hand tools of various types. Crabbe chanted pule to the various manifestations of Kū that preside over the upland forests and carving. Nākānelua and some of the other leaders explained that these weapons and the wood we were working with were the body forms of Kū and that when we carved and used these weapons we would at once be invoking that mana and adding our own to it. The men paired off so that they could work together on the production of each other's pieces and at the same time learn from one another's achievements and mistakes. Those who were more experienced in woodworking and crafting guided the less experienced ones, who had either never used an electric bandsaw or never seen an ihe. Nākānelua and the other leaders provided lunch, and others also brought food and drink to add to the table. After pule, eating, and talk-story, everyone returned to work, and the workshops ended at four or five in the afternoon.

It is in the workshops that the men received the "pedagogy of Kaʻai." Kaʻai repeatedly told us that we should make three spears first, and then on the fourth we would know how. However, since time, money, and materials were limited, one would have to do. He actively defined the context of our activities as one of passing on men's knowledge by sharing stories of how he learned carving from his uncles in Kaupō. Over the course of many years he first watched, then fetched and carried materials, learned to sharpen and tie the adze, and finally began to carve the wood. "You guys are *jumping* way ahead of da game," he told us. "We got shorter period to *teach.*" He reminded us that our material culture would die unless we gave it life, and to do that we needed to make and use it, not purchase it and steal someone else's mana. We marveled at his uncle's stone and metal adzes, which he showed us, and awkwardly fumbled with his various mallets and chisels when there were not enough power grinders to go around. He made us feel the wood with our hand and trained us to identify the dips and ridges that needed to be transformed. When our inexperience threatened to do more damage than good to the wood, he barked and yelled at us sharply; just as quickly, he took the misused power tools from our hands and in a few quick strokes corrected the mistakes.

At the end of each workday, we cleaned up Kaʻaiʻs shop and sat down outside to talk story. Those who had worked with him over the years understood that he was one of the few individuals alive who had learned the craft from the old-timers in a traditional manner as passed on in the family, and thus to be in his workshop and listen to his stories, which he was equally renowned for, was a privilege. Topics of conversation ranged from what we experienced and learned in the workshop to the politics of the day to the latest goings-on in each personʻs life. Just as he carved wooden logs into implements imbued with the mana of the gods, so too did Kaʻai craft moʻolelo about the Hawaiian people, culture, and history from the fragments of his own life experiences and the pieces of our own that were shared in the circle. At a 1999 papa kuʻi ʻai (poi pounding board) workshop I recorded, he explained that when they were first getting started in the early nineties, one of the men wanted a spear to hang behind his desk. Kaʻai replied,

"Thatʻs not da right question, so I not goinʻ address da subject. . . . I will not teach you to steal your mana. Desire is talking the talk. Gettin da tools ready, datʻs walking da talk. Sometime along da line we goin know your skill level, letʻs walk da walk." Datʻs what Puʻukoholā about. The idea is dat, Hawaiians should not be fighting over heirlooms dat "so-and-so took to da mainland" and "aunty so-and-so get, [so] our side of da family no moʻ [taro] poundah"—dat should stop. The original Hawaiian *made his own world*. . . . And so itʻs part of also owning da material culture. You gonna walk around and say "Nā Koa" you bettah know how to use a spear!
And we reach dat point, so dis is da thing—to honor Hāloa. And why should we honor Hāloa? For da Christians, Jesus Christ gave his life to save da earth. Hāloa gave his life to bring hā to da world—oxygen, breath. They needed it, they made it, it becomes part of da culture, you possess all da knowledge, you tell da story— itʻs gonna be slightly different from my story, and datʻs okay. Thatʻs what produce da culture, when there are fifty-four versions and eighty percent sounds like da same. Then weʻre a people, we own da material culture (Kaʻai 1999b).

Kaʻaiʻs narrative points to a number of important themes that are reproduced in the Hale Mua, oftentimes inexplicitly. They have to do with the juxtaposition and elevation of traditional Hawaiian modes of belonging, behaving, acting, relating, and understanding and those produced in the modern, capitalist, Christian, American order. A number of the men want a

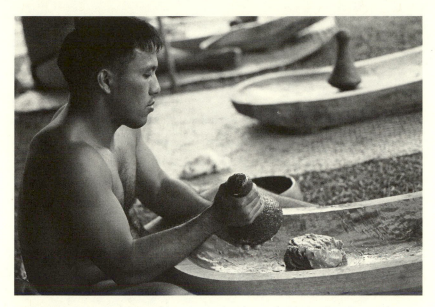

FIGURE 17. Author learns to pound taro into poi on the papa kuʻi ʻai (poi board) using the pōhaku kuʻi ʻai (stone poi pounder) at the East Maui Taro Festival, Hāna, Maui, 2000. PHOTO BY MASAKO CORDRAY.

spear because it offers them a chance to possess the ultimate symbol of Hawaiian identity and masculinity, one that is a particularly difficult commodity to come by. Kaʻai rejects the very basis of such an idea and posits instead the notion that it is only real when one produces it through work and gives it life by learning to use it. Moreover, the embodied practices of carving and storytelling work recursively to create meaning and identity.

The poi board (figure 17), and indeed all material culture, produces the life and hā (breath) of the culture and the people when it is used; thus it physically manifests the prayer of Hāloa, the taro that sprang from the stillborn fetus of Wākea and Hoʻohōkūkalani and became the staple crop of the people. As the foundation for extending life by literally pounding taro pieces into the solid mass, the papa kuʻi ʻai allows the men to ritually perform the unification and sustenance of the people and culture by making poi and feeding people. The same holds true for a spear: its primary importance lies not in its *representation* of identity, though this is undeniably important, but rather in its use in perpetuating the cultural and spiritual practices of the people. An integral part of the life-giving process is the emergence of the creativity and "innate" knowledge of the carver. Though Kaʻai provides a basic template to follow, each man shapes his piece differently and produces a unique project that is at once the embodiment of his own self and the creation of a new entity. As we shall see in the next chapter, this process is formative in Kūkona Lopes's narration of finding community with the men after carving his first weapon. At the same time, his experience is one in which individuality becomes a site of slight distress, a dynamic which speaks to some of the inherent tensions between individual achievement and group affiliation that are expressed and then worked out in moʻolelo.

In 2002, those working at Cliff Alakai's house (the majority of the group) did so under the direction and leadership of men like Nākānelua and Alakai, who had learned from Kaʻai over the years, thus affirming that his teachings indeed lived on in his students, who were themselves able to pass it on. Alakai reflected on Kaʻai's teachings:

I think we as Hawaiian people need to get back to what's real in our culture and get away from the mysticism, and that's what I learned from Sam [Kaʻai] and appreciate, you know. Make the thing, make it forty times, and after you've made it forty times, you'll know how to make. And, you know, sometimes people will make it once, and they create like paddles, you know. They'll make a beautiful paddle but they'll never paddle it . . . so they never really know what it's like. They should make a couple, paddle it, and get real comfortable with it, so they know. And that's one thing Kyle Nākānelua preaches, and I think came — comes from Sam [Kaʻai], about learning it, and knowing it inside and out, and using it. You know, it's not living culture unless you practice it, and I think we need to do it. (Alakai 2002)

Hawaiian objects, once valued for their utility within particular historical and cultural contexts, have now become valued commercially and socially precisely as symbols of Hawaiian history, culture, and identity. Specifically with regard to spears, the objects represent and embody warriorhood and manhood. There is an implicit critique here of the commodity fetishism noted by Marx, wherein a mystification of social relations is effected through the "appearance of potent, free-floating objects detached from labor" (Gordillo 2006, 163–64). By contrasting the "real" with the "mysticism," Alakai comments on the ways in which Hawaiian "things" (objects, practices, knowledge) are perceived to be imbued with mana or spiritual influence and are thus accessible to only a few experts who claim status via these things. The "need to get back to what is real" is to also work against Hawaiians' alienation from culture, which creates deeply felt ambivalences when novices in cultural realms must reckon with the strangeness of the practices and objects they encounter, including carving spears and carrying them on a heiau. Finally, there is a need to demystify the processes by which invocations of culture reproduce inequalities in the community by privileging only particular kinds of knowledge and discursive authority (Dominguez 1992).

HAWAIIAN EDUCATION AND MASCULINITY

When asked what led him to join the Hale Mua, Puka Ho, a thirty-seven-year-old Maui County lifeguard, pointed specifically to the equalization of statuses that might not otherwise be (re)produced in an "educational project" located in a classroom. At his first practice in 1999, Nākānelua told him, "I dunno all da answers, brah, but I can find you one means fo get your answer." Ho recalled, "That's what got my respect for Nākānelua." After getting to know the others, he decided that "this is good braddahs, I no mind hangin wit dem." Being interviewed with Pākī Cabatingan, a forty-five-year-old county worker in the horticulture division (see chapter 5), Ho frequently responded to comments made during the conversation the three of us had. While discussing the impact of the Hale Mua and his identity, he echoed Cabatingan's statement that his interest in Hawaiian culture and history had been piqued: "It's like Pākī said, it increased, yeah, made my desire fo learn more. And now I know, get one addah way of learning. It's not just readin' out of one book it's doing . . . Fo me, I get . . . hard time learning outta one book, I get easy time doing, yeah. When you make da mistake, you see da mistake you do, eh, instead of jus doin em on paper. You know you write em down, and den 'Oh, I cannot figure dis out, I cannot figure dis out,' but if you doin em, and you make da mistake, you like 'Oh, das what I did wrong,' cause it's deah in front of you, yeah, instead of on paper . . . I learn that way *easier.* . . . I guess that's da upbringin, eh: you do em wrong you catch cracks [get whacked]" (Ho 2002). The Hawaiian proverb "ma ka hana ka 'ike — knowledge / learning comes from work," captures the role of practice in making him feel that he could learn his culture and identity.

Ho also expressed a feeling, held by many men, that the process of learning Hawaiian culture "outta one book," that is, taking Hawaiian language and studies classes at the community college or university, is an alienating experience. One of the strongest appeals of the Hale Mua is its contradistinction to formal Western educational institutions. Many of the men felt that the classroom was an elitist, haole, and alien space and often a feminine one as well. Hawaiians as a whole struggle against a history in which colonial discourses of "stupid" and "lazy" Hawaiians were (re)produced in the classroom, a process on which others have written (Ah Nee-Benham and Heck 1998; Meyer 2001). Yet the gendered patterns of education involve different processes for male and female students. In the context of "learning" to be boys and men, schools are sites where "'real lads' are formed in relation to the feminized world of schoolwork and are characterized by toughness, sporty prowess, and resistance to teachers and education" (Swain 2005, 219). The informal peer groups are particularly important sites for the making of masculinities, wherein "the aim is to be the 'same as the others,' for this provides a certain protection from teasing and, perhaps, even subordination" (ibid., 217). Boggs notes that the ways of speaking and relating that Hawaiian children in Nānākuli learned at home and in peer groups in the late 1960s were at odds with the routines and participation structures of the classroom; such was especially the case for the boys, whose "struggle for equality" within peer groups was a formative experience (Boggs 1985 chaps. 4, 9). Gallimore et al. (1974, 194–207) note that for these reasons,[5] these same boys were more prone to come into conflict with teachers, and overall they performed more poorly than girls. Rather than seeking to understand the underlying social, cultural, and economic causes, many point to this as affirmation for the stereotyping of Hawaiian men as lazy, stupid, and violent (see Nunes and Whitney 1994, 61).

Having gone through such an educational experience, many of the men in the Hale Mua refuse to return to the university to take Hawaiian language or culture classes. A further disincentive for many of them was their perception of the feminization of Hawaiian educational space, a view supported in no small measure by Trask's assertion that "women lead our Hawaiian Studies Center" (1999, 191). The change in leadership that saw Jon Osorio become the first male director of the center in 2004 did little to shift that perception. Kalani Makekau-Whittaker, an educational specialist at the Kīpuka Native Hawaiian Student Center at University of Hawaiʻi Hilo, notes that men constituted only 22.3 percent and 34.7 percent of the fall 2005 enrollments in Hawaiian studies programs at Hilo and Mānoa, respectively (Makekau-Whittaker, email 1/17/07).[6]

With its egalitarian ethos and its exclusive focus on men, the Hale Mua creates a safe, comfortable space for men to learn and not feel stupid or overwhelmed by women. The ability to show vulnerability is especially important because men who do so are then able to discuss and work out issues pertaining to male violence. As we will see below, Ho's embodied learning in which he would "catch cracks" when he did things "wrong" was a part of a larger pattern of domestic violence experienced in the home. Many men have forged their masculinity out of violence (Bowker 1998), so this is one of the primary elements that the Hale Mua both builds upon and seeks to transform through ritual and training (see also Ito 1999, 105–07).

Kū Rising: Gender Ideology in Practice and Performance

Inspired by the ceremonies at Puʻukoholā, the Hale Mua's Wehe Kū (Opening of Kū) ceremonies on Maui take place at the historically and spiritually deep heiau of Pihanakalani (Gathering Place of the Chiefs) and the chiefly complex Halekiʻi (House of Images). Though its history goes back at least to the thirteenth century (Beckwith 1970, 333; Kolb 2006; Wilson 2006), the men of the Hale Mua chose the site for its association with the eighteenth-century high chief Kahekili, who worshiped, resided, and trained his warriors there. Also like Puʻukoholā, these structures became objects of state power when they were named the Halekiʻi-Pihana Heiau State Monument and added to both the National and State Register of Historic Places in 1985.

Memorializing Kahekili has played an important role in the way the Hale Mua defines itself as a specifically Maui group and localizes Kamehameha's narrative of Hawaiian nationhood. Before Kamehameha's rise to power, Kahekili was the foremost chief of the archipelago and had brought all islands except for Kauaʻi, whose chief was his ally, and Hawaiʻi under his direct rule when he died of old age in 1793. It was through a mixture of war and intermarriage with high-ranking Maui female chiefs, including Keōpūolani and Kaʻahumanu, that Kamehameha finally took over Kahekili's domain, and only after his death. Genealogists and historians have long debated the true paternity of Kamehameha, some arguing that Kahekili was his father, not the formally recognized Keōuakupuapāikalani (Desha 2000, 32; Kamakau 1992, 68). Such a historical context provides fruitful grounds for a remembering of Kamehameha's "Hawaiian" nation through a Maui lineage.

Kahekili figures prominently in the Hale Mua's identity in numerous ways. As I mentioned in the introduction, the men of Nā Koa chose to jump into the Pō at one of his favorite cliff-diving points during a protest march in 2001. The Mua also adopted the hoaka, a crescent moon symbol associated with Kahekili and the Maui chiefs, as its own design (seen on the shirts worn by Hale Mua members in figure 14 on page 120). The hoaka is also a military formation called Kahului that the Mua assembles in to conduct prayers; coincidentally, Kahului is the name of the main town on Maui and the site where practices are held. Finally, the hoaka is also the second taboo night dedicated to the worship of the god Kū, who on Maui takes the form Kūkeoloʻewa.

The Wehe Kū ceremonies officially began the year's cycle of activities starting about March and ending in September with a closing ceremony (see the appendix). On March 30, 2002, we gathered 4:00 a.m. on Pihanakalani and Halekiʻi heiau, which sits on a bluff overlooking the Wailuku Industrial Center and Kahului Harbor on one side and the Paukūkalo Hawaiian Homes, through which we drove to arrive at the gate leading up to the heiau, on the other. We wore only our malo and kīhei and carried the ihe and neʻe we had carved at the workshops. We chanted to open the ceremony and then proceeded down to the ocean, a five-minute walk, to ritually bless and name our weapons. We returned to the heiau to silently wait for the sunrise and to contemplate our goals for this year. As the sun came up, we watched the night turn to day, pō to ao. It was during this transition that we chanted "E Ala E (Awaken/Arise)" to greet the sun.

We then assembled under a traditional thatch house that was constructed in 1996 by the master builder Francis Sinenci and his group from Hāna, along with help from some of our men. At this time we shared ʻawa and spoke about the names of our weapons and how they reflected us individually and our group collectively. Crabbe, Kaʻai, and finally Nākānelua all took the opportunity to once again explicitly state the purposes of the Hale Mua and the significance and necessity of men learning their responsibilities as Hawaiian men. This included being a good husband and father, protecting and providing for one's family, and perpetuating the Hawaiian culture. We then ate ritual foods in an ʻaikapu (sacred eating; see chapter 3) and ended around noon. The season of Kū had begun.

In the Hawaiian pantheon of akua, the Kū/Hina pair represents the male/female duality of the sexes that organizes the universe in the cosmogonic genealogy chant the Kumulipo (Beckwith 1972; Kameʻeleihiwa 1999, 2–4; Valeri 1985, 12). Kū, whose name means "standing, upright, erect," encompasses all the male gods (and their properties) and represents the male generating power; Hina, whose name means "to fall, topple, or lean over" and references the moon (mahina), presides over the female akua and represents female fecundity and the power of growth and (re)production (Beckwith 1970, 12–13; Pukui et al. 1972, 2:122; Valeri 1985, 12). As Kameʻeleihiwa (1999, 4) remarks, "The Hawaiian world was . . . divided into female and male domains of work, and was considered *pono,* correct and righteous, when there was a balance between the two. When there is balance in the world, the ancestral *Akua* are pleased, and when there is perfect harmony in the universe, people are protected from all harm." Not only is Kū defined with and in opposition to Hina (and vice versa), but also if either is missing, the whole of society suffers. As Pukui et al. (1972, 2) explain, "*Kū,* the masculine, is always accompanied by *Hina,* the feminine" (128), and together the two "symbolize the balance embodied in well-being" (147).

Kanaka Maoli seeking to return balance to the self and society have used the metaphors of duality and balance between Kū and Hina as models for thinking. One of the primary philosophies of the lua seminars was that of understanding how the balance of Kū/Hina guided not only attacks and counterattacks, but also embodiment of both the masculine and feminine in each individual; indeed, the word "lua" itself means "duality" or "two, second" (Paglinawan et al. 2006, 9). As the ʻōlohe (lua master) Richard Paglinawan explained in an interview when the classes began, "Lua is in harmony with nature. You go with the flow of things, and you use it to your advantage. Lua is fluid, like hula. Hula and lua at one time were almost one and the same because men were the dancers. Lua was the 'hard' part, hula is the soft. So you could relate it to yin and yang, or Kū and Hina" (Clark 1993, 10). In this frame, the masculine lua complemented the feminine hula. Though the ʻōlohe do not make this distinction in their 2006 book (Paglinawan et al. 2006), it seems to have been quite explicit at the time that Kyle Nākānelua, who was in the first class, entered. He credited much of what he learned about Kū/Hina balance, and his subsequent focus on the Kū, to his experience in the pā lua. Importantly, the connection to the mana of Kū comes through the physical embodiment and performance of it in ritual and in training.

As a gendered project, the effort to reinvigorate Kū ritualizes resistance and contestation to the perceived colonial emasculation of Hawaiian men and the Hawaiian nation. As Nākānelua described it, "Because we're a male, masculine oriented group, our 'imi 'ana (searching) is towards the masculinity of the culture because there's been so much femininity. And again, not that femininity is bad; everything has its place and its time. No laila (therefore) . . . if you believe, everything has its place and time, then it should hold true to da fact that there should be a place and a time for the mana Kū. There's a time for healing, there's a time for building mana" (Nākānelua 1999).

The idea of building is important here, for if decolonization entails healing, it also demands an active rebuilding of nation, place, and hale. Yet in the name of cultural reclamation, the project of revitalizing the mana Kū runs the risk of inscribing the Kū/Hina and male/female dichotomies with the valences of strong/weak and dominant/submissive that work to support the structures of Western patriarchy. Arguably, Hawaiian history has numerous examples of strong, dominant women figures, and thus the Kū/Hina duality should not be seen as absolute or even applicable in all situations. I will discuss this tension further below; here I note that invocations of Kū and Hina index strategies for balance and pono in society and in individuals as well as the perceived imbalances and needs for restoration.

Kū is also the akua of governance, productivity, work, industry, upland forests, deep-sea fishing, and, of course, war. Unfortunately, the common rendering of the Kū, and most notably his manifestation of Kūkā'ilimoku (the island snatching god), exclusively appends to him the dubious distinction of being the god of war. The efforts of Ho'oku'ikahi included refiguring that depiction, so influenced by colonial and missionary outlooks. After interviewing Ka'ai in 1991, Steve Friesen wrote, "Western historians have focused on this militaristic aspect of Ku [sic] because of their own imperialist interests. But Hawaiians, according to [Ka'ai], worship the deities like Ku who care for them. The full measure of the god's care is recognized in the full measure of names, and must be understood in that broad context" (Friesen 1992, 22). These tropes of Kū the war god are also used to change colonial subjects into savages and bloodthirsty male warriors. The primary goal of Nā Koa was to restore courage and discipline, not violence (see chapter 2). As Ka'ai and Nākānelua sought to decouple the concept of Nā Koa from violence and war, so too have they sought to place Kū in the larger context of his multitude of being. As men remembered the mana of Kū, they too would be upright members of the community ready to rebuild lāhui.

Hoʻoikaika Kino: Strengthening and Embodying Identity

If the Wehe Kū gives primacy to the ideological aspects of identity formation, the weekly meetings focus on the body and action. These practices usually go from 5:30 to 8:00 p.m., alternating between Wednesday and Thursday nights depending on Nākānelua's work schedule. Since many of the members of the Hale Mua are also in the Royal Order, meetings are held at Hale Nanea, a harborside property in Kahului leased by the Royal Order and comprised of an old meeting/party hall and an open grassy area (which was seeded and manicured by joint members of the Hale Mua and Royal Order).

Like all other activities of the Mua, training sessions are circumscribed by prayers and chants meant to separate our time together from our work and family lives "out there." A number of men also wear pāʻū (waist wraparounds) as they do at Puʻukohloā (see chapter 3). This embodied practice further contributes to the demarcation of the time and space as a specifically Hawaiian one. For many of the men, this is an important expression of their Kanaka identity.

In 2002, the workouts were done with the spears and fighting staffs we carved in the workshops. We began with stretches and warm-ups and then shifted to a more vigorous routine of hoʻoikaika kino (body-strengthening exercises) that was based primarily on hula and lua moves. Each exercise carried the name of a wave, which itself was a carryover from the lua philosophy of nalu (waves) and fluidity (Paglinawan et al. 2006, 10). When the nalu workout was finished, we practiced various hula, haʻa (ritual dances),[7] and martial sets that were specifically aimed at developing proficiency with our weapons; many of the moves to these routines were embedded in the basic exercises done at the beginning of practice. One form we trained in was the pig dance "Mahaʻū," which we would be doing in unison with Keʻeaumoku Kapu's group of Nā Koa at Puʻukoholā.[8] Also a product of the pā lua (Paglinawan et al. 2006, 42), the Mahaʻū honored Kamapuaʻa, a chiefly ancestor who could take the form of a man, a pig, or a variety of other plant and animal forms (Charlot 1993; Kameʻeleihiwa 1996). The dance was based largely on a Marquesan pig dance and thus reflects a larger Polynesian identification as well as a more specifically Hawaiian one.[9]

The last part of practice ended in sparring practice, which was in preparation for our upcoming sham battle with Keʻeaumoku Kapu's men (see chapter 4). We trained with helmets, gloves, and other protective gear as we went into full contact spear fencing (kākālāʻau) with padded spears. At the end of the practice we gathered again, closed in prayer, and exchanged breath in the pressing of noses through the honi. Afterward, people made announcements, discussed upcoming events, evaluated the workouts, and talked story about anything else that came to mind.

Hoʻoikaika kino primarily works to achieve pono by strengthening the body, mind, and spirit. American ideals of beauty and health shape the ways in which preoccupations/obsessions with the body are articulated by Hawaiians today, especially since the dominant sexualized images of Kanaka men and women in the tourist industry are those that conform with Western standards of slim but shapely physiques, straight hair, and facial features that are "Polynesian" but mixed with those of Anglos and/or Asians (Desmond 1999; Imada 2004). Yet for ʻŌiwi (as is the case with many other indigenous peoples), the colonial experience of decimation from diseases and epidemics continues to attack the cultural and psychological immune system of the Kanaka body politic and far outweighs any concern over appearance.

The colonization of the body manifests itself not only in culturally defined regimes of sexuality and propriety, but also in more viscerally distressing ways through obesity, diabetes, cancer, and other health-related problems. These often culminate in high mortality and suicide rates, which for Hawaiian men approach epidemic proportions (Blaisdell and Mokuau 1994; Cook et al. 2005). Likewise, the structures of late capitalism and Hawaiʻi's dependence on imported foods and goods maintains this bodily malaise to such a point that for many Hawaiians dis-ease has become something endemic to their culture. Thus, as Marshall (Marshall 1999; 2006) argues, the project of *de*colonization can proceed only by recovering and healing the body.

In the Hale Mua, as in other Hawaiian health organizations that Marshall describes, the health of the Hawaiian people includes as its core component the health of the culture, and as such many of the activities are culturally based and include a metapragmatics of healing the nation through healing the culture, identity, and soul of the "sick" people. In addition to the process of healing, the more aggressive projects of anticolonial and nationalist resistance require assertions of strength and power, both culturally and bodily; thus the emphasis on rebuilding. For the Hale Mua, these are gendered as inherently masculine and essential for the remaking of Hawaiian men.

Nākānelua urges members to stand up and take charge of their own health. He speaks with a conviction and authority that earn the men's respect not only because he is articulate, but also because he literally embodies those qualities, ethics, and attributes that he urges others to take up. Years of training in sports, the military, martial arts, and the fire department and working in the taro patches have given him a muscular, tanned physique. Through his training as a firefighter and other training in health care, he had taken as his kuleana (area of responsibility) the health and welfare of Hawaiians on the personal, professional, and political levels; in fact, when he was a member of the sovereignty organization Ka Lāhui Hawai'i, he was in charge of the Maui Island caucus's Department of Health (Nākānelua 2002b). He also wears a number of traditionally designed tattoos that represent his ancestral lineage and visibly mark his body as a Hawaiian one (see figure 18). This becomes even more impressive when one discovers that Keone Nunes, a Hawaiian tattoo practitioner who uses rituals, protocols, and handmade tools and needles, placed these markings on Nākānelua in a manner that was more painful and meaningful than if done at a tattoo parlor with a machine.[10] Many of the men come not only to respect but also to identify with Nākānelua through the life experiences he shares in talk story (see chapter 5). Two particular aspects as they relate to bodily experience and performance are worth extended discussion here: violence and dance. It is through the gendered remaking of these practices that Nākānelua is most successful at lowering men's defenses and opening them up to new experiences.

THE VIOLENCE OF MODERNITY

The problem of violence and unusually high incarceration rates among Hawaiian men has long been a topic of great concern in the Kanaka Maoli community. Hawaiians between the ages of twenty and forty-four have the highest rates of suicide among the major ethnic groups in Hawai'i (Kana'iaupuni et al. 2005, 113). The rates of confirmed child abuse or neglect cases are three to four times those of the other major ethnic groups, and Hawaiians were

FIGURE 18. Kyle Nākānelua cleaning out the fibers used to strain the ʻawa root when mixing the drink, East Maui Taro Festival, Hāna, Maui, 1999. Clearly visible are the tattoos on his left arm and leg done by Keone Nunes. PHOTO BY MASAKO CORDRAY.

twice as likely as others to report physical, sexual, or emotional abuse on a Department of Health Survey (Kanaʻiaupuni 2005, 63–64). While representing about 20 percent of Hawaiʻi's population, Hawaiians comprised 38 percent of the in-state prison population and 41 percent of Hawaiʻi inmates housed in out-of-state facilities (OHA 2006, 171, 173). There is a danger in reproducing such data without accounting for biases in collection and other possible flaws in methodology, and I do not seek to present this as proof of endemic Hawaiian violence. Nonetheless, these are disturbing figures that unfortunately correspond to given notions of Hawaiians, which themselves serve as the source for looking for alternative ways of healing and transforming (cf. O'Nell 1996). It is also relevant because, as many studies of masculinities elsewhere have shown, violence is one of the most fundamental and problematic ways in which men define and embody subjectivity (Bowker 1998; Connell 2005b, 81–86).

One of the most promising aspects of the reemergence of the pā lua, Nā Koa, and the Hale Mua is their potential to provide men a place in which violence born of hurt, pain, and lack of cultural identity can be transformed into a more productive form of energy. It is also a place where they can see and meet other men who can help in the process of both healing and constructing a different idea of masculinity. Such a theme was prominent in the interviews I conducted with Puka Ho. While contemplating the increase in his desire to learn about Hawaiian history and language, he also discussed his new understandings of being a man:

HO: A lot of values dat Kyle [Nākānelua] puts out there fo da guys in da Hale Mua is, you know, basically take care your family, take care your stuff . . . do what you gotta do, do what you tink is right. And I tank him fo dat, because if . . . I nevah run into dis bunch of guys, I probably would be still drinking beer aftah work every day, and instead of tinking about what I do and how I do it.

TENGAN: So you feel it's had a real positive impact on your life?

HO: Well, yeah, real positive impact, because when I was younger, I grew up, my dad would drink every night, come home bust up my maddah, bus me up, you know, send my maddah to one hospital. So you know da kine role models, that's how you figure, oh, well, I goin get oldah, I goin work, come home drunk. And Nākānelua wen show dat there's anadah path fo take (2002).

Significantly, Ho describes seeing a different vision of mature Hawaiian masculinity that contradicted his own previously held and embodied notions. Though I would not consider Ho's experiences the norm for most of the men, he certainly was not alone. Three others in the group told me they had grown up in homes where beatings were more common than not, and one of them even left home when he was seventeen and lived on the beach for a while before he had a stable job. He didn't blame his father for that behavior for he knew that "life was hard," acknowledging that, in addition to individual or cultural factors, larger structural forces were also responsible for his fate. He also credited Nākānelua and the Hale Mua for helping to alter his perspective.

Rick Bissen, a prosecuting attorney (see chapter 5) also grew up in a family where violence was "natural," though in his case it was usually among the older men, who would get into fights with each other. Family violence was even seen as predestined since his mother's maiden name was Nākoa. Like Ho, he spoke of the way Nākānelua helped to change his ideas about warriorhood and violence:

There's varying interpretations of [Nākoa]. The way my mom had interpreted their name . . ."the warriors" . . . was, like "the fighters" because there was a lot of fighting within the family, I mean a lot of hard-headed Hawaiians who . . . were stubborn, and resorting to physical violence was a natural thing. . . . But when Nākānelua explained it he said, "You know, it doesn't have to mean 'the warrior' meaning, like the violence." The way they wanted the term to be understood was "the courageous." And, the best example they gave, which is what has stuck with me is, the courage to be a young, Hawaiian, male, and to wear a malo in public, and to say "This, I am not ashamed of who I am or what I stand for." And it's that you have the courage to live your belief (2002).

Those familiar with the feature film *Once Were Warriors* (1995) might find parallels in the discourse of transforming violence by recourse to warrior cultural traditions that inculcate discipline, pride, and self-esteem, thereby transforming violent energies into productive ones. Indeed, many men in the group find hope in the Mua for the younger generations precisely on this basis. Along these lines, Nākānelua has spoken to inmates at Maui Community Correctional Center and staff members from Child Protective Services. Others, such as Ka'iana Haili on Hawai'i, have used the hale mua concept to develop full curricula for the domestic violence, substance abuse, and prison programs. Among other things, Haili holds that "our male ancestors were warrior/healers" and "to be either you had to learn the balance; in order to kill we learn to heal — Kū and his many forms are balanced in both death and life" (email to author, 12/26/06). While rooting the men in the cultural practices of land stewardship and taro culture, he also advocates a political and structural understanding "that as long as we allow others to determine the fate of our 'āina (land) we will be at the top of the lists" (ibid).[11] Sally Engle Merry noted this sort of discourse in the program of a Native Hawaiian pastor (also in Hilo, Hawai'i) who "talked about the ideal warrior as a person violent in war but not at home" and "discussed male violence from a perspective of the Hawaiian sovereignty movement as well as Christian ideas" (2006, 46).

While the possibilities for positive transformation of violent masculinities are there, they are limited and rely largely on the tailoring of the Hale Mua model to the needs of the group. The majority of the men who have come to our Hale Mua are older men with steady jobs and, as Alakai (2002) frames it, "have structure in their lives"; they are not the "at-risk youth" or otherwise marginalized men who would perhaps benefit most from the community and identity the Hale Mua offers. Moreover, Nākānelua is quite clear, as Ho noted, in stating that you need to "take care your stuff" first before dedicating your time to the Mua, and he does not present the Hale Mua as the panacea for all the social ills and problems that Hawaiian men face. The issue of gendered violence will not solve itself overnight and will require approaches on multiple levels. While part of that may involve a return of sovereignty and land, it must also include interventions into the structures of domination in the domestic space.

Within the group, though, the men's embodied experiences suggest that the most effective means for reforming masculinities defined through violence is by refiguring warrior and masculine subjectivities through body-reflexive practices. Connell defines this as a process wherein bodies act as "both objects and subjects of practice, and the practice itself forming the structures within which bodies are appropriated and defined" (2005, 61). This is precisely the appeal that lua, warrior arts, and the whole regime of physical training (hoʻoikaika kino) hold for remaking masculinity in the Hale Mua. As Nākānelua explains of the training routine, "[It] is very Kū oriented. . . . It makes men feel really good — No different, no different from the formation of the karate dojos, no different from shoto-kan, or kung-fu, or anything like that. It just, it's a way for men to develop their physical prowess, and their thinking abilities, their strategic abilities, to practice their leadership roles" (Nākānelua 1999). Through such body-reflexive practices, men come to perform and know themselves and their bodies in a new way. Some have familiarity from previous experience in (as well as popular stereotypes of) the martial arts, and this works to also make the process of coordinating ʻŌiwi ideals and movements into redefined practices of "fighting." The other primary area this is worked out in is dance.

DANCING AS MEN

One of the most notable changes brought about by the Hawaiian renaissance in the 1970s was the rebirth of men's dancing, largely tied to the revival of the ancient (kahiko) form of dance. Kanahele contrasted the "authentic" ancient form to the "modern or hapa-haole (half-foreign)" one, which had become "an accommodation to the tourists" used to "advertise the charm of the islands" with "a smiling *hula* lassie" (Kanahele 1982, 15). In ways similar to the Hale Mua's reclamation of "real" cultural traditions of warriorhood, the "return of the male dancer to his rightful place" (Kanahele 1982, 15) was a refuting of the colonial feminization, commodification, and "prostitution" of the modern form in the tourism industry (Trask 1999). In 1977, Kanahele remarked, "I remember as a kid no local boy would be caught dead dancing the *hula* for fear of being called a sissy, but now you're likely to get popped in the mouth if you imply that a male dancer, who may be on the football team, is a sissy. Something must be happening to change this deep-set attitude" (1982, 3). Two years later he added, "Male dancers have also become favorites of local audiences, both men and women, although the squeals of glee I hear when the men come on stage wearing a modern style *malo* come mostly from the *wahines*. John Lake tells me that invariably it is the male dancers who get the biggest applause" (1982, 15). It's notable that Lake, who had a Hawaiian club at the all-boys Catholic St. Louis High School, was a part of this movement, as he later came to be the primary ritual specialist at Puʻukoholā (see chapters 2, 3). Lake, along with others such as Darrel Lupenui and John Kaʻimikaua, did much to change the image, and today men are very prominent in hula competitions such as the Merrie Monarch Festival held annually in Hilo, Hawaiʻi, which is televised statewide and streamed live on the Web.

However, many of the men in the Hale Mua still associated hula with women and māhū (effeminate males, gay men, and/or transgendered women),[12] as have other scholars (Robertson 1989). Nākānelua was one of those football players dancing hula in school (Maryknoll, a Catholic School), but he felt that it was *only* because he was a starter on the team that nobody teased him. Coming from a working-class neighborhood in downtown Honolulu, he hung out with boys who defined their masculinity through toughness and fighting. He recalled that when he was invited to join a hālau, he declined because he felt he would have to "duke it out every day" with the "rugged" guys he hung out with.

Many of the men in the Hale Mua still associate hula with effeminacy. Jacob Kana (figure 19), a thirty-one-year-old power plant worker who was

FIGURE 19. Jacob Kana (foreground) and Elama Farm, Hāna, Maui, 1999. PHOTO BY MASAKO CORDRAY.

raised in the rural taro farming and fishing village of Kahakuloa, recalled that while witnessing the various cultural activities that women were taking part in, he had always sought something for the men: "I really liked the group because, first of all it's like, ah, just a bunch of men, eh, just all local braddahs just gettin' togeda and stuff. That, to me, dat's what we need, dat's what was missing, all dis time. Cause like everybody else, like da wahines li' dat, dey had hula and stuff li' dat, but to me was, I dunno, I nevah like hula. Hula wasn't my ting, was more, I dunno, I used to tink was *soft*. Was, and, I dunno if dat's wrong or what, but da's what I used to tink, so I nevah did like join hula. But to me nevah have notin' fo' men" (2002).

Keenly aware of this perception, Nākānelua tries to emphasize the masculine and strong aspects of dance, often by highlighting the martial aspects. He also focuses on the ha'a forms, which are understood as more sacred, serious, and rigid and thus less secular, playful, and soft. The term is also the cognate to the indigenous Māori dance form of the haka, commonly thought of now as a "war dance." This form has come to be a national symbol and global commodity through its performance by the New Zealand All Blacks rugby team and its use in the marketing campaigns of the corporate sponsor Adidas (Jackson and Hokowhitu 2002). For many Hawaiians (and other Polynesians), the haka represents the archetypal performance of Polynesian warrior masculinity, and thus some cultural organizations and local football teams have begun to perform haka (Tengan and Markham n.d.).[13] While inspired by the haka, Nākānelua chooses not to appropriate the form since for him it would represent a stealing of another people's mana and a diminishment of our own.[14]

In choreographing haʻa, Nākānelua emphasizes the lua strikes and fighting techniques embedded in the dance steps. This works extremely well for Ho, who remembered "the first time we had to dance one hula, I was like, 'Oh, brah, I no dance hula!' I mean, nothin wrong wit hula, but dat's not fo me. But when I seen them doin em, I was like, 'Whoa, dis buggah get plenty martial moves,' I could see in em. And dat's what wen' kinda attract me to dat. . . . I mean I no like dance da hula, but oh, dat buggah look like one good technique or sometin'" (Ho 2002).

The concerted effort to redefine dance is a reaction to the continued appropriation of the hula as a commodity spectacle and the consequent performance of it as such. The latter includes a cultivation of homogeneity of body types, appearances, and movements in groups that perform in tourist venues and in local competitions. At sites such as the Merrie Monarch Festival, which has become a spectacle visited by tourists and locals alike, both male and female dancers are heavily sexualized. The young, muscular males evoke the "squeals of glee . . . from the *wahines.*" This body type corresponds to the touristic image of the domesticated and sexualized beach boy and Duke Kahanamoku (see chapter 1). For the middle-aged, heavier men who come from a tough upbringing and contest touristic images, the "deep set attitude" against the popular visions of hula remain.

While many of the men may keep their distance from what they consider feminine dance, Nākānelua nonetheless maintains hula forms in the repertoire of movements he teaches, though with a "masculine" emphasis. Such is the case with the Molokaʻi Kuʻi. Nākānelua learned the dance when he was in intermediate school at Maryknoll, where he performed it as a courting dance in which the boys would chase the girls across the stage. In the Hale Mua, he changed it to reflect more of the tough, aggressive positioning that would speak to other men: "If you talking about, you know, trying to impress a woman, then your movements are, you know, kinda gallant, yeah, and prancing. . . . If you're a man, and you wanna make an impression on a man —

whether it be a boss, or a coach, or guys on a team dat you wanna be a part of and stuff, you know—den you gotta crank up yo' testosterone, you know, you gotta show up yo' balls, you gotta be there. So, when dat 'a'ano [attitude] comes out of you, yeah, your attitude changes, your body motions change, you tend to stiffen up at different points along da way. A different emphasis on da hand. . . . your mana is projected different" (Nākānelua 1999).

Thus Nākānelua does not disavow the hula but rather seeks to reclaim it as a practice done by and for Hawaiian men, not for tourists or for women. Again, the focus is on remaking masculinity and doing so through traditions and practices that are real. Reflecting on the spear dances we had been learning, Nākānelua explained their significance for cultural and historical consciousness: "We come from a culture that was, nothing was written. So history was in the song, history was in dance, history was in the prayer. And, the commemorations of things that happened, are brought forth, are brought back to life, are relived . . . through the dance. . . . We thought . . . why not do a pahua (spear dance) with a traditional Hawaiian ihe? . . . So we made em, and den we danced wit it. And dat was it. No great show, no grand performance in front of throngs of people, just for ourselves. Just to say, we participated in it, just to say we did it, and it was done, it can be done, just for ourselves" (1999).

Nākānelua was not entirely forthcoming in his statement that there is *no* show in our activities, for the ritual performance of the dance at Pu'ukoholā is certainly done in front of an audience (see chapter 3). Yet his main point about *whom* these activities are done for is valid: the ritual performance of dance is meant to bring about a transformation of the self by reconnecting with history and with the fellow performers of that collective mo'olelo. As I mentioned in the introduction, the visibility of Hawaiian male bodies played a central role in the effectiveness of the Lele i ka Pō. As men jumped from the cliff, the sight of their bodies falling into the ocean from the land became a powerful bodily enactment of identities in transition, a performance that is also carried out in the telling of life stories that speak of multiple life transitions and returns (see chapter 5). The ritual and embodied processes of the men work to further the goals of cultural and political transformation in the Hawaiian community, a society that is itself undergoing important changes and transitions.

The Politics of Hawaiian Masculinities: Struggling to Balance Kū and Hina[15]

While the project of transforming and remaking masculinity through ritual holds great promise, it also presents a set of important issues that need to be dealt with. Messner (1997) notes that a variety of men's movements in the United States, such as the mythopoetic men's movement, the conservative white Christian revival of the Promise Keepers, and the African American men's Million Man March are backlashes against feminism that utilize essentialist discourses to reclaim traditional (patriarchal) roles that have been lost. In racialized masculinity politics, the struggle against race and class oppression often supersedes the struggle for gender equality, and women of color suffer most. Messner argues that the transformative potential of masculinity politics is severely limited insofar as many of the movements end up working to reconstitute patriarchy (1997, 73). As Native Hawaiians move forward in the collective pursuit of reclaiming lāhui, it is imperative that we take seriously the gender politics that threaten to divide kāne and wāhine. In an effort to situate the personal and political project of the Hale Mua within the larger context of gender imbalance, I evaluate the extent to which the Hale Mua serves to (re)inscribe a patriarchal order that is not Maoli. A critical aspect of this evaluative project is to interrogate how masculinity is performed and toward what ends in the contexts of exclusive ritual space, mixed ritual space, and secular space. Throughout, I ask the question: What does balancing Kū and Hina mean in these different sites?

When the Hale Mua gathers for workshops, ceremonies, and training, it provides men a safe space for learning and practicing Hawaiian identity and community in ways that would not be possible in other educational institutions, workplaces, or at home. In this way there is some resemblance with the mythopoetic men's movement, which Michael Schwalbe argues is essentially a search for communitas among middle-age, middle-class white men who have experienced a type of spiritual bankruptcy as workers in the American capitalist society (Schwalbe 1996; 1998). In the Hale Mua, the activities and discourse focus on men's relationships to each other and to the family and community more generally. Invocations of Kū are meant to strengthen cultural identity, reconfigure pasts marked by violence, and encourage responsibility and upright moral behavior and leadership as Hawaiian men. The Hale Mua spaces are ritually separated from the normal work and family spheres — the space of (partial) liminality between neocolonial society and the vision of a traditional indigenous one. Ritual process reorders status relationships and allows men to relate in ways that might otherwise not occur given their differences in class, education, geographic mobility, and cultural knowledge. In this context, restoring Kū is about re-membering various qualities of masculinity and manhood he represents that are inclusive of the diverse men that come to the Mua.

At Puʻukoholā, both Kū and Hina are present in bodily and ideological form, though the balance is a negotiated one. While men dominate the site, women do take part in ceremonies, workshops, organizing, and decision making. The Hale Mua's relationship to the larger assembly has at times been tense, as our establishment of a kapu preventing women from entering the pavilion has been contested by women who see it as sexist and patriarchal; other women have supported the creation of a men's space, which provides us the opportunity and safety to expose ourselves bodily and culturally as we work to establish relations with men from other groups, particularly those from Keʻeaumoku Kapu's Nā Koa (see chapter 3). Our ʻaikapu ritual eating, for which other men from Nā Koa and Nā Papa Kanaka join us, has also been criticized, especially as it takes place concurrent with a community dinner. I personally have felt torn on this issue because I enjoy the company shared with men and women at such communal events; yet it is the only time that we are able to come together, share a meal, talk story, and bond as men of Puʻukoholā, and it helps to bridge the gaps in status, age, experience, and geography that separate the men of our groups. The challenge of allowing women warriors onto the battlefield remains unanswered. All of this suggests that despite our shared occupancy in the ceremonial space, we do not all agree on what the balance between Kū and Hina means or how to enact this balance in this historically male ritual space. At Puʻukoholā, Kū comes to be equated with men and Hina with women, rather than masculine and feminine qualities that both may possess. Thus in this context, patriarchy is inscribed insofar as the binary between masculinity and femininity is enacted as a binary between men and women with men as dominant.

Leaving both the Hale Mua and Puʻukoholā, men reenter a neocolonial order where ritual and ceremonial meanings are vacated. The tense gender relations which are ritually subdued on the heiau are laid bare outside its walls, and Kū clashes with Hina. In one particularly relevant example, Hawaiian men (not of the Hale Mua) involved in the construction of a traditional thatch hale (house) as part of an urban development project prohibited women from participating since house building was traditionally a male activity. Maria Kaʻimipono Orr, who holds an M.A. degree in archaeology/ anthropology and was an invited guest at the groundbreaking, noted that she and another Kanaka Maoli woman who was one of the regular construction supervisors felt "put out." She exclaimed in an email, "Barring women from building hale or participating in building one, is not only a waste of potential energy, etc., but an act of oppression . . . first this seemingly innocent kapu . . . then what next! The White, Protestant, males weren't/aren't the only beings on this planet to be oppressive in their dominant thinking and behavior. I feel like we're taking a giant step backwards!" (email, 3/20/01). What this example represents is a patriarchal assertion of power and authority, for it prevents the participation of women who contributed to the project. The rules of kapu only make sense when they operate as a part of a whole structure organized by the logic of Hawaiian kapu (Saussure's point that meaning is given by frame, rather than by element). When taken out of that system and implemented only in decontextualized and abstracted pieces, friction emerges because the other pieces that made it pono (correct) are not there to support it.

Noenoe Silva, an associate professor of political science and the director of the indigenous politics program at the University of Hawaiʻi, asks, "Does mana kāne (men's mana) have to exclude or oppress women, or be perceived as excluding or oppressing women? What's interesting from my point of view is that the late 19th c. Kanaka men did not seem so very invested in oppressing women — they supported and appreciated the Hui Aloha ʻĀina wahine, and went on to support women's suffrage. And they wrote down those awesome stories about [goddesses] Hiʻiaka and Papa" (email to author, 5/3/01). Silva's remarks are accurate, and the historical record does in fact demonstrate that women had access to mana, rank, and power in ways that complemented men's (Kameʻeleihiwa 1999; Linnekin 1990; McGregor 2003). It is also useful to note that the case of the Hui Aloha ʻĀina, the men and women each had their own separate organizations and kuleana (responsibilities). I would suggest that this is one of the reasons their leaders *could* work together when it came to making decisions and organizing the mass protests.

Ideology aside, the problem for men of the Hale Mua who are being "cast forward" as leaders is whether or not, or to what extent, their assertion of authority and mana requires a diminishment of women's. Does Kū rising depend on Hina's lying down? Do they need to be separate categories? When I asked Nākānelua directly, he responded, "Does the Mua advocate for total male dominance of the society, and the suppression of females? . . . This Mua doesn't advocate for that. What . . . the mua advocates in regards to the male sex is, it's very important for a male to have a duty and to have a responsibility. . . . It gives him a sense of well being. That's what we're advocating. That a male pick up his responsibility . . . the advocacy is not for the suppression of the female spirit" (2006).

Though this practice sounds good in theory, we must be wary of the contexts in which "responsibilities" are defined, understood, and practiced. There are echoes here in the discourse found in the Promise Keepers, who similarly advocate for men to pick up their responsibility as men and leaders. This call then gets taken up and used by individual men in a political fashion to support antifeminist and antigay projects through fundamentalist reading of the Bible and a call to return to "traditional" family values (Messner 1997, 22–35). Such a model cannot serve to cast our people forward. I find some comfort in the fact that there is no fundamentally patriarchal or homophobic discourse in the invocations of Kū and Hina, though calls for "restoration" of Kū can easily morph into "elevation above" Hina.

J. Kēhaulani Kauanui, an associate professor of anthropology and American studies at Wesleyan, has posed the following critical questions: "I guess it bothers me that the Hale Mua are attempting to reach for a moment in our genealogy that is seen as more 'culturally pure' and measuring it to their status now without accounting for ways they were more empowered under the colonial system than Hawaiian women. Why such a selective genealogy? . . . Am I sensing a sort of defensiveness on the part of Hawaiian men? If so, it makes me wonder about potential resentment that may be brewing. . . . Is it that men are contesting arguments that posit that Hawaiian women are seen as the primary leaders? Or, that the men agree that women are the leaders and are contesting that leadership and asserting their own?" (Kauanui and Tengan n.d.). The selectivity comes from the present context of the cultural nationalist movement as one that privileges identity and knowledge from the re-membered precolonial period, precisely as a means for addressing the current malaise of the neocolonial present. The issue of how or if men have benefited from the patriarchal bargain of colonial modernity is an important one; some have, some have not. Most of the men in the Hale Mua come from working-class families, even if they are currently middle class. Yet for many who now occupy that position, their status has come with (or created) a deep sense of alienation from the community. It is this struggle to reestablish connections with other men and community that leads most of the men to look to older forms of being and acting, one in which men could still relate in the hale mua of old.

However, Kauanui is correct in identifying a certain level of resentment brewing. In part, this is a response to women leaders' discounting of men's leadership (see discussion of Trask in chapter 1). The level to which discourses in the Hale Mua manifest this sort of reactionary tone varies. Most talk about male leadership tends to be along the lines of claiming responsibility in family and community, and men are less concerned with discrediting women than they are with validating men. There have been times, however, when men have made statements such as "Wāhine need to step aside." This discourse assumes that leadership in the community is a zero-sum gain, wherein the emergence of male leadership requires the removal of female leadership. This amounts to an assertion of patriarchy and reproduces the same structures of oppression and hierarchy that disempower individuals along the lines of race, class, gender, sexuality, age, body, and so forth. When it emerges, it suggests that patriarchy is what is needed to right society. In my experience, this kind of talk is less frequent than the concern with work, family, and community, but its presence is a cause for concern.

The oppositional nature of discourse on gender works against the establishment of balance and complementarity that we need. On the part of the Mua, one of the shortcomings of only focusing on Kū in the men's discursive practices is that the Hina in each of us is disavowed. The space of the Hale Mua is almost completely heteronormative. In response to my query on the issue of homophobia in the group, Nākānelua responded:

I've seen serious cases of homophobia, and I have not seen that in the mua. . . . We've had homosexuals in the Mua, bisexuals in the Mua, we have metrosexuals in the Mua—we got a pile of them in there and that's ok too. And I haven't heard anybody speak against it. I'll tell you what though . . . there was certain issues addressed in regards to understanding homosexuality and certain individuals had a need to understand it, personal issues. . . . We discussed it, and it was addressed from a cultural point of view utilizing certain kinolau [manifestations] of certain akua [gods]. For example you got this whole māhū thing going on, like taro is one male plant, but yet get babies. . . . Well what I look at is culturally . . . our kūpuna looked at that as one higher state of being. So, if we're studying this and we're taking a look at this, how is there a fear for homosexuality? You know I don't see it, I don't see it. (2006)

His mention of homosexual men in the group surprised me, though the fact that they remained closeted suggests that the openness is more individual than collective. At the 'Aha Kāne 2006 (see introduction), one of the key-note speakers was Hinaleimoana Wong, a māhū (transgendered woman) who has emerged as a vocal and visible leader in the Hawaiian educa-tion movement and other realms of activism and politics. I was glad that Kamana'opono Crabbe and the rest of the committee brought her in to physically remind the five hundred men gathered there that Kū did not need to exclude Hina. Yet the reception was mixed; some were enthusiastic, oth-ers were put off and walked out. The issue of homophobia (as well as trans-phobia) in our community is real, even if it is not as pronounced in other areas that do not share a (transformed) tradition of acceptance (Tengan 2003b).

The 'Ōiwi community has a long way to go toward achieving a real balance of Kū and Hina. We need to get away from the discourse of who has been oppressed more; both men and women suffered, and differently. The strength of the Hale Mua lies in the work it does with men and the transfor-mations of self in a social context of and for men. The extent to which new understandings of the balance between Kū and Hina may emerge is ques-tionable. Perhaps the metaphors we use are the wrong ones to begin with. Kū and Hina were only two of the forty thousands gods. The hale mua of old was in fact dedicated to Lono, the god of peace and fertility. He too took many forms, including Kamapua'a, the pig god and chief we dance of. In practice and in ideology, the Hale Mua has begun to also look toward the different models for thinking offered by male deities other than Kū, such as Lono, Kāne (god of life and freshwater), and Kanaloa (god of the ocean). Hopefully we will begin to celebrate female deities such as Pele and Hi'iaka as well. The Hawaiian community as a whole has always recognized and celebrated the diversity of being that is manifested in the kinolau (body forms) of the gods, people, and land, and the fact that moves have already been made in the Hale Mua to explore this diversity is encouraging. Kū and Hina are useful to the extent that they help us to reflect on the ever-present struggle to seek balance and complementarity. True, many men feel there is a long way yet to go before men's places or roles are restored, however the lāhui defines them. Perhaps when the work of rebuilding Kū is done, we will be ready to move on to a new embrace of Hina.

NARRATING KĀNAKA

....

Talk Story, Place, and Identity

> Sometimes cameras catch things, but some things only men's stories catch.
> So have we gone forward? Yes, there are more stories to be told, more kōrero
> (oratory) and moʻolelo (stories), more things for the sparkling eyes and open
> ears of our moʻopuna to hear. Yes, we're going forward.
> — Sam Kaʻai

In this chapter I focus on one of the most important ways that the men remake connections with each other, the land, the ancestors, and the larger Hawaiian lāhui through the sharing of moʻolelo — stories that are fragments of narrated life experiences. Life stories are a very powerful vehicle of reflection on one's personal subjectivity and on how one is part of a larger collectivity shaped by culture, gender, race, class, and place. Just as they use the larger discourses of moʻolelo as historical narrative, such as that of Puʻukoholā (chapters 2, 3), Kānaka ʻŌiwi Maoli use moʻolelo of life stories as "cultural tools" (Wertsch 2002) to "create meaning within a social ecology of meanings" (White 2000, 498). I look at the occurrence of life narration in two main contexts: those produced in interviews and those given in a large group discussion in 1999. I argue these enactments are typical of an entire area of narrative self-construction for the men of the Hale Mua — an area best labeled by the phrase "talk story." Through the telling and hearing of life stories, the men come to know and enact their identities as members of the Mua and of the larger lāhui Kānaka Maoli — nation of real people.

Mo'olelo: Storytelling and Self-Making

I became aware of the importance of mo'olelo when I first joined the group in 1997. After our Wednesday night practices, people who had time would usually stick around and talk story. Boggs describes talk story as a communicative event that is usually done in Pidgin (Hawai'i Creole English) and "involves a search for, and recognition of, shared feelings" and solidarity that is accomplished through a number of verbal routines such as "recalled events, either personal or folktales, verbal play, joking, and conversing" (Boggs 1985, 7). Ito (1999, 12) writes, "Talk story is a relaxed, rambling, sometimes intense commentary or conversation. . . . The accuracy of details . . . is less important than enjoyment of the social interaction. The point of talk story is not an accurate transfer of information but a social exchange, affective enjoyment of one another's company." As Ito (1999, 9) notes, the sharing of life stories in talk story sessions among her Hawaiian "lady friends" living in Honolulu during the 1970s was fundamentally an instance of *emotional exchanges* that represented "the heart of Hawaiian culture" and reaffirmed and reproduced the ties of affect that held together and defined Hawaiian communities. I too have recognized a naturally occurring mode of talk among men in the Hale Mua (talk story) and focus on that in a number of related contexts ('awa circle talk, for example), as well as my own interviewing, which extends and modifies talk story styles of speaking by eliciting narratives of personal and collective histories through nondirective interviewing techniques.

Like the Hawaiian families Ito describes in her book, the Hale Mua maintains its "ties that define" through the sharing of affect-rich life stories in a variety of contexts. The men would regularly talk story after practice in ways that were common to any social gathering; often, it was done in more typical settings of having a few beers after the workout. In addition to this, a similar but more formalized talk story occurred at the end of any group endeavor, for example, at the end of a spear-making workshop (chapter 4), on the last day of Pu'ukoholā (chapter 3), or at the final meeting of the year (appendix). Through the telling of their mo'olelo, the men would situate their participation in the Mua in the context of their own lives and speak of how they grew personally through their participation in the group project. In so doing, they create an opportunity for other members to relate through shared experiences. All of these speech events bore a strong resemblance to one another and led me to pay close attention to the ways in which moʻolelo work. The new members who are unfamiliar with the group's routines become socialized not only through the process of watching and learning, but also by hearing and *feeling* the stories of other men and finding points of commonality and shared emotional understanding that serve as entrees for their own personal narrations. As most men are used to talking story in similarly affective styles, the sharing of life stories flows easily from established forms of discursive practice.

Moʻolelo, as fragments of narrated life experiences, place speakers and listeners alike in a succession of personal, social, historical, and spiritual events, and thereby actively form individual and group subjectivities in the Hale Mua. Through the moʻolelo, the men I interviewed both contextualize their participation in the Hale Mua and actively work out issues of identity that extend into other areas of their lives. Thus I examine the ways in which the men articulate their reasons for joining, the time in their lives when this occurs, and the desires and anxieties that preceded and serve as the context for their subjective experiences in the Mua. In narrative practice individual subjectivities are culturally constituted (White 2000) — that is, shaped by and fed back into a larger discourse on Hawaiian masculinity and identity. During interviews, a number of the men spoke of how they did not actually know what it was that was missing until they found it in the Hale Mua. Like narration in therapeutic settings such as Alcoholics Anonymous (Cain 1991; Swora 2001) and religious testimonials of conversion to Christianity (Stromberg 1993; White 1991), telling stories in the Mua *does* something for one's sense of self, especially when performing identities in transition and transformation (Watson-Gegeo and White 1990). It is by learning to place their stories in a larger succession of talk that the men come to a new understanding of subjectivity.

One of the most important sites for this kind of identity work is the ʻawa circle, where men are obliged to "share their moʻolelo" (see the appendix). This typically involves a narration of their personal experiences, reflections, and evaluations of the topic being discussed over the ʻawa, usually a project or activity undertaken in the Mua. The format of speaking to the past, present, and future is followed, though the subjects addressed vary with the individual. The men usually express their gratitude to the other men of the

Mua for their fellowship and pledge their continued commitment to the group and to the larger struggles of the Hawaiian people. They often speak in testimonial fashion of loss, struggle, survival, and reclamation in their own lives as Hawaiians and as men, a project that is furthered through the very telling of their moʻolelo. Many of these testimonial life stories follow patterns that I argue are both learned and performed through communicative events such as the ʻawa circle and the ceremonies at Puʻukoholā I have already analyzed (chapter 3). Men who enter the Mua hear a number of different moʻolelo about the traditional role of Kanaka Maoli men in the ʻaikapu period, the detrimental effects that colonialism has had on the kāne, and the need to learn and reclaim their responsibilities as ʻŌiwi men today. They in turn learn to tell their own personal moʻolelo as stories shaped by and within these larger moʻolelo, at times repeating very closely some of the metaphors and rhetoric employed in the "defining" moʻolelo. In sharing their moʻolelo with the group, they enact their subjectivity as one remade by the collective production and interpretation of knowledge, memory, history, and identity (Cole 2001). The ʻawa circle is a context-creating practice that establishes a safe place for men to talk in a therapeutic fashion with others they trust and feel comfortable with. In part, the safety is created through the exclusivity of a male-only space. Their moʻolelo often become testimonies, acts of naming and identifying a historic pain that can be transformed and healed only by giving voice to it.

The ceremonial protocols followed give this event an added spiritual, moral, and pedagogical dimension that adds to the discursive authority of the speech, and thus identity, produced therein. At the same time, these protocols establish a clear participant structure (Phillips 1972) that members are meant to learn in order to be competent members and speakers within the circle and within the group (and hence reproduce aspects of the social organization of the group). The creation of hierarchies and structures would at first glance seem to be antithetical to fostering egalitarian relations in the Mua, which is one of the central characteristics of the group (Brenneis and Myers 1991). As I discussed in chapters 3 and 4, the creation of a distinctly egalitarian modality of social relations, what Turner (1969) calls "communitas," plays an important role in the ritual remaking of specifically Hawaiian ties of community and collective identities. The enactment of such relations in the sacred ritual space contrasts the stratified, class-based relations of production in the late-capitalist society of neocolonial Hawaiʻi, in which Hawaiian men, at least symbolically, are often at the bottom of the ladder as a collective whole. This same class system has also severed ties between Hawaiian men of different class backgrounds, a situation that the Mua seeks to remedy by reaggregating the community of Hawaiian men in the ritual space of the Hale Mua.

Thus the establishment of a new rank system might threaten to weaken the ties of community among the members. Yet knowing one's place is precisely what many of the men are looking for, and locating oneself in a hierarchy does just that while also giving one the kuleana to speak and to participate in the collective production of identity involved in the ʻawa circle. It also identifies those who are most competent speakers as a result of their age or their position in the group, thus providing the model of speaking to those who are younger and less experienced in telling moʻolelo. The physical environment and the protocols of who gets served and who speaks in what order provide a bodily and spiritual experience of knowing one's place in a succession of ancestors, people, and stories.

Out of respect to the sanctity of the ʻawa circle, I have never recorded any of the ceremonies that were kapu (prohibited), though I was able to record a less formal one in 2005 that marked the closing of the season, part of which I reproduce in the appendix. Here I would like to look at a talk story that took place at a meeting on October 13, 1999. As it was the first meeting for the attending prospective members, Nākānelua discussed the history of the Hale Mua, and older members shared their stories in ways that strongly resembled the narratives of ʻawa ceremonies (as in the closing discussions at Puʻukoholā cited in chapter 3). The fact that this collective act of producing a succession of stories occurred outside of the ʻawa circle indicated the importance of moʻolelo in the formation of group subjectivity.

"You Belong Here": Talk Story and Subjectivity

After explaining the philosophy and purpose of the group, Nākānelua let the new guys know that there were others who weren't there that night but who came when they had time; indeed, the overall policy was that everyone in the Mua was free to come and go as they pleased. Kamika Nākānelua, Kyle's cousin, raised the question of eligibility for those who did not know, and Kyle Nākānelua told them to bring any friends or family that may be interested, as long as they were Hawaiian. If they were not Hawaiian but had Hawaiian children that they wanted to pass the information on to, that was also okay; the main thing was to be wary of non-Hawaiians (usually haole) who were just "nīele" (nosy). After a bit of group discussion regarding spear making, Peter Vanderpoel (see figure 2 on page 12), a firefighter and one of the younger members of the group, offered his thoughts:

I've only been doing this for about a year and a half now, but, uh, I don't know if you guys feel a little bit weird coming in here with a bunch of braddahs holding spears (Vanderpoel holds up the one in his hand, pretending to look threatening). Um, first time I came out was four o'clock in the morning on the heiau [temple], and I had to wear a malo. It was *cold*, and uh, only good thing about it was *dark*, and nobody could see my 'ōkole [butt]. But uh, I've found that after coming a bunch of times, this is the place for me; I mean, it may not be the place for everybody. I paddled, I didn't get into hula, I just wasn't into it, [Kāwika Davidson, standing next to him, nods and smiles] but this is a place where I could explore my Hawaiianness. So if this is the place you want to be at this time, by all means, we're all here, to help you go forward.

Nākānelua asked if anyone had anything else, and Keoki Ki'ili spoke up: "Just that my door is open every day, Monday through Friday. Come any time. You like talk story, we talk story." Martin Martinson, a retired army chief master sergeant who was wounded in Vietnam, raised his hand, in which he held a book that was the translation of Samuel M. Kamakau's work (see the introduction for a discussion of Kamakau). Perhaps motivated by Vanderpoel's invocation of the cold, Martinson began by talking about his introduction to the Mua through the filming of a documentary titled *Ancient Warriors* in 1995 and the subsequent commemoration march of the Battle of Nu'uanu (see also Sam Ka'ai's story in the conclusion):

I got one thing to say. When I came into the group about five years ago, we made a movie, that's how I got into the group. And I just retired from the military, and uh, I was told if I wanted to "Come look around." I said, "Okay." And the first thing we did, we had to walk from Waikīkī to Nu'uanu [some of the older members laugh knowingly, and Nākānelua looks down and smiles] and by the time we got there, it was cold. It was *so* cold, some of the guys, they actually locked up on the spears, they locked up on the kāhilis, and stuff li' dat, it was *that* cold. And as things went along, I didn't come all the time, but there was always more knowledge they had here, and that's why I'm always here—for the education. Ah, if you asked me about five years ago about this guy [holding up book], I'd say "Who da hell is that?" 'Cause I didn't know anyting, about [Samuel M.] Kamakau—I always wondered how these [Hale Mua] guys got so smart. How come dey knew all dis stuff, and I didn't know anyting. And I started learning about all the books they were reading, and everybody shares this information. And it doesn't matter what walk, what background you have; it's that you're Hawaiian, so you come here to learn. And that's why we're here, to share this information. And everyone's full of information, you'd be surprised. You cannot say that, "Wow, nobody cares," cause I tell you what, I kept comin' in here sayin "What dat? What they talkin' about?" And that's how you feel right now, I think, but it takes awhile, and there are guys that are older than Kale Boy [Eldridge] and myself, I think [people start naming others not present and joke about some of the older ones there]. But you be really surprised. So don't feel that you're gonna be left out. It doesn't matter who you are, as long as you're Hawaiian you're invited. You *belong* here, if you want to be.

Martinson's talk then elicited speech from Carl "Kale Boy" Eldridge, a new addition to the group and then near sixty. I met Eldridge (and found out we were related) in 1996, when I was doing research for my undergraduate thesis, which looked at Hawaiian cultural nationalism in the group he was president of—Hui o Wa'a Kaulua (Society of the Double-Hulled Canoe) (Tengan 1997). Discussing his reasons for joining the Hale Mua, he stated,

The thing that really, really impressed me about this group here, was not the martial arts, but the concept of learning what we as Hawaiian men supposed to know as a matter of fact. . . . The hard part for me is . . . all the knowledge and history we had as small kids, it was taken away from us, us guys lost that. . . . A lot of our kūpuna died with a lot of knowledge, and it shouldn't have been that way, cause now we gotta go look for it. . . . The last person in my family to know this was my grandfather, but he nevah taught to his young sons, and it never came down to us. So now I gotta go to a younger man in order to learn dese things. And I want that to be handed down to my grandchildren, and I want them to get it from somebody in their family. So mahalo to you, Kyle [Nākānelua].

Oftentimes men will speak of the ways in which their participation in the Mua has filled a gap in their lives, in the case of Vanderpoel a place, community, and identity. Others, like Martinson and Eldridge, talk about the knowledge and education they have acquired here that they could not find elsewhere. Many of the stories take on a testimonial form in which individuals talk about the experience of loss or disconnection they have felt as Hawaiian men and their subsequent or current struggles of recovery and reclamation. In many ways, the narrative structure of these stories resonates with those of conversion narratives (Stromberg 1993; White 1991); both forms of narrative practice are potent identity markers and makers, especially in their practice, performance, and enactment in large groups understood to be safe places where like-minded and feeling persons will listen and empathize.

The project of articulation is accomplished in part by connecting to others through the telling of moʻolelo. This occurs when the other men in the group respond through verbal and nonverbal cues (laughing, nodding, and smiling), commenting on the story (discussion of who was older than Martinson), or by telling their own stories that pick up and expand upon events or themes others have mentioned; in this way, a succession of talk is created between men that affirms and validates the individual stories and their interlocutors. Individuals will highlight commonalities with others in the group, either through generational experiences (Martinson and Eldridge did not have an opportunity to learn until after retiring) or shared experiences in the Mua (Kāwika Davidson understood Vanderpoel's lack of interest in the hula). The latter often involve overcoming an initial physical or emotional discomfort with the help of others in the group in order to arrive at a deeper understanding of and comfort with one's identity as a Hawaiian. Both Vanderpoel and Martinson spoke of enduring the cold of the heiau and the march, which others laughed at because they too were there. I myself remember standing on the heiau with Vanderpoel in the midst of the rain and wind thinking I would never come back. Eldridge told of the regret he felt as an older man looking for the knowledge that passed with his kūpuna. Yet through the help of Nākānelua and the others who share the knowledge and the pain, the group moves forward, and each person commits himself to helping and sharing with newcomers and with family and friends outside; a perfect example was Kiʻili offering the opportunity for anyone to come and talk story. Thus the new members come to know what it means to be a part of the Mua, and old members relive experiences that have defined their participation and growth in the group. Finally, these feelings are all reaffirmed by the sentiment articulated by Martinson: "You belong here."

A Succession of Interviews

When I first began interviewing individuals about the Hale Mua in 1999, my questions were aimed at finding out how and why they joined and what role the Hale Mua had played in their life. Not surprisingly, many of the stories I heard were familiar because I had heard them before in ʻawa circles or in other talk story sessions. At the time I was not asking life history questions, but I found that almost all of the men responded in ways that drew in personal histories, desires, and quests that "brought" them to the Mua. Thus when I did the majority of my interviews in 2002, I also included a life history component in order to better understand the life stories that emerged when men talked about the Mua. Finally, I asked men their opinions on their views of the "predicament" of Hawaiian men in general today.

Between 1999 and 2002, I recorded interviews with seventeen members of the group, about 60 percent of the active members in 2002.[1] They had been active with the Mua for varying lengths of time, the shortest being three years. Each man could claim at least one other ancestry in addition to Hawaiian; most could claim two or more. Their ages ranged from thirty-one to fifty-eight, the average being about forty-four. (One exception was Sam Kaʻai, who was sixty-four, but his status as the group's elder put him in a slightly different category). All of the men said they were heterosexual. Ten were married at the time, and seven were single or dating. Eleven had children, and three had grandchildren.

In terms of occupation and education, there were three firefighters, three county workers (a lifeguard, a wastewater plant operator, and a laborer in the horticulture department), the Maui County chief prosecutor, a financial administrator, a doctor, a retired police officer, an out-of-work artist (Kaʻai), a small business owner, an air traffic controller, a tugboat operator, an electric plant worker, and two doctoral candidates in psychology. Eight men, one of whom was a Vietnam veteran, had some military service. Ten were public high school graduates, and seven went to private school, a meaningful distinction because of the highly uneven, two-tiered education system in which the high school one graduates from often is a cue to race and class relationships. In terms of higher education, eight of the seventeen held a bachelor's degree, and six of them had obtained graduate or professional degrees. These rates are considerably higher than the percentages of 12.6 and 3.2 for all

Hawaiians, respectively the lowest and second-lowest rates of all the major ethnic groups in the state (Kanaʻiaupuni et al. 2005, 126–27). In general this is a fair representation of the makeup of the group generally, primarily educated middle class with some representation of blue-collar workers. Significantly, most of the men were upwardly mobile (i.e., they had better jobs and more education than their fathers) and almost all came from working-class or lower middle-class family backgrounds.

The issue of place was also less than straightforward. At the time of the interviews, fourteen lived on Maui and three on Oʻahu. Six might be considered "Maui Boys," in that they were born or raised or both in Maui, though all but two had spent considerable time on Oʻahu or the U.S. continent or both. Of the remaining members, nine were from Oʻahu, one was from Hawaiʻi, and one was from South Carolina. Even these numbers are misleading, though, for all of the men had experienced travel, movement, and relocation in some form, even the Maui Boys. Of the total, only three grew up in rural areas, but all came to eventually live in town (on Maui) or in the city (on Oʻahu or the continent).

In the following pages, I will first lay out an extended discussion of the narratives of Sam Kaʻai and Kyle Nākānelua, for it is their knowledge and experiences that have most profoundly shaped the Hale Mua o Maui. Much of the cohesion of the group rests on the degree to which the other members want and are able to relate to these men. This sets the stage for a discussion of the relations of the others, which I spend a considerable time discussing through the moʻolelo of an additional five members whose life stories articulate them one with the other.

In Search of the Eyes of Hema: Re-membering the Navigator's Song

ʻO ke ānuenue ke ala o Kahaʻi;	The rainbow was the pathway of Kahaʻi;
Piʻi Kahaʻi, kōī Kahaʻi,	Kahaʻi ascended, Kahaʻi pushed on,
ʻAʻe Kahaʻi i ke koʻiʻula a Hema;	Kahaʻi tread the rainbow-hued trail of Hema;
Hihia i nā maka o ʻAlihi.	The eyes of ʻAlihi gazed in bewilderment.
ʻAʻe Kahaʻi i ke anahā,	Kahaʻi tread along the reflected light;
He anahā he kanaka ka waʻa;	The man like a canoe on the reflected light;
Iluna o Hānaiakamalama;	Above was Hānaiakamalama;

'O ke ala ia i 'imi ai i ka makua.	This was the pathway to seek the father.
O hele a i ka moana wehiwehi	He went over the deep, dark ocean
O halulu i Halekumukalani;	That roars at Halekumukalani;
Ui mai kini o ke akua,	The myriad of gods inquired,
Nīnau Kāne me Kanaloa,	Kāne and Kanaloa asked,
Heaha kau huaka'i nui e Kaha'i?	"What is this great journey of yours, Kaha'i?"
I 'imi mai au i nā maka o Hema.	"I am searching for the eyes of Hema."
Aia i Kahiki i 'Ulupa'upa'u,	"There in Kahiki at 'Ulupa'upa'u,
Aia i ka 'ā'aia a hāhāmau i'a a Kāne,	With the 'ā'aia bird, the hāhāmau fisher of Kāne,
Loa'a aku, i Kūkulu o Kahiki	[They] will be found—at the Pillars of Kahiki"[2]

Hema (literally "south" or "left") was a famous chief of Hawai'ikualuli, Ka'uiki, Hāna, Maui. When his wife Luamahahoa was with child, Hema traveled to Kahiki, the far-off lands, to find a birth gift in the form of the 'ape'ula—a red tapa cloth used to wrap the images of the akua Kū. In the land of Kapakapaua he was killed by the 'ā'aia, a legendary fishing bird of the akua Kāne. Kaha'i, son of Hema, was born at Kahalulukahi, 'Īao, Wailuku, Maui. When he grew to manhood, he voyaged to Kahiki, treading the ko'i'ula (rainbow pathway) of Hema to search for his father. There he encountered the akua Kāne and Kanaloa, who told him that the eyes of Hema were to be found at the "Pillars of Kahiki"—the edge of the world, the horizon of the ancestors.

Kaha'i (the break, fracture, joint) is the name of many voyaging chiefs in Hawaiian history. Another bearer of the name is Sam Kaha'i Ka'ai Jr. (see figure 20). Born in Hāna on April 17, 1938, to Edward and Caterina Marciel, Sam was given in adoption (hānai) to Edward's childless sister Christina and her husband, Samuel Kaha'i Ka'ai Sr. of Moloka'i.[3] Not until he was nine did Sam discover that "what was an aunt and uncle were really [his] biological parents." Ka'ai spent his early years on the Marciel homestead in the rural sweet-potato growing and fishing village of Kaupō on the southeastern side of Maui. During World War II, his grandmother Kealoha "Pake" kept her grandchildren safe there and away from any wartime "conflict or unpleasantries." When his parents separated, Ka'ai lived with his father, who married Eliza Kapukini Apo from Waihe'e, Maui, and Ka'ai helped to raise the five

FIGURE 20. Sam Kahaʻi Kaʻai Jr., Hāna, Maui, 1999. PHOTO BY MASAKO CORDRAY.

children born of that union. He later attended intermediate and high school on Oʻahu, but dyslexia hindered his academic achievement even as it augmented his artistic skills.[4] He eventually earned a certificate of completion in 1957 from McKinley High School, or Tokyo High as it was called owing to the predominance of Japanese American students there.

After winning an art scholarship, Kaʻai spent two years at the Honolulu Academy of the Arts. Having entered with considerable experience using adzes and chisels to make wooden boards and boxes while living in Kaupō, he taught in his second year the woodcarving class he had taken the year prior. After finishing his art studies, he was hired to work at the International Marketplace (a tourist market in Waikīkī) to carve human faces. He also served in the Army Reserves for a few years.

Kaʻai began to feel that "something was missing in Honolulu," so he moved back to Maui in 1960 and eventually opened a shop on Front Street (Lāhainā) called Ka Honu (The Turtle), where he sold carvings he made and imported crafts from thirty-eight Pacific Islands. At twenty-three he married a schoolteacher from Michigan, and they had three daughters. At this time he also began to visit his great-uncle Līhau Kaʻula Kaʻaihue in Kaupō and talk about "Hawaiian subjects," which "were not popular at the time." His growing sense of unease and dissatisfaction — that missing thing he first felt in Honolulu — and a divorce in 1985 led him to a crossroads:

When I got separated, I took a reappraisal of what I was doing. . . . The satisfaction for the Western world is you should be paid a salary . . . there was no spiritual satisfaction. [There was] just about a two and a half year dark period, and, after that I just made up my mind—that Hawaiian culture was orientated towards tourism. It was not really to be done for itself. . . . The kūpuna [elders] had another set of values, yeah. I remember elders being frustrated because they had all these kind of sayings that our Hawaiian was not good enough to understand, and therefore we couldn't enjoy that humor . . . [and] that philosophy. . . . And then, you know, like most Hawaiian parents there's arguments over heirlooms, taonga [Māori word for "treasure"]. You know, some aunty somebody took the pounding stone to California as a Hawaiian memory, and of course nobody pound poi. . . . So the theme "A 'oe maoli? Are you real?" became clear. (2002)

This answer came with "the realization" that Hawaiian "material culture was missing." In his view, things considered Hawaiian were either adaptations of foreign objects (e.g., the 'ukulele, which was the Portuguese *braguinha*) or Hawaiian-looking items produced elsewhere (e.g., kukui [candlenut] lei made in the Philippines and lauhala [pandanus leaf] mats made in Sāmoa and Tonga). He summarized Hawaiians' collective alienation from their material culture in his maxim "When you eat poi from plastic bags, you burp foreign sounds." He argued, "Hawaiian things will be in Hawaiian hands when Hawaiians pick it up, and you can't pick it up in the store, you gotta make it."

All of this "became clear" to him in 1988 when he went to Aotearoa / New Zealand on a Fulbright scholarship to study carving with Māori artisans. He recalled an incident in which he witnessed a young man being scolded by some of his elders for his "Rastafarian hairdo." The tohunga (master carver) told them to leave him alone, for it wasn't the hair that needed defending. What mattered was "A 'oe Māori? Are you real?" He explained, "To a Māori . . . accident of birth did not make you who you were. The fact that your parents got together don't make *you,* it made a *human being;* now what made you *Hawaiian?* or made you Māori? So they would say, 'A 'oe Māori? Are you real? Do you go in the street with your father's good name?' And . . . that hit as a kind of a clear answer to the things that you kinda not put your finger on at home." Ka'ai lamented the fact that instead of doing the things that make us Maoli, we look to written accounts by foreign observers like Cook, who themselves never did the activities they wrote about.

In contrast, he spoke of what and how he learned "in the doing" when he was growing up in Kaupō:

My tūtū (Līhau) used to say, "Kālai kālai, nānā ka maka, hana e ka lima (carve, carve, the eyes watch, the hand works). Your hand coordination, your eye coordination was you, but the sharpening of the adze before you started was the foundation, and the binding, the making of the handle. . . . And then you have to allow for this little extra. It's for the blisters, cause as you concentrate on your carving and you shaping the wood, the adze on the other hand is shaping the hand, shaping the tolerance, shaping the judgment, shaping the 'uhane [spirit]." . . . So by doing all of dese tings increases our familiarity, and then you can feel the same pain of the people before you and have some kinship that its not measured by this time and that time, but time in work. (2002)

Kaʻaiʻs familiarity with the material culture led him to carve the stern images for the Hawaiian voyaging canoe *Hōkūleʻa*'s maiden voyage in 1976. On one stern was a female image, that of Kiha the moʻo (lizard) who represented the kūpuna and the guidance and care of the heavens.[5] On the other side was a male holding a mother-of-pearl disc above his head. Kaʻai explained that he was "an effigy of our time, reaching for the hōkū, the stars. . . . Some people were crying in their heart that they were born too late, see. The trouble is . . . when they pray, they wen look down, they nevah look up. Cause if you get up before dawn, the heavens have not changed. . . . Their relationship to each other is there, so if you lost your way . . . on the land because the streets are changed and the bulldozah making new alanui [road], well, ʻaʻa ke alanui o ka lani (brave the path of the heavens), the heavenly roads are still there. [pause, eyes tearing] Look up, see your star, *remember* where your kūpuna said the island was. . . . So, choose the right star, set the course, give your life to eternity, ma mua, go forward." As has been noted elsewhere (Finney 1979; 1994a; 2003), the voyages of the *Hōkūleʻa* were instrumental in stimulating cultural revitalization in Hawaiʻi and the revival of ocean voyaging throughout Polynesia. For Kaʻai personally, the *Hōkūleʻa* "taught many lessons" that "allowed probing. . . . Everybody looking at oriental and occidental ideas; Hawaiians only had to look south to other islands."

Over the years Kaʻai had been to such places as Tahiti, Sāmoa, Rapa Nui, Rarotonga, Fiji, and Aotearoa/New Zealand. In Aotearoa, he saw a people who had maintained the rituals and songs that kept their ties of family, clan, and tribe together throughout the years of change. "Simply by his forgetting" these things, Ka'ai observed, one "rejects his family." Their primary institution for cultural re-membering was their marae (ritual meeting places and houses), where "you must sing the song of the tribe, of the hapu [clan], and if you cannot, then your child will not belong. . . . That belonging is driven home. Today we do it in hālau, but that kind of support, marae is everything. They have their institution; they zealously stand and protect it. It is a big financial burden to everyone to have those things, but *not to have* [it] is to be *lost* in the wilderness of change." Ka'ai himself was "adopted" by a family (and thus by their whole tribe) and "integrated" as one of their own. Reflecting on his experiences there, he brought them full circle to Hawai'i and the Hale Mua: "If they go to the field, you too will go. And if they go to the church, you too will go because *we* go as the hapu, the iwi, the family, the clan, the tribe. So that kind of stuff we see, we admire, and once you know, you know it's absent here. So I have a tribe. Do you know it's name? Hale Mua" (2002).

Ka'ai's life story is exemplary in the ways that he connects family, work, society, and cultural practice to create a sense of coherence in his life (Linde 1993). He links the dissonance in his personal and work life to the cultural and social malaise he perceived (and still does perceive) as characterizing the Hawaiian people and culture. In Ka'ai's case, practicing the real Hawaiian culture brings order to his own disrupted models for family, work, production, and community — those things that define him as a man. In his life story, he draws connections between the failure in his marriage, his lack of fulfillment as a producer in the culture industry (both on O'ahu and on Maui), and transformations (degradations?) in Hawaiian culture, which include missionization, the adoption of Western cultural practices and laws, the loss of language, values, and philosophies, and the eventual commodification of culture for tourist consumption (Desmond 1999; Halualani 2002; Merry 2000; Osorio 2002; Trask 1999). He also notes how all of these processes have led to the fetishization of cultural objects by Hawaiians, which is both a cause and an effect of the disintegration of familial ties as people became further removed, both physically and culturally, from the old ways.

It is the breakdown in family relations that frame and are understood by the breakdown in cultural practices and relations. Not surprisingly, it is through a reassembled understanding of family and work that Kaʻai sees the answer to cultural degradation. It is here that the genealogical chants offer a mode of Maoli theorization of Kaʻai's life. Like Kahaʻinuiahema, Sam Kahaʻi Kaʻai followed the rainbow-hued path in search of nā maka o Hema—the eyes of the South, the eyes of his father. "Hawaiians only had to look south." Memory is, then, both a context for and a subject of reconstituting self and society. His journeys to Aotearoa opened his eyes to what he was missing—the ritual practices of belonging that maintained identity in the family, clan, and tribe. More specifically, it is through a revaluing of the man's role in cultural (re)production that Kaʻai asks, "A ʻoe maoli? Are you real?" It's not the "accident of birth" that determines identity, but rather what one does to *make* oneself maoli and to carry his "father's good name." These lessons he was taught by his uncle Līhau, whose instruction in carving taught him that blisters of hard work allow one to "feel the same pain of the people before you and have some kinship that it's not measured by this time and that time, but time in work." Thus Kaʻai testifies to his ability, and the ability of all Hawaiians, to recover from the historical and cultural loss that became reproduced in the family and in the individual. Significantly, this is done through a process of re-membering life occurrences and narrating a remembered Hawaiian culture. His moʻolelo places him back in a succession that experienced a haʻi, or a break; through his reclamation work, he made that haʻi a joint, a connection to the next generation.

Replanting Keiki: Masculinity in Family, Place, and Practice

The first time I interviewed Kyle Nākānelua at his loʻi (taro patch) in Wai-luanui, East Maui (see figure 21), he crouched down and pointed to a large, old-looking taro and explained that it would not be replanted again; instead, he'd plant the keiki (children) that were the offshoots growing from the parent (makua) plant. Pointing to a small group of young shoots growing in what looked like a neglected patch of mud off to the side, Nākānelua explained that after one harvests the keiki, you must first poke them into the ground and let them sit; the strong ones that survive are taken out again and replanted. If you tried replanting the top of the older, mature taro, the corm would be small, more susceptible to disease, and likely to die. He pointed to one such plant, with its wilted and torn leaves. "See dat baby? See how da

FIGURE 21. Kyle Nākānelua and his grandmother Helen Nākānelua in the loʻi (taro patch) at Lākini, Wailuanui, Maui, 2000. PHOTO BY MASAKO CORDRAY.

blight wen hit em? If dat doesn't survive, it goes back into da hua [corm], and dat's where you get dat pocket [rot]. Dat's what I found. UH [University of Hawaiʻi] guys get their own manaʻo [ideas], but dey nevah did come here and look."

Fortunately, I was one of the "UH guys" that went to look, and what I found in the moʻolelo of Kyle Kaʻohulani Nākānelua was the hope that the keiki can survive the blight. His father, Paul Hānaialiʻi Nākānelua, had left the taro patches of Wailuanui in the 1950s for a construction job on Oʻahu with his uncles. There he met and married Barbara Rodrigues, and Kyle was born in Honolulu on September 10, 1959, the second of three children. Unlike their parents, Kyle and his sisters were brought up "in the midst of the construction *explosion* . . . of downtown Honolulu." He recalled, "Da sound I distinctly remember growing up to was pile-drivers, *every day* man, just BOOM-CHH BOOM-CHH . . . I can never remember a day wit'out that stuff going on" (2002a).

Nākānelua received all of his schooling at Maryknoll, a Catholic school in Honolulu. He admits that he "wasn't a good student" and "required a lot of attention and help," which he did not often receive. As was common in those days, nuns and brothers were swift to brandish rulers and launch chalkboard erasers if there was any disruption in the classroom. This, however, was nothing compared to the "furious" beatings he would get if his father came home after a twelve-hour workday to find that Nākānelua was slipping in school. "It's tough, you know, but it makes you *resilient*" (2002a). Nākānelua spent more enjoyable times during the weekend with his dad at Little League baseball games, where his dad "would go all out" and bring snacks and drinks for all the kids, even those on the opposing teams.

Hawaiian tastes and communities were maintained in the home, where "there was always a bowl of poi on the table," and at the Veterans of Foreign Wars center where his father's construction crew (the "uncles") cooked pigs regularly in the imu (underground oven). During summer and Christmas breaks, Nākānelua and his sisters stayed with their grandparents in Wailuanui, Maui, playing and working in the loʻi. At Maryknoll he danced hula and participated in historical skits for the "annual Hawaiian program." Because hula was associated with women and māhū, and he often felt he had to "muscle through" them, though no one ever said anything to him since he was a starter on the football team and had a reputation as "a scrapper."

After graduating in 1977, he enlisted in the U.S. Air Force in the fire protection field to get training for a job in the fire department. When asked about the role his service played in his growth, he responded, "The military experience in itself, you know the whole chain of command, the rigors of discipline, well that's all a part and parcel of being a man. You eitha get wit da program or you know, you get run ovah. . . . They give young people *major* responsibilities, and you own up to it." (2002b). While stationed in Japan, he met two Hawaiian-Filipino men who shared with Nākānelua their "plantation style" of Kaji Kempo (Kajukenpo) fighting; here he began his training in the martial arts.

After returning to Oʻahu from Japan, Nākānelua got a job in the Kahului airport fire station and moved to Maui in 1982. When he was thirty he married Oʻahu-born Lolita "Ola" Cole. Though he had always been interested in "Hawaiian things," that interest became a "search" after a white woman who was a tour guide asked him if he knew what the word "haole" meant. He told her "white," which was the understanding he grew up with, and she said, "No," it meant "without breath." He thought to himself, "Son of a bitch. I get one *haole*, and one *woman*, tellin *me* about *my culture*! Sshhiit! How da hell does *she* know dis and I *don't*?" This motivated him to do "more book work, more academic stuff" (2002b). The "major breakthrough" for

Nākānelua came in 1988, when his wife bought him David Malo's *Hawaiian Antiquities* for his birthday. It "opened the door for everything," and ever since he "read every Hawaiian book about everyting out dea" (2002b).

Nākānelua also acknowledged that in large part his personal development in the culture could proceed only after his promotion to captain allowed him to dedicate more time to his search. "I had set myself up financially through the occupation of being a fireman, and I pretty much could grow no further in that realm. . . . So it afforded me now the opportunity, the time to research this thing, to learn this thing. Cause if you wanna do anything Hawaiian, it goin' cost you: goin' cost you financially, goin' cost you in money, goin' cost you in time" (1999).

Nākānelua did intensive research into his genealogy, and he took over his grandparents' loʻi in 1989. His grandmother Helen Nākānelua was a taro farmer who had become involved in a water rights group, Hoʻāla Kānā-wai, and the sovereignty organization Ka Lāhui Hawaiʻi, which Kyle joined after attending some meetings with her. Though he learned much from the groups, he grew much more from the "mundane work" of farming taro with his grandmother, who "implanted" in him her thoughts, behaviors, and memories.[6]

The more mundane it is, the more of a fuller memory you'll have . . . Play baseball wit your kid; the more you play baseball wit em, girl or boy, da more dey goin have dat memory when you ain't around. . . . When dey goin through their psycho-motor skills, that's the time fo hit em wit whatever philosophy you wanna impart on them. . . . They tired and . . . had enough already; when a person is in that kind of state, they so wide open to hōʻupu, that thought implantation. . . . Whatever you tell em at that point in time, it's goin stick. . . . And how I've learned this is just being with my grandmother . . . pulling weeds, pulling weeds, pulling taro, cleaning taro, planting taro. . . . She don't stop talking! Eight, ten hours straight, just on and on and on, the same stories over and over again. . . . And I can tune her out, but just because you can't hear her physically doesn't mean all that stuff isn't going into you. And you find yourself making the same judgments that they've made on other people, which is what you gotta watch (2002a).

Nākānelua's efforts to re-member Hawaiian ways led him to Puʻukoholā heiau. In August 1991, he was on duty at the airport and ran into Earl "Mo" Mollar, a fellow firefighter and activist, and Sam Kaʻai, whom he had heard of but never met. After being introduced, Kaʻai asked Nākānelua if he was going the Hoʻokuʻikahi. Since his daughter was just born and his taro patches needed tending, Nākānelua was doubtful. Kaʻai told him, "Oh well, if you real, you'll be dea; if not, you won't be." Two weeks later, after overcoming his anger and receiving encouragement from his wife, he jumped on a plane and attended the first Hoʻokuʻikahi. Though profoundly moving, it took some time and additional understanding of Hawaiian ritual practices before he could reconcile them with his Catholic beliefs, which he eventually did by finding similarities between the two. The next few years for Nākānelua "was nothing but a whirlwind," as he completely immersed himself in his cultural research. Despite his wife Ola's apprehensions, Nākānelua decided that their children would be put in the Hawaiian language immersion schools, and he taught himself Hawaiian from books and by speaking with his grandmother: "Nowadays we have Hawaiian language, and its basically a [UH] Mānoa ʻano (style) or it's a [UH] Hilo ʻano. . . . So you get this kind of thought process. . . . The elders have a language based on living. . . . And so fortunately my grandmother is a native speaker, and they have a whole different way of thinking, and the language brings life to da work, and den da work gives life to da language, and when you separate da two, you *lose* something in da process" (2002a). Unlike many learners today, Nākānelua received his Hawaiian education outside of the classroom on his own and found sources that were literally grass-(or taro)roots.

The other major area he worked to reinvigorate was the lua and Nā Koa. For him, it was just another phase of his own "self-searching" since he carried the name Nākānelua, which itself could be translated variously as "the lua (fighting) men" or "the lua (dual/two) men." As I mentioned in chapter 4, his prominence in the lua schools and at Puʻukoholā culminated in his founding with Sam Kaʻai of Nā Koa o Maui, which became the Hale Mua. As the group grew, men from the Royal Order of Kamehameha took notice, and soon members of the Mua were recruited for the Royal Order. Using the language of the loʻi, Nākānelua explained, "It's just like the taro you saw there. It was a bunch of mākua [mature adults] . . . just being planted, and nevah have any shoots, and da huas [corms] was gettin smallah and smallah every yeah. So, you know, we needed to get some young hulis [taro slips] in deah. . . . We planted em and it's flourishing" (1999).

Nākānelua discovered that to be a visible figure in the community entailed responsibilities, something he inscribed on himself with traditional Hawaiian tattoos (see figure 18 on page 148). He recalled an instance when, after being invited by some coworkers to have a few beers at the beach, he thought twice because of his doubly marked body: "I gotta always be conscious of what I'm doing, because of what I represent, and because of who I represent. You know, 'Aw SEE! Just one naddah braddah ackin' up, wit' all dat shit on, tinking dey be all dat!' Da's da judgement go' come out. So I gotta make sure that, you know, I don't afford them the opportunity for that judgment . . . that's what you gotta live wit,' you know, once you put dat ting on" (2002a).

All of this growth did not come without a cost. Time spent in the taro patches or with the Mua soon was time away from home, and this put a strain on his family life and his relationship with his wife. The tension was ongoing, but he legitimated it by explaining, "Whenever I come back, I was always a better person. It wasn't that I come back and beat her or [was] more impatient. I always come back more patient, more open, more reasonable, more calmer. . . . There were times when [she said,] "You gotta go back already. You gettin on everybody's nerves" (2002b). He also mentioned that Ola continued to find books he had not yet read while also ensuring that the children's English language skills were maintained. In the end, Nākānelua felt that the culture had brought about an important growth in his own self and in the family:

It's helped me to be more of who I truly am. . . . You know, some people no feel comfortable as females and males, and all of a sudden dey make one flip in their life and you know all of a sudden dey comfortable. Well, I nevah felt comfortable in my life being Western. . . . And now dat I have dis, I feel really comfortable wit who I am, and because I am comfortable, I'm a better husband for my wife. I'm a better father fo' my children. The stories and the songs that I sing to them are Hawaiian ones, and I seen dem grow in dis, and they are more solid in who they are as human beings. . . . And again, it's an attribute to the mākua, to the parents, because the parents provide this kind of environment . . . because the parents feel this way. . . . It permeates the children, and the children permeates back to da couple, and now da family becomes *thick,* and *grounded* (2002b).

Like Ka'ai, Nākānelua articulates indigenous masculinity by narrating cultural activism and personal growth as a man in terms of work, family, travel, and place. If Ka'ai represents the transitional generation that saw "culture" become an heirloom to be mourned and fought over, Nākānelua's time was the "explosion" of change, the postwar statehood period that officially began the month before he was born. Transplanted from the taro patches and driven into manholes, country people found that their lives became even tougher in the city. Yet even in the urban loʻi, the taro took root, feeding off of streams now covered by concrete, but still producing keiki (children) that would themselves one day be transplanted back into the taro patch that the father came from. Like the taro offshoot that was poked into the harsh environment of the metropolitan muck, Nākānelua developed a masculinity based on the "toughness" and "resilience" that was required in an environment where there was no room for mistakes or weakness. This hindered his participation in the hula, which was seen as feminine and weak. Instead, he found connection in what he now calls his "first exposure to the hale mua" — working in the imu with his father and uncles. The other major grounding he got was during his visits to Wailuanui, where he drank of the waters in Lākini.

His father, Hānai (which literally means to "feed"), passed on to his son the importance of work and the ability to put food (especially Hawaiian food) on the table. This was reinforced both in the loʻi and in the Air Force. By the time Nākānelua was settled on Maui, the experience of travel, urbanity, and lack of further growth in the workplace compounded his discomfort at being Western. It was women who gave Nākānelua the initial impetus and ability to "delve deeper": the haole woman highlighted his ignorance of language, his wife bought him the books and encouraged him to go to Puʻukoholā that first year, and his grandmother worked him like a slave and implanted all of her characteristics and thoughts in his head. Indeed, his grandmother taught him that "the language gives life to the work, and the work gives life to the language." Thus when he speaks in metaphors of taro, it is an organic source of knowledge and wisdom, one he has both come to know and live through the doing. It then extends to his family with values and knowledge "permeating" the keiki from the makua, creating a "thick" and "grounded" ʻohana, a family, whose roots are in the loʻi.

Taken together, the life stories of Kaʻai and Nākānelua articulate a number of important experiences that other men have gone through, and they also provide solutions and answers for others. Telling of such stories establishes a place for Hawaiian men in the family and community, both in time and space.

This is particularly relevant at a time when the Hawaiian cultural nationalist movement has occasioned an intense, heavy critique of Western capitalism and patriarchy in Hawai'i and of the roles Hawaiian men play in perpetuating these systems of domination (see chapter 1). At a time when feminist critiques question the place of men's productivity, the connections one can make with work, cultural (re)production, and family in narratives of reclamation and redemption are vitally important for maintaining a valid sense of self and identity. For these stories to be validated, they need to be heard; in many cases, they need to be learned. The Hale Mua provides a forum for both purposes. In the final section, I complete the hale by connecting the mo'olelo of other men to the centerposts in a succession of discursive beams, poles, and thatching. This hale mua is one made of mo'olelo that bind the life experiences, historical occurrences, cultural flows, status transformations, and spiritual summons together through multiple tellings and hearings.

The Work of Men's Mo'olelo: Connecting History, Culture, and Memory

One of the prominent themes of the life stories shared among the men was the importance of the Hale Mua addressing the search for knowledge about being Hawaiian as well as what it means, both historically and culturally. Many expressed a feeling similar to Ka'ai's, namely, that "something was missing," or like Nākānelua's, that he wasn't "comfortable being Western." Most were quite explicit in stating that they didn't know what it meant to be a real Hawaiian. The institutions of work and education were held up as the primary sites in which loss occurred, either through removal from or failure to impart culture.

The mo'olelo of Keoki Ki'ili and Kūkona Lopes most clearly highlight these themes. Ki'ili left Maui in 1967 as soon as he graduated from Baldwin High School and moved to the U.S. continent. There he entered what was to become a long career in the military, both in active duty and in civilian status. In 1990, Ki'ili became associated with an Office of Hawaiian Affairs (OHA) project to establish a "blueprint" of all the Hawaiians on the U.S. continent. A kupuna named Aunty Rena Nelson took him under her wing and introduced him to her friends as her "coconut hānai [adopted son]," that is, he was "brown on da outside, white on the inside." This statement triggered "assimilation" anxieties he had previously felt, the first being a realization at a meeting that all his coworkers and closest friends were white, and the other being a telephone conversation with a Sāmoan who told him that he sounded "very, very, white." All this "opened up" in him what he describes as a "yearning to be what I really am, a Hawaiian man that was educated and wanted to return home to find my roots" (2002). He returned in 1993 and through sovereignty activities, lua, and the Royal Order, he became an original member of the Hale.

Kūkona Lopes (see figure 22) characterized his arrival at the Hale Mua (upon invitation by Ki'ili in 1998) as guided by a "sense of discovering why I was born Hawaiian . . . something that always just played around in the back of my mind." Like Ki'ili, Lopes had landed a career (as an air traffic controller) after serving in the Air Force. A "city boy" from O'ahu, he graduated from the Kamehameha Schools in 1972 as part of what he called the "lost generation" produced by a curriculum of "making Hawaiians into haoles." When Lopes moved to Maui to find work, an "essence coming from the land" that he had never felt before led him to realize that he too was a "coconut" (1999).

Both men found reconnection through the nexus of historical, ancestral, and interpersonal relationships created in the Hale Mua. Ki'ili's narration of his first experience at Pu'ukoholā heiau articulated a number of important narrative themes: "The thing that really got me was getting on to the heiau, me and the men, going around in malo and swimming around in the ocean, and touching the stones [pōhaku]. . . . We would stop in the back of the heiau, and we would put our hands on the pōhaku and we would try to touch the mana of our kūpuna who put that stone there. . . . If you remember the first time you went down there and you come back and it's almost like you're empty, it's like, 'Wow, what happened?' As if you took a step in the timezone, and then we came right out of it, and it's like 'Why did I have to come out of it?' Guess you might say, you know, walking with a suit on and a malo on at the same time, you walking in two different lives" (2002). Embodied acts of "going around in malo and swimming in the ocean" and "touching the pōhaku" are shared experiences done with "the men." Together they feel "the mana of the kūpuna" who placed the rocks there and perhaps swam in the same waters of Kawaihae. Ancestry is important, for it is through their mo'okū'auhau, their genealogical connections as Hawaiians, that they are able to link their stories to the larger histories of the lāhui, as well as to the personal stories they share with one another. Combined with their coparticipation in the ritual process, the mo'olelo that emerge from

FIGURE 22. *Left to right:* Keʻeaumoku Kaʻiama, Kūkona Lopes, Keaweʻaimoku Kaholokula, and Andre Perez prepare for the beginning of a sham battle, Puʻukoholā, Hawaiʻi, 2005. PHOTO BY SHANE TEGARDEN.

their experiences of ritual transformation are powerful tools for narrating and remaking self through society, and vice versa. Thus, the assumption of my own shared memory ("you remember") leads Kiʻili to make a statement about his and indeed all of the men's spatial and temporal experiences ("you took a step in the timezone . . . we came right out . . . Why did I have to").

In practice, the weekly meetings of the Hale Mua aimed to maintain these connections of men with each other, ancestors, and place. Lopes's recollection of his first meeting, at which he initially stood back and just observed the routines, resonated with Kiʻili's moʻolelo. When I asked him how it felt to watch that practice, he responded, "Like, even now when you just asked me that, I get the tingle again right, because it was like ʻYeah, this is something that calls to me.' You know I won't say that, in reliving past lives or anything, you know this is what I did, no, cause I don't know if that really exists, but then again I do [chuckle]. I dunno, what I'm tryin to say is that, it was something that touched a part of me that just said, ʻYeah, this is what you should have been doing all along.' . . . You know, looking back now this is what Kamehameha Schools should have been for me" (1999). The memory sparked a physical response ("the tingle") that he felt the first time he saw the embodied performances of the men, who at the time were training with the ihu aʻu (marlin-bill daggers) at an open-air basketball court at the

Paukūkalo Hawaiian Homes community center below the Pihanakalani and Halekiʻi Heiau. It also served as another frame for reevaluating his experience at Kamehameha and his life as a Honolulu urbanite, which shortly after that meeting he regrettably had to return to because of being relocated in his work. At the time of the interview, he and I had just attended our first Puʻukoholā after a year of commuting between Oʻahu and Maui to train with the men (see figure 14 on page 120). Lopes longed to go back for good, but the demands of work dictated that now was not the time. This led him and Kiʻili to discuss how "everyone has their journey," and his move back to Oʻahu was a "test" of his commitment. He found that every time he returned to Maui he was "recharged" after being "drained" on Oʻahu. This sort of geographic tacking mirrors the cultural crossings between the urban/rural, work/nonwork, Western/Hawaiian spaces the men inhabit.

Men's Work in Moʻolelo: Connections Across Class and Occupation

The other most commonly discussed theme in the men's stories was the joyful experiences of brotherhood, fellowship, and camaraderie as men, regardless of educational, occupational, or class differences. The group offers identity and community to the men, especially those who are middle-aged and come from a middle-class background (like Kiʻili and Lopes), who are searching for a way to take part in the cultural projects of re-membering lāhui. It also serves as a place for less economically mobile men as well as those who are not necessarily looking for their Hawaiian "self," but rather for a Hawaiian group of and for men.

Hanale Amaral's life story captures a little of each of these elements. Born in 1944 on the island of Oʻahu, he grew up in the Nānākuli Hawaiian Homestead community and moved to California when he was twelve after his father took a job at the Long Beach Naval Shipyard there. Not finishing high school, he enlisted in the navy in 1966 and spent four years in Vietnam repairing gunboats and working on a rescue ship. Through the military he was able get his GED, and when he returned he worked his way up from a mechanic for Firestone to a facility manager at American Honda in California.

When his father passed away around 1988, Amaral and his wife moved back to Maui, where both she and his father were originally from. Employment opportunities were few, and he recalled, "It was a shock to be making that kind of money you making on the mainland and you gotta come home and my first job was driving a tour bus for $7.50 an hour." On top of that, he had to listen to the tourists "grumble about Hawaiians . . . all the time." He quit that job, worked in construction for a short period, and then eventually got a county job as a wastewater plant operator. At his stage in life, he wasn't out to "impress anybody" but "just [to] do my thing, keep everybody happy, keep my family happy," and teach his grandchildren (2002).

Though his return home led to a "downgrade" economically, his cultural growth was tremendous. "I didn't realize how much Hawaiian meant til my father died and I came home, and then I realized that being Hawaiian is a gift." In part this came from his association with the Hui o Waʻa Kaulua, a community organization in Lāhainā working to build a Hawaiian voyaging canoe and a cultural park. It was also a product of the deep interpersonal connections he made with other Hawaiian men such as Carl Eldridge, whom he considered "closer than my brothers." From their participation in working on the canoe, the two of them came to join both the Hale Mua and the Royal Order together. In reflecting on his participation in the three organizations, he linked his newfound pride in his heritage to the welcome he felt in the Hale Mua and the need to keep local children home and stop the brain and culture drain.

You gotta be proud of what you are. And that's why I got involved with Carl Eldridge . . . and all the guys, because I always felt welcome. You know it's nice to come home and never feel out of place. . . . You go the Hale Mua, you have different talents, different education skills. We have doctors. We have attorneys. All different men in different fields, but all come to one place and enjoy each other, and no one tries to be better than anybody. . . . That's what makes me feel good. That's why I say being Hawaiian now is important. . . . We gotta take the younger generation like [how the Hui o Waʻakaulua was working working with children on the canoe] and teach them. Our kids today, here in Hawaiʻi, suffer because their parents work so many jobs to make ends meet so dat these kids can have a good education, and they don't wanna stay. They wanna go to the mainland cause they wanna make the money, and it falls back to the same thing I did. (2002)

Here the teaching of canoe building and navigation is seen as a means of instilling pride and rootedness in the children, a quality that Amaral sees as inversely related to aspirations for economic wealth and mobility, which threaten to lead them away when they grow older. It is significant (perhaps ironic) that the object for this discourse is a voyaging canoe, for it is precisely the rethinking of travel and discovery that Amaral is a part of. Relatedly, the Hale Mua creates a place for these diverse men and a network for men and boys to "come home" to and "stay."

Though the general pattern for the men has in fact been one of "coming back," there are a few who never left. If the stories of Kiʻili, Lopes, and Amaral are those of the "routes" of Hawaiian male mobility, Pākī Cabatingan's is that of the "roots" of Kanaka locality. Born (in 1957) and raised on Maui, Cabatingan attended Baldwin High School and came from a working-class neighborhood in Wailuku. At the time of our interview in 2002, he worked for the Maui County horticulture division, a job that coincided with his passion for native plants. When he joined in 1996, he was working at night in guest services at a hotel that catered to Japanese tourists, which prevented him from attending Puʻukoholā that year. Cabatingan was also taking Hawaiian language at the local community college and making Hawaiian crafts in his girlfriend's hula implement shop. At the same time, he was enrolled in Japanese classes for work, and he laughed as he contemplated, "That was kind of interfering with my Hawaiian!" This conflict of job training and personal growth led him to see the Hale Mua (actually Nā Koa at the time) as an avenue through which he could continue his cultural education, deciding "I bettah get to dis Hawaiian, you know, class, or this program, or whatevah you like call it" (2002).

However, the transition was made difficult not only by his work commitments, but also by his initial lack of interpersonal connections with group members other than his friend Kalei, who invited him:

I was tinking, "Ah, dese guys. I wonder if dey know what dey doing." You know what I mean. Anyting, you know, you kind of skeptical about people who tinking about old kine stuff—talking bout old stuff—but I nevah know none of dese guys—Nākānelua, Sam Kaʻai—I heard of dem, but I nevah did meet dem. . . . So I wen' couple practices in '96, I nevah went to Puʻukoholā, but I kind of was kind of interested, so I wen' quit da hotel. '97 was my first year I wen go all da way. . . . And den when I met Nākānelua, Sam Kaʻai, and I seen da dedication dey had, [and] Kamanaʻo [Crabbe]. . . . And I seen dat dese guys was sincere in what dey was doin.' . . . Nobody was out there to . . . prosper off another. [They] just like to share all da knowledge. What dat person have, dey can share. What you don't know and somebody else get, you can ask, and you know, dat person willing to give you. So dat was one big reason why I stayed too, cause of dat attitude. [It was] not all [about] only tryin to find ways to take advantage of somebody, eh, to make a dollah off of somebody; dat wasn't da case. So da's da kine group I can trust (Cabatingan 2002).

What is striking here is the way work experiences and work relations serve as the larger frame against which Cabatingan judges and feels out the group. Although Cabatingan doesn't state it as such, part of the difficulty in establishing community with the other men lay in overcoming class divisions. On the one hand this was a structural matter, as he worked two jobs and had less free time than some of the others, who could more easily dedicate their time to activities and take vacations to go to Puʻukoholā. Indeed, Cabatingan had to quit his second job in order to fully experience and enter into the Hale Mua. This decision was likely facilitated by a dissatisfaction with, or at the very least a lack of passion about, working in tourism.

The decision was also cultural in nature, as he was at first suspicious of the motives behind people who are "talking about old stuff," that is, the less familiar (because not commodified) forms of ancient knowledge and practices. This suspicion seems to be less about the Christian Hawaiian fears of paganism, though there certainly is a connection, and more about the possibilities of class exploitation and individual advancement under the guise of cultural affiliation. As noted by others, the fact that Hawaiians devote great energy to developing and maintaining affective interpersonal bonds and relations of reciprocity simultaneously leaves them vulnerable to exploitation, manipulation, and deep emotional pain (Howard 1974, 31–32; Ito 1999, 100–02; Linnekin 1985, 135–63). This produces a wariness within individuals such as Cabatingan, who must first make sure that the motives are true and that this is a real Hawaiian group — not only in the subject being taught and learned, but in the *ways* in which people relate and "share." This verification process can only be done in face-to-face interactions and identification with men who, despite their real or perceived class differences, are "willing to give" and thus can be trusted.

Of Men and Crabs: Status Anxieties and Resolutions

Lopes noted in his interview that what he missed the most after leaving Maui was the feeling of acceptance and family when he was "doing the work-out" with "the guys." That feeling was "anchored" when he carved his first weapon—the ihu aʻu. A la Kaʻai, he stated, "In shaping it . . . I could relive the way things were." Yet at the same time, he carved his "a little differently" from the others in the Hale Mua; rather than "look down on it," the men "seemed to like it" and thought it was "innovative." He recalled, "That made me feel good . . . that I wasn't doing something that somebody would look at and say, 'Aw, brah, what you tryin to do?' It was just like, yeah, this is your creativity, this is what you feel, do it. That's great, and that's what I like about our group too. It's really cohesive, there's no jealousy" (1999). Anxiety over potential jealousy begins with an expression of individuality (in contrast to group identity) and revolves around a material object, itself an apt metaphor for the larger dynamics of capitalist material relations conflicting with indigenous interpersonal relationships. His initial worry about the group's construal of what he was "tryin to do" comes from both a desire to be accepted and fit in and a fear that he'd be seen as pretentious.

Both Lopes's concern about jealousy and Cabatingan's wariness of being taken advantage of are two sides of the same coin of the embodied ambivalence that arises when Hawaiian men attempt to remake subjectivities across class and status divisions which are themselves produced by colonial capitalist society. Frequently the conflict arises when individual achievement in work and education conflicts with or even damages group affiliation among Hawaiian men (and women) and their peers (Howard 1974; Boggs 1985). Hawaiians and non-Hawaiians alike use the shorthand of the "ʻalamihi [black crab] syndrome" to explain this dynamic. Here, Hawaiians are likened to crabs in a bucket who pull down those that try to climb to the top to escape. Karen Ito explains it as an outcome of Hawaiian notions of self that are "grounded in social relations" and "the reciprocal exchange of emotions" (1999, 80–81). While the ideal self is characterized by aloha (expansive generosity of love, empathy, and hospitality), cultural failings manifest in jealousy. Ito's lady friend thus explains the crab in the bucket behavior as a result of Hawaiians being "a jealous people" (ibid., 86). Hawaiian staff members of the Queen Liliuokalani Children's Center (QLCC) in the 1970s argued that it was more than a blanket denigration of all achievement, but rather it depended on "how the ones who made it got to the top" (Pukui et al. 1972, 2:310–11). If the "top crab stepped on all the others" and did not "help fellow Hawaiians in need," then he was not "really Hawaiian anymore" but "turned *haole.*" Others have convincingly argued that the use of this trope works primarily to mask the larger colonial processes that have created and are also perpetuated by divisions among Hawaiians (Perry 2002; Trask 2001). However pernicious it may be, this idea remains one of the most self-debilitating for Hawaiians today (Kanahele 1986, 450–51).[7]

Though neither Lopes nor Cabatingan explicitly refers to the "crabs in the bucket syndrome," their misgivings give voice to its presence. Sam Ka'ai, however, was quite explicit in identifying and critiquing the concept as one that the Hale Mua is defined against. When I asked him to characterize "the average Hawaiian man," he argued that the only thing "average" is the modern capitalist society we live in, or the "galvanized bucket":

The trouble is that the bucket is galvanized; if it was a basket they crawl in and out . . . I don't think it's the fault of the crabs as it is the fault of the environment. And so there's some galvanizing stuff in Hawaiians, but Hawaiian men are trying to raise their families, some cope well, some don't. . . . I think there is a deep philosophical difference. Society is preparing you to be in a capital economy, but many Hawaiians want to be in a subsistence economy. The ones who have been educated enough to make it in a capital economy become the leading edge because they have spendable income. The one that is growing taro is admired because he is "native" in a sort of childlike quality, rather than being the cardinal part of society. . . . When you talk to Hawaiian men, they tell about when they went hunting, they went fishing, all that reminiscing — except that the prime movers sell lands . . . for higher values than the native can ever own, so you're alienating the native population. So the average Hawaiian man is coping, dealing, and handling all those problems. . . . There are men coping at every level. . . . The only thing "average" about Hawai'i is the galvanized bucket. Rules and restraints of society on man and how we handle it. Some handle wit aloha, some handle wit anger. Hopefully wit thoughtfulness and discipline, is what the Hale Mua is for (2002).

Ka'ai's analysis is an insightful one. His characterization of Hawaiian men "coping" echoes the observations made by Howard and others (Gallimore and Howard 1968; Howard 1974) of Hawaiian men in Nānākuli during the 1960s who were coping with competing cultural paradigms (Ka'ai's "deep philosophical difference") present in the transitional community. One of the Polynesian-Hawaiian attitudes Howard identified as particularly challenged was "status assent," or accepting one's position in society (1974, 212). Steve Boggs notes that "the ambiguity of statuses in a culture conflict situation decreases the likelihood of status assent" (email, 1/15/07), thereby foster-ing feelings of resentment that Hawaiians must cope with.

My contention here is that the Hale Mua, and the formation of commu-nity and identity within it, helps to produce a shared understanding and acceptance of differential statuses as not diminishing the Hawaiianness of individual members. The frequent invocations in my interviews (and in other forms of discourse) of the "different backgrounds" of the men, fol-lowed by the "doctors and lawyers" examples, work to discursively legiti-mate these different class positions. The structure of the 'awa ceremonies, wherein all are open with their life stories and status is recognized by age first and then by activity in the Mua, also helps to diminish resentment of sta-tus ascription, particularly because it is determined by the protocols of the group rather than by occupational or class identities. This allows for an imagined reintegration, vertical or otherwise, of Hawaiian society in the body of the group, a process which is itself seen as hindered on a larger scale because of the 'alamihi syndrome. In the context of the Hale Mua, individual achievement (which in other cases might be seen as haole) is validated as Hawaiian *because* it now feeds into a group endeavor, that of casting men forward. This integrating process takes place in the sharing of mo'olelo in ritualized 'awa ceremonies, tape recorded interviews, and informal talk story sessions.

Perhaps the best example of remaking community across class divisions comes in the mo'olelo of the Hon. Richard Thomas Bissen Jr., now a circuit court judge but at the time of my interview in 2002 the chief prosecutor of Maui. Bissen was thirty-five when he attended his first practice in 1997, which he thought was going to be more of a discussion group. He was surprised to find not only that the men were training in martial arts, but also that they were called Nā Koa, which was his mother's maiden name. He attended the practices for about two weeks, mistakenly thinking that Kyle Farm, who was leading the practices in Kyle Nākānelua's absence, was the Kyle everyone referred to as the head. When Nākānelua finally attended, Bissen was surprised because they had been friends from before, and he was even more surprised to discover that Nākānelua knew he was coming all along. In trying to figure out the ambiguity that shrouded his entrance, Bissen reflected, "I think part of it was . . . they thought, you know, maybe, was I gonna stick with it? . . . Did I think this is something I'd be interested in doing? I guess some had made an assumption that I wasn't gonna be there because, 'Naw, the guy is an attorney' or 'He does something in the public eye, he's not gonna come hang out with us,' I think that's the impression. It's the same underestimation that I've been met with since high school, college, law school, you know it's the same thing, just, people thinking, 'Oh, he's not gonna wanna get down in the dirt with us,' because people have an image of what they think the county prosecutor does or is made of. But nobody knows that I grew up feeding pigs" (2002).

The "underestimation" Bissen felt his whole life was precisely the general expectation of low achievement that most Hawaiian males face, especially those who, like Bissen, come from a working-class background and look Hawaiian (i.e., are big and brown). Growing up, he worked in his grandfather's catering business, collecting slop for the piggery and serving food and drinks at catered parties that his family also performed music at. Given this background, it would be quite easy to see him as the happy-go-lucky Hawaiian, a depiction that was only compounded by his quick wit and love of joking. Yet he was in fact a serious student, and he went from St. Anthony High School to Santa Clara for college. When he went to the University of Hawai'i Law School, his classmates wrongly assumed he was on a special "preadmissions" program developed to help Hawaiian students adjust to law school by giving them an extra year. Ironically, the assumptions made about him when he first came to the Hale Mua were based on quite disparate premises, namely, that he was too "high up" to want to be physical or "get down in the dirt" with the rest of the guys. Bissen remembered that "they were surprised that not only did I come the first time, but that I kept coming, and that became an instant part of my life."

Bissen also surprised himself to a certain extent when he took part in his first ceremony, a greeting of the *Hōkūle'a* at Kahului Harbor (see figure 15 on page 127, second from right): "If you'd have told me that I would be wearing a malo in public, at the arrival of the *Hōkūle'a* . . . as the county prosecutor, with other county officials walking by, I would have bet you every penny and dime I had that 'no way.' But the group was such that—especially from Kyle Nākānelua who obviously sets the tone and goes, 'If you wanna come, come. If you wanna participate, fine. If you wanna wear a malo, fine. You don't have to.' It was a real low pressure sales, and I was like 'aah, how bad can it be? OK, I'll come'" (2002). This atmosphere that Nākānelua and the group created led him to continually return to practice each week and attend Puʻukoholā each year. He enjoyed "the camaraderie" and "the knowledge," and was "really impressed by the guys that commit to this," including doctors and guys who write books about it. "I don't know of any time in history," Bissen says, "where something like this has ever happened, any time in history, where we are able to step out of our modern, complex, sometimes when we get too complex lives, and it would be, just men, doing some things of old, enjoying it, passing it on, you know, living it."

Though said somewhat in jest, the acknowledgment of my writing was a sincere one. Indeed, much of my ability to be writing this is precisely because I have entered into the bonds of trust, affection, and reciprocity as a member of the Mua — and one brought in by Bissen himself. Articulating their stories with mine has been a profoundly emotional experience of great joy and great pain. The reality of our galvanized and galvanizing bucket persists, as do the divisions that separate us along multiple axes. Nevertheless, the ability to sit and talk story with the men is one that produces a profound sense of communion and community, and it gives some hope that our lāhui can be re-made, if only in moʻolelo.

Conclusion: Talk Story, Place, and Identity

In this chapter I have argued that the men of the Hale Mua actively create connections with each other, the land, the ancestors, and the larger Hawaiian lāhui through the sharing of their moʻolelo. As fragments of narrated life experiences, moʻolelo place speakers and listeners alike in a succession of personal, social, historical, and spiritual events, and thereby actively form individual and group subjectivities. Many of the men highlight life transitions, whether in occupation, family situation, residence, social activities, education, or cultural awareness. The members of the Mua thus often use spatial tropes in their narrations of self and perform identities in transition and transformation. The telling and hearing of moʻolelo helps to bring coherence, connection, and completion to individual and collective lives that have either "gone out" and are now seeking to "come back," or are forced to tack between the cultural and economic spaces of "living in two worlds." The narrative practice of talk story becomes a way of rejoining those elements of self and society that have experienced disjuncture as a result of colonialism and modernity. One of the most significant ways is to refigure class and status disparities as understood in a Western capitalist frame as much-needed diversity that lends to a fully integrated model of Hawaiian society, localized in the Hale Mua. When members gather in ritual spaces of transformation and collective production of identity, the men of the Hale Mua come to a deeper understanding of themselves, their communities, and their place therein. Through the mutual creation of knowledge and exchange of emotion, the men begin to heal the fractures of colonialism and remake who they are as a people.

....

The Journeys of Hawaiian Men

"I goin tell you one story." Sam Kaʻai shifted his weight in his chair, gripped the top of his hand-carved cane, which lay resting on his chest, and launched into a moʻolelo. I had been interviewing Kaʻai in his garage for over an hour and a half. He was telling me his thoughts on the "galvanizing bucket" of late-capitalist Hawaiʻi (see chapter 5) through moʻolelo that were personal, historical, mythical, and political. I strained to hear him over the clangings and bangings of our bucket — the roar of automobiles driving by on the busy Pukalani road, where he lived. Kaʻai recounted the experience of leading a predawn commemoration march in 1995 that retraced the path from Waikīkī to Nuʻuanu that Kamehameha took in his epic battle against the forces of Kalanikūpule, the son of Kahekili who was ruling on Oʻahu in 1795. Kamehameha's defeat of the Oʻahu forces at Nuʻuanu brought the domain of Kahekili under his control and represented the single most important military victory in his campaign to unite the islands — that is, the most significant after the slaughter of Keōua and his men at Kawaihae. The Battle of Nuʻuanu, like Puʻukoholā, became a site for re-membering lāhui and masculinity, and its commemoration was led by Nā Papa Kanaka o Puʻukoholā and Nā Koa. Men in the Hale Mua such as Martin Martinson and Keoki Kiʻili (see chapter 5) related their embodied memories of the cold as tests of endurance, identity, and masculinity. Kaʻai had another memory:

As we left Waikīkī, we passed a bar. . . . One girl came out and said, "The Hawaiians are coming!" — and the Hawaiians *were* coming; they were all in malo, it was night, torches were burning, and there were hundreds coming. And this Hawaiian man ran out from the bar, and he was excited that it was *Hawaiians* are coming and he was saying, "Eh! The *Hawaiians* are coming! UP da Hawaiians [gesturing with fist in the air]!!" When he said dat bout da third time, I told Kamana'o [Crabbe], "You go tell him something; you go say next time he says 'up,' we go pay him one visit!" You know . . . what is this "*Up* the Hawaiian"? You know, he was goin like that with his hand [gesturing with fist up in air]. . . . So finally, you could see he was getting more and more excited, the guy must have been about forty or fifty years old, and he didn't know what to say in Hawaiian; he needed to show da people in da bar he drinkin' [with] dat he Hawaiian, he needed to show us he Hawaiian, so what did he yell? "AH, AH, up da Hawaiian, Ah, *MELE KALIKIMAKA* (Merry Christmas)!!" [gesturing with fist in air] Dat's da only ting he could remember in Hawaiian. Dat man—galvanized; dat bar galvanized him, that man, that bar *stole* his soul, took away dat ting in him that made him a *Kanaka*. . . . You laugh because he said "mele kalikimaka," but when you gave thought and empathy to him, you knew, he was *desperately* searching around for something to *say*. . . . All he could pull out at this time of, expression and continuity, was "mele kalikimaka"—dat, was sad. But eh—he said hi, eh? [grinning] "Aloha e ka po'e kanaka, ma mua [Greetings, Hawaiian people, go forward]." So Hale Mua, ma mua, goin' forward. (2002)

The bittersweet tone that Ka'ai ends on is an appropriate one to end this book on. The contrasts and resemblances are profound and unsettling: the stereotypical image of the Hawaiian male drinking all night confronting Hawaiian men who have taken up an idealized notion of ancient warriorhood *precisely* as a means of walking away from what he represents. Confrontation evokes an immediate response of preparedness to fight—the "visit" that Ka'ai referred to would not have been a friendly one. But "when you gave thought and empathy," violence was not the way to respond, nor was a complete denial of kinship with that man. Despite our desire to move past the alcoholism, abuse, violence, and displacement that have come to be seen as Hawaiian, we know it is a product of the bucket, and we also sometimes find ourselves drinking in the bar or at someone's house with fathers, uncles, brothers, and friends. But there is hope; we are moving forward, if not always as fast as we like and not in an environment that allows us to move freely.

All areas of the Pacific have witnessed the gendered implications of colo-

FIGURE 23. Sam Kaʻai blows the pū (conch shell trumpet) at Ka Lae (South Point) as the *Hōkūleʻa* retraces the voyage made by Keōua Kūʻahuʻula from Kaʻū to Kawaihae, Hawaiʻi, 1991. PHOTO BY FRANCO SALMOIRAGHI.

nization, whether it be the substitution of traditional Chuukese male warrior activities with alcohol abuse and violence (Marshall 1979), the loss of culturally appropriate roads to masculine prestige and the concomitant instability of community life in the Eastern Highlands of Papua New Guinea (Dickerson-Putman 1998), or the failure of Tongan men to achieve a satisfactory sense of manhood and thus turn to practices of femininity like fakaleiti (James 1994). Many of the colonial experiences encountered by men in Hawaiʻi articulate with those of Māori men in Aotearoa / New Zealand and elsewhere, especially in the realm of the military and sports (Tengan 2002).

The comparison with the Māori case also speaks to the parallel trajectories of colonialism in Hawaiʻi and Aotearoa in which settler colonies appropriated lands and enforced a cultural hegemony that disrupted and marginalized the indigenous populations. These histories are similar to each other but different from the colonial projects carried out in other parts of Oceania, where cultural imperialism seems to have been far less complete and oppressive. Since the 1980s, Hawaiian and Māori groups have actively engaged one another and other peoples involved in the transnational indigenous movement. Common experiences of marginalization in English-speaking settler societies have helped them reconnect through their shared Polynesian genealogies to exchange strategies of cultural revitalization and self-determination in ways they have not pursued with other Pacific Islanders. In part, such transnational indigenous discourse informed the way in which Pu'ukoholā and the Hale Mua became sites for re-membering masculinities and Kanaka Maoli subjectivities.

As I detailed earlier, a product of this transnational indigenous discourse has been the direct influence of Māori modes of resistance and aggressive cultural assertion on the ways that Kānaka Maoli have launched anticolonial projects. One of them has been the reformation of cultural masculinities and the remasculinization of culture, especially through gendered tropes of *strength,* as a means of reclaiming identity in the face of global tourism and its concomitant representations of a feminized, domesticated Hawaiian body. The "warrior" masculinity established at Pu'ukoholā and elaborated on in the Hale Mua has been forged partly in relation to Māori men. Yet at the same time, Hawaiians have influenced Māori politics and cultural forms as well, a fact sometimes forgotten in our impulse to measure ourselves against the Māori other. As we were to find out, Sam Ka'ai was one who actively contributed to this intercultural dialogue and modern-day diffusion. Thus it should come as no surprise that the largest single endeavor carried out by the Hale Mua was a trip to Aotearoa.

Huaka'i Māka'ika'i a Aotearoa: Return of the Elder Brother

Between April 28 and May 11, 2004, thirty men between twenty-five and eighty years of age and seven boys ages eight to fourteen, all members of the Hale Mua, toured the North Island of Aotearoa, also known as Te Ika O Māui—the great fish caught by Māui. In Aotearoa the voyager, trickster, chief, and demigod Māui is known as Māuitikitiki; in Hawai'i, he is Māuiki'iki'i (Māui who fetches or procures) or Māuiakamalo (Māui of the loincloth). While the first epithet links the stories of the Māori and the Maoli and reminds us of our larger Polynesian identity, the second reminds us that mana kāne (male power and potency) resides in the malo, for Māui's conception came when his mother girded the loincloth of the chief Akalana. This concept of malo making men is reproduced in the traditional and modern hale mua when boys and men who are kā i mua receive their first malo and begin to walk the path of becoming Hawaiian men. The Hale Mua o Māui honors Māuiakamalo by performing a dance (ha'a) choreographed by Nākānelua which tells how he fished up the Hawaiian islands with his magical hook Mānaiakalani and snared the sun to slow its pace so his mother's tapa cloth could dry.

For a number of years, Nākānelua and others in the Hale Mua had dreamed of making a journey to Aotearoa. In our shared Oceanic genealogies, 'Ōiwi Maoli are considered the elder brothers to the Māori, and so ours would be a reunion of siblings. Sam Ka'ai told many stories of Aotearoa (see chapter 5), and thus many of us wished to return with him to visit the people and places he spoke of so frequently; we also wanted to do so while his strength was still with him (diabetes, the disease of colonization, was beginning to take its toll on his health). Also in our group was one of our Māori "younger brothers"—Glen "Puhi" Gibson, who was a member of the Ngāpuhi tribe of Waimate on the North Island. As he had been on Maui for a number of years and come to be a part of our family, we would accompany him in what was a long-overdue homecoming.[1]

There were also some very concrete objectives (and objects) we had in mind. The New Zealand Museuem Te Papa Tongarewa held the feather cape, helmet, and image of Kū of the high chief Kalani'ōpu'u, the reigning monarch of the island of Hawai'i when Cook arrived. (Cook tried to abduct him). There were two men in our group who were descendants of that lineage, and as a group we would go to Te Papa to pay homage to these objects and their genealogies with an 'awa ceremony. There was also the matter of a certain taonga (treasure) that we currently had in our care—the carved stone named Māuiroto (inner Māui). The ritual expert (tohunga) Rangitihi John Tahuparae from the Whanganui area hosted Ka'ai when he was in Aotearoa as a Fulbright scholar. Tahuparae came to the Ho'oku'ikahi 1991 to support Ka'ai's efforts, and he gave Māuiroto to the advisors of the ceremony as a source of inspiration and mana when they needed guidance (see chapter 2). Ka'ai felt it was time to take Māuiroto back for a visit to his home of origin. Finally, many of the men hoped to meet and train with members of the Whare Tū Taua New Zealand National School of Māori Weaponry founded by Dr. Pita Sharples, a former professor of education who held a PhD in anthropology and linguistics. Such a meeting, if conducted properly, might even result in an exchange of weapons and knowledge and would be the ultimate test of the training we had been carrying out over the years.

Indeed, the trip was seen, if not explicitly stated as such, by many of the members as a measurement of the Hale Mua's growth as a group and how well we could represent Kanaka Maoli as men; Nākānelua later called it "a graduation for us." This indeed was our rite of passage, as individuals and as a group. In part, we were motivated by the question posed by different Māori leaders at different points in time, a question that in part led to the establishment of Hoʻokuʻikahi, Nā Koa, and the Hale Mua — "Where are your men?" (see chapters 2, 4). Hawaiians too were asking themselves that same question in various ways, the most well known phrasing of which came in the lyrics of Ernie Cruz Jr.'s song "Where Are the Brothers?" (see the introduction). Our trip, then, was meant to provide our answer: "We are here." Nākānelua explained, "The mission was to look at ourselves in the mirror and to see how much of who we 'are' we *were*. . . . The ultimate judgment, actually, is the guy on the other side . . . especially if he's the epitome of that image, yeah, of a person who is culturally clear and connected." In other words, it was also meant to answer Kaʻai's oft-asked question, which he himself learned in Aotearoa: "A ʻoe maoli? Are you real?" (see chapters 2, 5).

The first "reality check" occurred even before we left. Kāwika Kiʻili, the youngest of the four men (of whom I was one) who carried the name Kāwika (David), observed that the number of Hawaiian first names from the original list diminished dramatically when the final list was published with names corresponding to tickets and passports. This served as a reminder of the fact that many of the men acquired their Hawaiian names only after entering the Hale Mua or one of the other sites for remaking identity. Sam Kaʻai recalled that moment and laughed. "It was a really painful rite of passage," he said, "and yet [names were] willing to be sacrificed for the unity of going. . . . I receive it as a warm kind of aloha, but of a courageous nature. Now when somebody doesn't mind standing in a malo and showing me his physical pros and strength yet worries about revealing his palani (white) name, there's something to laugh about and joy about, maybe even sing about and someday chant about. It's maoli, becoming real" (2006).

Of course, we were paying with more than just cultural capital to attend. The total cost for each person was about two thousand dollars, and it would require almost two weeks off from work and being away from family. At least one member needed to raise funds, and a number of men were unable or unwilling to make that kind of sacrifice. Those who could were also required to read a seventy-six-page "Training Manual" that included the words to all the chants, prayers, genealogies, songs, martial arts sets, and dances we would be performing, as well as a six-page-history of the Māori people (downloaded from the Internet) and an academic journal article on marae and urban tribal identity written by the Māori anthropologist Paul Tapsell (2002). Finally, a number of men were asked to carve extra weapons and other forms of material culture such as fishhooks that might be needed for any cultural exchanges we engaged in there; others were tasked with learning new chants, one of which was the section of the Kumulipo that told of Māui's deeds. Thus, after a year of preparation, the Hale Mua went south in search of the eyes of Hema (see chapter 5).

NGĀ TAPUWAE: EXCHANGING OLD AND NEW SONGS

On April 30 we arrived in Auckland and were hosted by the Stirling family at the Māori language and cultural immersion primary and secondary school Nga Tapuwae, which they founded and ran in Mangere, just outside of Auckland International Airport. The patriarch of the family, Te Kēpa Stirling, was a prominent Māori educator and elder whose parents were the subjects of three books by the anthropologist Dame Anne Salmond (Salmond 1975; Stirling and Salmond 1976; Stirling and Salmond 1980). We were welcomed to their school with a pōwhiri (greeting ceremony) in which the voices of the students poured forth in unison. Many of the men were moved to tears as the children's songs and dances exuded a spirit and strength we sought to instill in our children. After an exchange of prayers and speeches, we had lunch and walked around the campus.

Thrilled to see a group of Hawaiians, a number of the young children standing outside their classroom broke into the chorus of "Hawaiian Roller Coaster Ride," one of two songs recorded by Mark Keali'i Ho'omalu and the Kamehameha Schools Children Chorus on the soundtrack of the Walt Disney animated film *Lilo and Stitch*. Ho'omalu, a California-based kumu hula, has blended modern and traditional forms in chant and dance (some think his beats sound more hip-hop than Hawaiian); this has earned him both praise and criticism in the Hawaiian community. In our group it was mostly praise, and in fact the ha'a we performed about Maui was based on the words of the chant recorded by Ho'omalu.

Rather than do that ha'a, we returned the favor by calling on our musicians and dancer to reciprocate with song and hula. Rick Bissen came from a family of entertainers and, as he always had at Puʻukoholā, came ready with his ʻukulele. His cousin Keawe Kaholokula had performed professionally before joining the Hale Mua, and he was one of the few men in our group that danced the ʻauwana (modern) form, a favorite at parties; it was also the same hula form that many of the men associated with māhū, though they always saw Keaweʼs performance as quite masculine. The third member of the trio was none other than Ernie Cruz Jr. Though he was not a member of the Hale Mua prior to the trip, he was friends with those of us on Oʻahu who frequented the Hale Noa ʻawa bar where he played music. It was a fortuitous set of circumstances that led him to join our huakaʻi mākaʻikaʻi — we needed at least one more musician to help carry us through the nonceremonial, though still ritualistic social exchanges that required guitars rather than spears, and he wanted to go to Aotearoa and learn more about the traditions we practiced, especially those pertaining to ʻawa. And so there we were, listening to Disney-Hawaiian songs with kiwi accents and cheering on Keawe as he danced hula.

After dinner, the performing arts (kapa haka) group composed of teachers, parents, and former students of the school invited us to attend their practice for the upcoming National Kapa Haka Competition. The prestigious event attracted the countryʼs best performance troupes and served as an important site for the perpetuation of Māori culture, somewhat akin to our Merrie Monarch hula competition (see chapter 4). Arihia Stirling, Te Kēpaʼs daughter and principal of the school, stated, "Our club is not really interested in doing great things at the Kapa Haka [Competition]. The kaupapa [idea, foundation, project, motive] behind our club is just to have good role modeling for our kids." She explained that as urban Māori "some of our children never even get back to their homelands until theyʼre actually adults themselves. So, this is one of the ways the school is able to maintain some sort of Māori culture for them in the city, and it keeps them off the streets." At Ngā Tapuwae, Māori culture was not just about learning the songs, but also "the stories behind them, why we sing them, and the messages in them" (see Tapsell 2002). She suggested that that was the reason we earlier felt the childrenʼs "wairua, their spirit, touch yours, because they understand what theyʼre singing about." The same sort of exchange of wairua was taking place at that moment in "what we call whakawhanaungatanga, having relationship time, with brothers of Hawaiʻi and ourselves and our families that connect us all." Cognizant that there were twice as many sisters as brothers in their group of thirty that night, Arihia explained that "a lot of our men are on shift work" and thus could not make it. No need to say more; conflict between work and culture was the story of our group also. The proportion of their men who did shift work spoke to the working-class background of most of the group.

Later that night we gathered with the kapa haka group to socialize over 'awa and music played by Cruz and Bissen. Not very keen on our grog, most of the Māori stuck to beer, which some of our men drank. This was the first of many nights of great music and fellowship we had with the three groups we visited, and we talked story and sang for many hours. If our scenario bore some resemblance to the (nonviolent) scenes of house parties from the movie *Once Were Warriors*, it was not completely imagined. The area we were in was South Auckland, the same lower working-class sector of the city—with its large Māori and Pacific Islander, primarily Sāmoan and Tongan, population—that the film and book were set in. Moreover, the Stirling family and representatives from the school appeared in the movie as extras and as performers, and Te Kēpa served as the choreographer of the haka performed. Before coming down, a number of our men had wondered how much life would resemble art; I doubt they expected this close of a match.

Beyond the setting, actors, and dances, the primary resonance with the movie was the message of drawing upon cultural identity as a strategy for self and community empowerment. Absent were the images of drunk and belligerent Māori and the intense gender violence and poverty portrayed by Alan Duff. Of course, we were all aware that the behavior we observed at Ngā Tapuwae was a product of our hosts' obligation to extend hospitality to us as visitors and present the best they had to offer. It is also impossible to know what sorts of lives they lived at home, or if the men on shift work would eventually find their way to a bar. Whatever the case, the time we spent at Ngā Tapuwae, including an extra three days at the end of our trip, was special and left a lasting impression upon us.

KORAUNUI AND TE PAPA: PERFORMING TAONGA

The next morning we flew from Auckland to the capital city of Wellington. Our forty-five-minute bus ride to the Koraunui Marae in the suburb of Stokes Valley (Lower Hutt), where we would stay, took us through beautiful open country with rolling hills, which our driver informed us was one of the locations in which the film *Lord of the Rings* was shot. In the late 1990s, while still working on his clinical psychology degree, Kamanaʻopono Crabbe had stayed at the marae with other Hawaiian doctors and health care professionals while visiting Māori health clinics. Mr. Ed "Koro" Puhia, the elder of the marae, befriended Crabbe and gave him a ceremonial cloak and an honorary title. Our stay there was an outcome and an elaboration of this previously established relationship.

Koraunui Marae was comprised of a meeting house, an open-air courtyard, an eating house, and a small multiuse chapel and schoolroom. Tapsell explains that the marae functions "as a central focus of any kin group's identity," especially during the welcoming ritual that "maintains the boundary between host and visitor until such time as it is successfully negotiated via oratory" (Tapsell 2002, 141–42). It is also at this time that "tribal leaders often empower and perform the kin group's *taonga* [tangible or intangible treasures passed down from ancestors]," which in Koraunui included a long dagger carved and gifted by Crabbe. As Tapsell notes, these deeply layered ceremonial performances of greeting "assist descendants and related visitors to relive their common genealogical ties to each other, to ancestors, and to the land" (2002, 142). Having prepared ourselves for this ceremony (in part by reading Tapsell's article), we did our part in the welcoming pōwhiri by chanting our genealogical creation chants and giving oratory that placed us in a set of relations historically and socially with our hosts. We ended with an exchange of honi, and then shared a meal as newly welcomed guests.

The next day, Tahuparae came to visit with us and Māuiroto at the marae. We sat in rapt attention as he spoke with great eloquence of the traditions of his people, who make annual trips down the Whanganui River. The year Kaʻai accompanied them, he blew the pū (conch shell trumpet) in a way that they had never heard, awakening an ancestral voice they had forgotten. Tahuparae thanked Kaʻai for that, and told of how they continued to maintain the tradition of the pū in their trips. He then placed his hand on Māuiroto, and after some time he told us that Māuiroto no longer speaks Māori — he speaks only Hawaiian. He was happy with us, and he would stay in our care. The things we were doing were pono, and we were to carry them on. We were deeply moved by Tahuparae's kōrero (speech), and we went to sleep early in preparation for our big day at the museum.

We arrived at Te Papa[2] early in the morning so that we could prepare; it turned out that it was the museum's staff who were unprepared. From previous experience with Hawaiian groups, they expected something along the lines of a hālau bearing lei (feather garlands) and were a bit surprised by the sight of us in our malo with spears and our 'awa bowl. Ka'ai blew the pū as we ascended a series of walkways up to the top of the building where the marae was situated. After participating in another pōwhiri, we set up the 'awa in front of the display of Kalani'ōpu'u's cape and helmet; the image of Kū, typically held in the back, was brought out for us. We gave our chants, and the two men whose genealogies linked them to the chief gave the offerings of 'awa in 'apu (coconut cups) they had carved especially for the occasion and were to be left there. When we completed the ceremony, we moved to the open foyer where a host of the museum's dignitaries were awaiting us. There we did an 'awa ceremony to sanctify our relationship with the museum, and afterward we joined them for a meal they had catered for us. Hema Temara, the marae coordinator, told us later that if we had asked for Kū, the cape, and the helmet, she would have been forced to give them to us since we had conducted all the proper cultural protocols. Next time we'll bring an extra suitcase.

During our free time before we returned, I came across an exhibit devoted to the rebirth of voyaging and the *Te Aurere* double-hull canoe carved by Hector Busby, who was inspired by the arrival of the *Hōkūle'a* in Aotearoa in 1985. As Finney has noted (1995; 2003), the *Hōkūle'a* has played a major role in a pan-Polynesian revival of canoe building and voyaging; the renewed interchange between Māori and 'Ōiwi has been a direct outcome of this development. Sam Ka'ai, who was associated with the *Hōkūle'a* as image carver and later as a crew member, had developed a fast and steady friendship with Busby, who also happened to be in attendance at our pōwhiri earlier. And there, in the images on display, was Ka'ai standing on the beach blowing his pū, as if he knew he would one day come back and blow it again in these very halls.

We returned to Koraunui in high spirits, and indeed a small group of us actually sought out some real spirits and returned to the Stokes Valley Bar we had visited, by invitation, our first night in. That night we had all gone over as a group, despite the fact that less than half of the men drink. We all had a good time singing karaoke and talking story, and it gave us a chance to hang out with a sector of the Māori community who were less interested in marae life. When our smaller contingent came back after the Te Papa trip, the owner, Matt, asked us, "Why didn't you tell us you were all doctors?" Puzzled, we looked at each other and said to him, "We got a few, but not all of us are." He then produced a copy of the latest issue of *Stokes Valley Times* (May 2004) and said, "Not according to this paper you're not!" It read:

Prestigious Visitors Coming to Marae This Week
Forty doctors from Hawaii and prominent Maori leader Dr Pita Sharples will be among the guests at Koraunui Marae from this weekend.
A FULL ceremonial Powhiri will be accorded the group from Hawaii. . . . One of the specially welcome visitors will be Kamanao Crabbe, a young doctor . . . [who will] conduct workshops and visit clinics here, along with the other doctors in the party. Mr Crabbe holds the title of Chief in his home area of Hawaii. (Prestigious visitors 2004)

After exchanging looks of bewilderment, we burst out in laughter. We couldn't have made up a funnier story if we'd tried, and we had to double-check to make sure Matt wasn't playing a joke on us with some fancy photo-shop work.[3] After establishing that it was in fact a real newspaper article, we explained more thoroughly who we were and what our purpose was; Matt and the small group of regulars that had come especially to see us had a good laugh. We then proceeded to play pool and darts with them, which unfortunately revealed our tremendous lack of pub skills and led one of the old ladies to remark, "Well, you *play* like doctors." They were happy to have us nonetheless, and before we departed Matt gave us an assortment of dish towels and coasters with New Zealand–based designs. Though not products of a museum or a marae, these modern taonga enacted the same processes of relating that we'd been engaging in throughout our time there.

HĪKOI: THE STRUGGLES OF INDIGENEITY

As for Dr. Pita Sharples, that part of the story was accurate, though to our great chagrin our time at the marae would not overlap. Sharples, due to come in the day we left, was among a number of Māori leaders involved with the organization of the Hīkoi, a massive protest march that began on April 22 at the top of North Island and would end in Wellington (the capital) on the day we were leaving Koraunui (May 5). The action was taken as a form

of resistance to the Labour government's attempt to extinguish Māori cus-
tomary rights and title to the foreshore and seabed, the area extending between the high-water mark and the outer limits of the territorial sea. The
Foreshore and Seabed Bill would vest complete ownership in the Crown and
would protect property rights of any private interests already established,
these being primarily held by foreign investors and speculators. Member of
Parliament (MP) Tariana Turia resigned her post on April 30, the day we
arrived in Aotearoa, rather than vote with her Labour Party for what was
seen as a declaration of war on the Māori community; notably, a number of
Māori men in government supported the bill. Though the bill eventually
passed, Turia and Sharples would go on to establish a new Māori Party that
took four seats in the 2005 elections. This was a direct outcome of the
collective Māori mana and political consciousness manifest in and created by
the Hīkoi, which brought approximately fifty thousand marchers into Wellington on May 5, 2004.[4]

We recognized the struggle of our Māori brothers and sisters as a shared
one. Back home we were concurrently undergoing the same kinds of fights
against efforts to dismantle Hawaiian entitlements, rights, and programs,
and many of us had taken part in the Kū i ka Pono protest march of ten
thousand people in Waikīkī seven months prior.[5] We had been told about the
Hīkoi before we left Hawai'i; Sam Ka'ai and Keli'i Solomon had arrived in
Aotearoa early and had marched across Auckland Bridge with the Hīkoi.
Folks in Koraunui were talking about it nonstop, especially as Pita Sharples
would be staying there. One of his students in the Whare Tū Taua, Robini
Peachey, was affiliated with the marae and in fact did a weaponry demonstration for us with his wife and daughter. A number of other visitors were
trickling in to stay at the marae for the Hīkoi, one of whom was a Māori
activist from Hapu (Clan) Sovereignty. He bore an uncanny resemblance to
our own Keli'i Solomon, who on Maui was also quite involved in political
affairs; it seemed we were destined to be a part of this march.

We chartered a coach to the town of Otaki, the departure point of the
penultimate leg of the march, on May 4. Our new activist friend joined us
and tied to the front of the bus a modified version of the sign he had brought
with him, which declared in red paint, "HAPU and Hawaiian SOVER-
EIGNTY." We arrived and assembled outside of the marae wearing our kīhei
over our street clothes and carrying our weapons. The streets were teeming

with Māori of all ages and backgrounds, some wearing traditional garb and carrying taiaha (Māori fighting staffs) and others wearing leather jackets and pants and holding flags and banners. The march organizers recognized us as a group requiring an acknowledgment and welcome, and an impromptu pōwhiri was held. They called out to us, and we responded with a chant and a performance of the Molokaʻi Kuʻi. We then greeted the front line of leaders in honi and joined the crowd, which on this leg numbered around five thousand.

Mana exuded from the collective assembly, and along the way rallying cries, chants, songs, and dances were performed. We even came across a young Māori man who was carrying a Hawaiian sovereignty flag and called out to us with a familiar Hawaiian protest chant, "I Kū Mau Mau." He explained that he had been in Hawaiʻi in 2002 with a contingent of Māori on a cultural exchange when a protest march took place. The cause that year was the Honolulu City Council's efforts to pass a lease-to-fee conversion bill that would have adversely impacted a number of Hawaiian trusts. Like the Hale Mua at present, his group took part in our march — and I remember because I was right in front of them with my family (and wondering who those Māoris were). Responding to this show of intercultural fluency, Cruz began leading the Māori song "E Papa," and the crowd joined in immediately. He turned to me and laughed and said, "You know, the 'Chant of the Islands' by Fiji?" I nodded and smiled, as I was quite familiar with the song made popular in Hawaiʻi by the recording artist who hailed from the Polynesian-Mormon town of Lāʻie on Oʻahu. Cruz blew the pū as we marched on.

We returned to Koraunui energized and alive with stories of the experiences and talks we had with fellow marchers along the way. Our Koraunui hosts stated, "We know! We saw you on Māori TV!" The newly established Māori Television network had been covering the march, and they had not only filmed our performance but also interviewed Nākānelua and Crabbe along the way. It was interesting to watch as the reporters used a mix of Māori and English in the questions, and both Nākānelua and Crabbe responded in Hawaiian and English. We were hoping to watch it again on the late edition of the news, but we had our poroporoaki (closing ceremony) that night.

The poroporoaki was a time for a final exchange of gifts and sentiments to affirm our relationships before we left. The monetary compensation for feeding and housing us had been determined and settled earlier in the form of the koha (offering) given at the pōwhiri. This particular time was set aside for sharing emotions and stories on the part of all; we also brought more personal, nonmonetary gifts such as carved spears, clubs, daggers, Hawaiian kauila wood, Hale Mua T-shirts and beanies, Cruz's CDs, and boxes of macadamia nut chocolates. We reminisced about the past few days, and an exchange of jokes and humorous stories produced much laughter. Many were teary eyed as they arrived at what would inevitably be a final farewell for many, though most vowed we would meet again here or in Hawai'i. Whatever the trajectories of individuals, our communities clearly had affirmed ancient connections and established new ones that would serve as the basis for future communion. Despite the efforts of nation-states to take them away, our shores will continue to be sites in which we welcome our kin and fight our invaders.[6]

Moving Forward: Maoli Stories of Self and Society

I conclude by returning to the larger themes of the book and drawing out some comparisons and contrasts with experiences in Aotearoa. In the modern configuration of culture and land in neocolonial Hawai'i, a commodified and feminized image of the islands is marketed to the United States and the world as an alluring, domesticated, and welcoming place for visitors. Meanwhile, Hawaiian nationalists contest these representations and work to expose the illegality of American occupation and the injustices of cultural imperialism (Kauanui 2005b; Sai 2004; Trask 1999). However, such challenges to the cultural and political order are often disregarded as fanciful imagination ("We're all Americans, get used to it!") or aggressively attacked by those who seek an end to all Hawaiian entitlements and the erasure of any signs of trouble in paradise.

In light of this situation, how precisely does close attention to language (as spoken narratives or official histories), culture (however one defines it), and ritual performance (such as the conducting of ceremonies on the heiau) lead to any sort of substantive change in the political or social status of 'Ōiwi Maoli vis-à-vis the state, U.S. imperialism, and global capitalism? I would argue that cultural movements enable new sorts of political and social action, especially in Hawai'i and the Pacific (and arguably throughout the world), where important historical transformations have occurred with the recoding of cultural categories, especially in the "contact zones" (Pratt 1992) of Western and indigenous islander encounters (Sahlins 1981; 1985). In the context of the Hawaiian cultural nationalist movement, any project of cultural assertion and decolonization aims to bring about societal changes by disrupting American hegemony and fostering a new sense of 'Ōiwi identity and politics. At a time when the meanings, definitions, and stakes of being Hawaiian are debated more hotly than ever, public enactments of Kanaka Maoli history and culture in critical spaces that work to solidify contested social realities have an important transformative effect that both imbues actors with a new sense of identity and subverts the dominant understandings of Hawai'i.

The Hīkoi is a particularly significant example, especially when considering that Pita Sharples entered Māori politics after participating in educational and cultural movements in Aotearoa, including that of the fighting arts. Not surprisingly, a number of men who came back to Hawai'i after that experience were likewise transformed politically, two immediately joining a broad coalition of independence activists called the Hui Pū. This was not a matter of wanting to be like the Māori, though certainly the comparisons were there. Rather, their renewed sense of political identity came from the unity and communion brought about when the Hale Mua moved as one to join the Hīkoi and did so under the leadership of Kyle Nākānelua. Our ability to then perform culture (chant, dance, and oratory) came about primarily because we could relate culturally to one another in the Mua as Hawaiian men and across class, generational, and geographic statuses. The ability to relate led us to a knowledge and trust in ourselves individually and as a group, and this in turn produced a mana that we were able to contribute to the larger Hīkoi (and indeed to all other undertakings in Aotearoa). The statement we made about ourselves was also a way of negotiating, relating, and communicating our friendship and alliance with our younger brothers, and so there was another larger set of transnational and pan-Oceanic identities and relations that were instantiated at that moment.

The Hīkoi, like the 1995 Battle of Nu'uanu March (see the beginning of the chapter) and the 2001 Keepers of Aloha March and Lele i ka Pō (see the introduction), were movements forward. As uniquely public, political, cultural, and historical events, these marches and the lele created contexts for multiple formations and performances of subjectivity and identity that in turn defined the larger significance of the events as ones that told particular stories and made particular statements about history, nation, and culture.

These narrations, both personal (recollections) and public (newspaper, radio, television), spoke to indigenous unity, strength, aggression, action, and continuity. They were important contestations of the dominant colonial narrative of the "disappearing/ed native," and the high visibility of Hawaiian men refuted the discourse of emasculation and absence that has so long configured notions of Kānaka.

Going Forward

Two years later, speaking with some of the men who had made the trip, I discovered that the feelings we had experienced were still fresh and the stories were full. In July 2006 I did a set of follow-up interviews with the assistance of Kāwika Kiʻili, who volunteered to help me with transcriptions. We sat down to talk story with Peter Vanderpoel, who was one of the few to travel with his son, who at the time was seven years old. Vanderpoel and I entered the Mua at the same time, and we endured the cold wind and rain on the Pihana heiau together; he was only four years older than I and thus closer in age to me than most of the others in the group. His story about Aotearoa became a story about our growth, individually and as a Mua, and I include it here at length:

The trip itself was a once in a lifetime kind of thing. . . . I can't even imagine a better trip. . . . For a Hawaiian cultural group, a men's Hawaiian cultural group with the history of some of its members, like Sam [Kaʻai] and Kamanaʻo [Crabbe], . . . to go down now with a group of men that they identify themselves with and to have everything go the way that it did, it's pretty incredible. . . .
For us, you know we're just this little group on Maui . . . started off with what, five guys? And then we [pointing to me and himself] came in, and gradually it started to grow and we did our thing. . . . End of summer we went to Puʻukoholā. . . . And in the process of doing our thing, other people in Hawaiʻi had kind of seen what we were doing, "Oh that's pretty cool, why don't you guys come and talk about it?" So the group would go and do these things, go to the Taro Fest and pound poi or go to the Ritz and do something there, whatever, talk about this, talk about that. Individuals would get involved with other kids or other groups and talk about the stuff that we do. So it started to be a little bit more than just a bunch of Hawaiians that got together and did their thing, right? So now . . . who is this Hale Mua?
Well eventually for me it was like the more you get involved, the more research you

do, the more reading you do, the more you think, "Wow you know, yea we're doing it the right way. We're pono." But . . . with today's world the Western pressures that are on you, and with one of my favorite sayings of Sam [Ka'ai's] . . . "if you eat from the buffet of life you start to fart foreign sounds," right? . . . You have to kind of wonder well, [is] what we're doing, is it really pono? You can read all the books, you can practice it and all this other kind of stuff, but in a lot of ways like what you're doing with your manuscript thing, you want to have outside validation for what you do, right? And it may not necessarily mean anything, but it does, it means something, some people may not see it as something that's important, but a lot of people do.

So in a lot of ways going to Aotearoa for us as a group was validation that we knew what we knew and we did what we did well. One of the things about it was that there has been a lot of groups that went to New Zealand to go and practice culture and do their thing. And that's basically what we wanted to do, we just wanted to go down there, see some of our cousins, see some of the family, have some cultural exchange on their terms, and do our thing. That's what we went there for. Go see our kūpuna. And the way that it turned out was, the validation that we had on virtually everything that we did was unbelievable. The feedback that we got was that we were the most solid Hawaiian group that's gone down there, especially a Hawaiian masculine group that's gone down there. So, wow, I mean, mission accomplished I guess. (2006)

It is significant that the "validation" of everything, from the growth of our reputation on Maui to my book manuscript to our performance in Aotearoa, is forged in a context of discourse — people talking about us, us giving talks, Vanderpoel comparing our practices to the historical documentation he uncovers, outside and inside audiences reading my book, and Māori feedback. Indeed, it is through discursive practice — ritual performance, talk story, book writing — that we come to know who we are and claim some semblance of (co)authorship in our lives as Hawaiian men.

In 2006, the Hale Mua was at a crossroads. Having experienced tremendous growth and success, and then "graduating" on the Aotearoa trip, many men wanted to take the Hale Mua to "the next level." Disagreement arose on precisely what that would mean and how it would be implemented. Some felt that they were no longer being "fed" sufficiently, and they began to drop off. Perhaps foreseeing a time such as this, Nākānelua told me during our first interview in 1999, "If we want this ideal of an idea to live, then all we

FIGURE 24. *Left to right, facing:* Richard Bissen, Kāwika Davidson, Peter Vanderpoel, and Keaweʻaimoku Kaholokula from the Hale Mua exchange honi and embraces with men from Nā Koa Kau i ka Meheu o Nā Kūpuna after a sham battle, Puʻukoholā, Hawaiʻi, 2005. PHOTO BY SHANE TEGARDEN.

gotta do is uku (pay) the manawa (time) and uku the mana . . . If we don't want it to, then all we gotta do is stop feeding it, and it will hala (pass) until the next group of courageous individuals decide that these are the stones they wanna pick up and the walls that they wanna build." The reconstruction of Puʻukoholā may present just that opportunity, or it may signal the end of this particular story.

There have, however, been exciting new developments that offer hope, especially with regard to training the next generation. On Maui, the Hale Mua has focused on inducting and teaching new boys; the increase in their numbers up to a dozen in 2005–06 has been encouraging. Those of us on Oʻahu also recently established a Hale Mua under the leadership of Ka-manaʻopono Crabbe and Kūkona Lopes, though we are still a part of the Hale Mua on Maui, and Nākānelua remains our head. Still in the formative stage, we had about twelve members in 2006, and most of our members are in their thirties. Perhaps what we're seeing in both cases is not the end of the story, but just the next chapter.

Whatever happens with the Hale Mua, I have had the great fortune of sharing the mana with the men and being a part of their lives, as they have been a part of mine. Taking on the role of the anthropologist has been a particularly challenging task, forcing me to constantly negotiate my status as subject and object of ethnography (see introduction) and make particularly difficult decisions about what and how to write.[7] For all who read the stories presented by the men of the Hale Mua, I hope they inspire a greater awareness of the struggles and triumphs of Hawaiian men, women, children, and the lāhui they have remade.

I end with a moʻolelo from Sam Kaʻai. While sitting and talking about Aotearoa, he recalled the stories he heard about our participation in the Hīkoi, which he had sat out on since he and Keliʻi had already participated in Auckland. Since six or seven of us carried digital video cameras, we could also give him a visual recounting of everything we saw — except our performance of the Molokaʻi Kuʻi. At that point, anyone who had a video camera put it down and went to dance with the group; most of us regretted not having the digital video memory of that moment. Kaʻai, however, had no regrets about his memory of the moment, which was forged in dialogue and discussion rather than gazing. It is good to re-member:

Perhaps my feeling of what you folks did . . . is more vivid because I've heard the story from at least twelve different guys. Like, you know if you said there was a "blunder" when they said "OK Molokaʻi Kuʻi!" and everybody to the *man* was moved to *be* the Molokai Kuʻi that nobody took a picture, for once. If you were programming it, you would give a guy a camera, but everybody was part of the company of the Nā Koa. And when they say "Nā koa" — hmmmmp [brings hands together as he imitates the sound of men assembling on cue]. That in *itself* is magic. So have we gone forward? At that time, yes. A whisper was a command. "Hoʻokuʻikahi! Kū!" ʻōlelo ka mākaʻi o ka Māui ["Unite! Stand!" said the marcher/guard of Māui]. All of that just fell together. What you didn't see is that sometimes the stories you come home with are more vivid than any camera can shoot. Sometimes cameras catch things, but some things only men's stories catch. So have we gone forward? Yes, there are more stories to be told, more kōrero [oratory] and moʻolelo [stories], more things for the sparkling eyes and open ears of our moʻopuna [grandchildren] to hear. Yes, we are going forward. (2006)

Hale mua, ma mua.

'Awa Talk Story at Pani, 2005

The following is a partial transcript of a semiformal 'awa ceremony conducted at the pani (closing meeting) on September 1, 2005, which brought to an end the season of work and began the four to five month period of moe (rest, sleep). Though normally marked by fairly high ceremony and ritual, this 'awa ceremony was more relaxed, and Nākānelua allowed me to record it. The men gave their final thoughts for the year, reflecting on Pu'ukoholā and their involvement in the Hale Mua. There were feelings of sadness and happiness, and a mix of joking and serious contemplation throughout. We followed our usual order of serving the oldest member (Carl Eldridge) first and ending with the youngest (Manu Gibson), and that is how we sat on the pandanus leaf mats. Then the members of the 'awa crew, Keoki Ki'ili and Hoaka Delos Reyes, drank, followed by Sam Ka'ai, and, last, Kyle Nākānelua. When each member was served a cup, he gave his mo'olelo, which ideally would reference something about the past, present, and future. When done, he drank, and a member of the 'awa crew, Keoki Ki'ili, called out "pa'i ka lima (clap the hands)," and all members clap three times to honor the speech and drink. This was our own style, based on traditional Hawaiian thought, Sam Ka'ai's innovations, larger Polynesian influence, and the needs of our men, which, as I have stated throughout, include the creation of a ritual space for transformation and sharing of stories. I present segments of this ritual talk story here in order to give the readers a sense of how the process looks and what is said, though this transcript represents less than half of what was spoken. Not included are the speeches of the children, about twelve, who drank first before going outside to play. Transcript here by Kāwika Ki'ili.

Hale Mua Members Served

CARL "KALE BOY" ELDRIDGE: It was great that the boys worked as one team, yea. Great seeing them at Pu'ukoholā and everything they brought to their sham. This is the kind of time I hate because now we go into moe period that's not involved in the Hale Mua, kind of lose track of each other. I kind of miss it, the boys kind of miss it

FIGURE 25. Boys from the Hale Mua and Kanu o ka ʻĀina Charter School take part in a sham battle. On flats to left stand the men of the Hale Mua, and to the far right is Nā Koa Kau i ka Meheu o Nā Kūpuna. On the raised knoll in the background on the right (above Nā Koa) stand the Alo Aliʻi. Puʻukoholā, Hawaiʻi, 2005. PHOTO BY SHANE TEGARDEN.

too, they always ask how come we don't have Hale Mua. So, I try to keep them active in other kind sports. I want to thank all of you guys for the strength that you guys had. Thank Nākānelua because you keep us together and you keep us going. And Sam [Kaʻai], he shares his wisdom with us, he's our resource person, our library. I thank akua for that.

Paʻi ka lima! (clap, clap, clap)

CORNE "CAPPY" KAMAKA BANCACO: Again I'd like to thank all the members of Hale Mua. Kale [Eldridge] covered much of my opinion. I am just thankful for everybody contributing. I just get so much out of it, out of the Hale Mua. Thank you Nākānelua, Sam [Kaʻai], from everybody. I get something from everybody . . . mahalo

Paʻi ka lima! (clap, clap, clap)

WILIAMA SMITH: This year's Puʻukoholā was an exciting one. I left part of myself on the sands of the field. Not sure about that one though, from both sides. It was definitely, definitely saw the need for teamwork. There are a lot of things happening to our people, the community. It takes education for us to understand. . . . We need to be educated so that we make the right decisions. This time of year after Puʻukoholā, it gets kind of sad that we go our separate ways, but I'd like to offer an opportunity for everyone that's interested to practice with me, to continue to practice. With that, aloha, mahalo.

Paʻi ka lima! (clap, clap, clap)

KĀWIKA DAVIDSON: . . . Puʻukoholā, I thoroughly enjoyed being on the field, I wish it would've been longer. I felt like we had the endurance and the discipline. It was truly a team effort, it was awesome. Good job. And if you noticed all of the health care systems, Hawaiian Health Care Systems, throughout the state were at Puʻukoholā this year and I talked to all three involved in this and they were extremely happy to be there, it's something that took so long to happen . . . Well I guess it's mahalo time, mahalo kākou.

Paʻi ka lima! (everyone: clap, clap, clap)

RICK BISSEN: . . . The most memorable thing for me this year were the kids and how they performed and how people were pretty astounded. Because these weren't just a bunch of kids that just came off of the side and started throwing spears, they were disciplined, they were trained, they were courageous. I was so proud of that. That's all due to Kyle [Nākānelua]'s work and all of you mākua [parents] here, and grandparents, who take care of the kids. I think for as long as anyone will remember, whoever was there this year, beyond the battle that we all were on the front page for, the kids deserved to be there. . . . Just one final thing, kind of touching on what Wiliama said about some of the things you face these days. . . . The battles we fight on the field, Puʻukoholā, is a metaphor for the battles we fight in our daily lives. I mean, we train as a Hale Mua, we go with a specific plan to show what it used to be like, to show how we fight with different weapons we make ourselves, try to be skillful at, try to show courage for. I was thinking about this, this same thing can apply to modern day, Hale Mua, how important it is for us to band together and fight other battles that need to be fought. Maybe with a pen. But we have a microcosm right here of so many parts. But what it comes down to is good leadership and discipline, people pull together, stay all paddling in one direction . . . Mahalo.

Paʻi ka lima! (clap, clap, clap)

CLIFFORD ALAKAI: . . . The year had many strengths and weaknesses. I also agree with Rick [Bissen] that watching the boys in their battle I was actually moved, and most of you think I have no feelings and no emotion; yes, I actually was moved. It was kind of interesting to watch them and the amount of mana and effort and energy that the boys put forward. . . . One of the disappointments I had this year . . . was the logistics of getting everyone there . . . if you guys wanna travel as a hui [group] that's fine with me, if you guys don't want to travel with the hui that's fine with me too. I think we're stronger when we travel as a group and we move together as a group, but I think if we're going to stay as a group I think we need to make the commitment early that we'll travel as a group. . . . The final thing I want to say, and leave on a positive note, the most important thing to me on this trip is sharing the fellowship with you guys. To me, whether we go to Hana, or we stay here or whatever, the fellowship that we share is the most important. The relationships that we have, and I think we've been through a lot together and we should appreciate the time. The period of moe, why do we sleep, we sleep to strengthen your body so that when the past ahead of you is presented you are ready for the test. . . . And with that note, thank you everybody, thank you for putting up with me, mahalo.

Pa'i ka lima! (clap, clap, clap)

KYLE "ELAMA" FARM: . . . Just wanted to mahalo everybody for coming out this year. . . . Not many things can compare to the birth of my daughter, witnessing that; but the only things that can compare to that is the things that we do in the Hale Mua. The first time, my first sham, my first year, [doing the ha'a] Imua Kamehameha on the heiau, I lost my mind; I thought that was the greatest thing in the world. Mahalo Nākānelua for that, for that seed that grew. This year I waited, seemed like I wait two, three, four years for this, a good challenge, something that's real. It's times like this, that moment in time however long it was, one minute, two minutes, I gotta say I truly feel alive. So for that feeling, mahalo to everybody and mahalo to Ke'eaumoku [Kapu] mā. As for the future, every year I always look for more of a commitment from everybody. I'm always watching for guys to step up more, and slowly we do, guys step up in a lot of ways. I'm looking for more of dat. One question I always ponder, you guys may want to think about it, is what is the Hale Mua to you. What does it mean to you? It's something that I think about all the time. So, always to Sam [Ka'ai], mahalo for your guidance, always. To the Hale Mua mahalo.

Pa'i ka lima! (clap, clap, clap)

JACOB KANA: I was one of the guys that was late [arriving into Pu'ukoholā]; sorry, everybody . . . This year I think we prepared really well for the battle that we do at Pu'ukoholā. I think that's why we won the way that we did. I like thank everybody over here for showing up at practice, and working hard, and just coming out and dodging all the spears and taking some hits too. As far as the future's thought . . . I got my youngest son involved, Mauliola. I never bring him tonight cause, I thought was only for us, the guys who went to Pu'ukoholā. Hopefully my other boys see and catch on and they like come too, that's what I like happen. But I'm happy with my youngest son, and I like try work with him for the future. And I guess next year, hopefully I can come earlier, but sometimes because of work we so busy, I get hard time. OK, next year I go try come earlier. Mahalo.

Pa'i ka lima! (clap, clap, clap)

PETER "LUPE" VANDERPOEL: . . . One of the big things for me was watching the boys this year. Mine wasn't so much the actual fight but it was the other times that they spent together. It made me think of, when I think about my childhood some of those times that really, you know, instantly come back to me, the really good fun times, this is gonna be one of those times, this year, for them. And if you look at the context under which it happened it's going to be something even more memorable for them, so that was one of the big things for me. This year was kind of a year of growth for me, personally. This is the first time that I actually have been put into a leadership role when we're over there. . . . I was able to get two of my brothers and a cousin to show up. One of my brothers . . . this was his first time actually being around real Hawaiian men and it was shocking for him, he didn't know how to act. But it was a good thing, I definitely believe that it was a good thing. My cousin was able to come and that was the first time that he'd ever seen anything like this, his exposure to it is going to be long lasting I believe. . . . I guess for the future, it's kind of the same thing I've always felt as far as the future of the Hale Mua and the future of us in our responsibilities. I think that it's definitely grown. It seems like ever since we went down to Aotearoa things have just been exploding, huge, and we've had to adjust how we look at things in a lot of ways, I think, [and] our responsibility to the rest of the world. But I think we're doing a good job of that. I just look forward to the future, I know it's going to be a good thing. Mahalo.

Pa'i ka lima! (clap, clap, clap)

HANALE LINDO: Well I'd just like to say, mahalo ke akua first for all the guidance and the support over this coming year. I'd like to give a big mahalo to Lupe [Vanderpoel] for talking to me over the past couple of years and finally getting me to see the light and come show up, with all the excuses I was giving him. Nākānelua, mahalo, mahalo for this experience. This is the first time that I have been part of a real Hawaiian organization. I never understood my Hawaiianess even though I went to Kamehameha Schools. . . . This past five or six months have just been the most unrealistic experience for me and my children, because we got to do something together as men . . . Was awesome. Pu'ukoholā, ho brah it opened my eyes to some unreal stuff. That was the meanest experience I ever had. I haven't gotten naked in front of guys since I was in high school [laughing]. I was kind of wondering, see everybody stripping, I was like whoa I thought we was going to change in the bathroom or something! [roaring laughter]. The first day it was kind of weird [more laughter] but after that it was good. Was an awesome experience, and I'm not ashamed show my 'ōkole [butt] any more. For the future, I look forward to many many more years with you guys, the Hale Mua. Brah you guys are awesome. Brah I just cannot explain all the gratitude and the aloha that I have for you guys, it's unreal. I really look forward to the coming years. Mahalo.

Pa'i ka lima! (clap, clap, clap)

MIKE LUATANGI VAITUULALA: It's good to be here with everybody and I'd like to say mahalo to Kamuela, Nākānelua, the leaders of Hale Mua for a great year. And I'd like to thank those guys who trained us all year, Lupe [Vanderpoel] and Elama [Farm]. Had a great time at the sham battle, although I didn't get to throw that much ihes [spears]. . . . But if I had known where the camera was I would've run by Hanale [Lindo, who was in the picture on the front page of the *West Hawaii Today*] over here [roaring laughter]. I think we won the sham; it wasn't because of Lupe's strategy but it was because of the meal we had Thursday night—chili with no chili powder [because someone forgot to buy it]. I think it should be a tradition from now on. Like Elama said what does Hale Mua mean to you? I don't know what it is about this group but there's something special about this group, something special and I'm happy to be part of this. I'd like to thank Kale Boy [Eldridge] for bringing me in because I know if I was a Hawaiian guy I wouldn't bring my Tongan son-in-law to a group of Hawaiians [roaring laughter]. Mahalo Kale Boy [Luatangi's father-in-law].

Pa'i ka lima! (clap, clap, clap)

KĀWIKA TENGAN: . . . I want to mahalo aku Kyle [Nākānelua] and Sam [Ka'ai] for the foundation that they have laid which is continued to be built upon by all of us and now is being carried out on O'ahu as we are forming our own Hale Mua there, and it is a testament again to the leadership and the wisdom and the pono of this papahana [program]. It's been a real exciting year for all of us to have brought in some new guys on O'ahu who are really hungry, who wanted to learn, and who wanted to be a part of this thing that we have. . . . Even Kūkini who got dragged that last time [in the sham], he went back to Hale Noa, the 'awa bar, and told everybody the story *(laughter)*. . . . We want to maintain this pilina [relationship] that we have with Maui, and even though we don't get to see a lot of men and perhaps only at the wehe and Pu'ukoholā we still feel that strong tie and connection to Maui and feed off of that and think about all of you every time that we meet up; and I think that showed when we came together at Pu'ukoholā, how things just clicked into place and how well everything worked out. . . . For those of you who don't know I'm also working on my book . . . and one of the things I wanted to do is to ask you all for permission to go ahead with the process of revising that manuscript and conducting more interviews and talking about what we've been doing here all these years and are continuing to do. Kāwika Ki'ili has also offered to help so if people are OK with it, we'd kind of like to do some more things, within probably the next few months going around kind of talking to people again . . . mahalo.

Pa'i ka lima! (clap, clap, clap)

KĀWIKA KI'ILI: I just want to thank everyone for another great year. Mahalo nui to Elama [Farm] for showing up week after week to work with us so we wouldn't get hurt in the battle, and I think for the most part we all came out alive so I'm grateful for that. I'm grateful for another great year at Puʻukoholā. . . . I stayed an extra day with a couple of guys down at Keʻei. Kupuna Bill Pānui was showing us around Keʻei, also Jeff Melrose was showing us the grounds. One of the things they showed us was some petroglyphs that were on the rocks, there was one over more by Kupuna Pānui's hale where I guess a Spanish couple had made their impression in the ground. They were stranded before Captain Cook's time, was the story, but they were taken in by the locals, the Hawaiians who were there. But they made a distinctive mark in the rocks over there. Also over more towards the battlegrounds of Mokuʻōhai, Jeff Melrose pointed out some kōnane [Hawaiian strategic game, akin to checkers] boards that had been made in the rocks and also some petroglyphs over there, some images that someone had purposefully left behind because they wanted someone else to see them; they wanted other people to know that there was a story that had been there before. I guess we have our petroglyphs today, Hanale [Lindo] immortalized in the newspaper; I think that's really cool. I really do think that's really cool, because there's going to be something there for your kids to see and to ask you about stories and for not just your kids but for everyone in Hawaiʻi and everyone in the world. You left your mark in the ground and I think that's really great. So I look forward to another great year with everyone. Ke ola nei.

Paʻi ka lima! (clap, clap, clap).

KAʻIEWE DAVIDSON: Mahalo ke akua no ke kuʻi ʻole ʻana iāʻu. Mahalo i nā kānaka apau. Aloha wau iā ʻoukou. First of all I'd like to thank God for not getting hit and spending all the good times with you guys, I have good fun. Good year. Hope to have more fun with you guys. Mahalo. [Kaʻiewe is Kāwika Davidson's son.]

Paʻi ka lima! (clap, clap, clap)

MANU GIBSON: I wanna tank everybody for being one good place to come to, if I get any problems I know I can always come back to you guys. I feel like I got to know you guys more this year and I just feel like I'm more with the men now and I wanna tank you guys for that. I wanna tank uncle Kyle [Nākānelua] for not getting too mad and uncle Sam [Kaʻai], all the kupunas for being there, and uncle Rick [Bissen] for coming back to play with me, and I sorry for hurting those small boys. Ok, thank you. [Manu is the son of Glenn "Puhi" Gibson, not present here.]

Paʻi ka lima! (clap, clap, clap)

ʻAwa Crew

KEOKI KIʻILI: I don't have too much to say but this year has been a hard year for me really since we lost Gordon [Apo, a middle-aged member who passed away suddenly]. . . . I'm always going to be there for all of you no matter what. Wiliama you know talking about still practicing. I'll be there, you know where my office stay.

Today I was telling a couple of nā kāne [the men] that the biggest test to do anything is on the cement. Especially when you just pau [finished] your ihe, because we did that at my house in Kahului, on the driveway, and ʻauwē to the point every time you scratch the ihe, ʻauwē [alas], and you're going to go like that all the time. To me it's like, you like practice, you practice at my parking lot, on the white grass, see so you don't wanna make ʻauwē so you gotta learn what you gotta do. So I'm there for you Wiliama if you wanna practice I'm open to that too, and anybody else. Mahalo Nākānelua for taking the leadership position, when he stepped up at the heiau and acknowledge Gordon, that to me cleared everything for me. I went back and I looked at all of my old stuff and I tell you what, powerful, we got plenty of good stuff, powerful, all the stuff we did the year before when we went to Aotearoa is still available now, still available for tomorrow . . . So, mahalo ka Hale Mua.

Paʻi ka lima! (clap, clap, clap)

HOAKA DELOS REYES: I would like to extend my mahalo to each and every one of you, the men of the Hale Mua for having me become a part of the Mua. For me the experience is learning from each and every one of you about being Hawaiian. I'm not the brightest but I draw on all of you for inspiration, motivation. I'm really thankful that I am a part of Hale Mua. It also makes me realize that if you listen to everyone speak I'm able to draw on strengths and weaknesses and I realize that when we come together as a Mua, as Rick [Bissen] was saying that it can be a key part in what we have for the future, and as Elama [Farm] was saying about what does the Hale Mua mean to you and I ponder that question in my head because the only thing that comes to me is let my actions speak for itself, whenever we need help I will be there always. Mahalo.

Paʻi ka lima! (clap, clap, clap)

Sam Kaʻai

Mua, mua, mua ka makahiki, mua nā Kānaka Maoli. Those of you who look at that photo saw what we were in '85. That picture reflects what people, Hawaiians thought of themselves. Everybody was hungry for this thing called "Hawaiian" but all our forms all come to us out of hula and out of Don Blanding. Aloha week is a passing review, it's different when men drill together, sing together, dance together, and above all when they mess it up on the field. When we first went to Puʻukoholā it was a field of kūkū [thorns] and doubt and kiawe [algaroba] and ʻopala [trash]. But they were trying. Today, what you see today is a well performed unit, there are specifics for the day of the kahuna nui, and the pule and going to temple. A new thing has been made paʻa [firm]. The aliʻis are not treated as a single unit. The kaukau aliʻi has given us some fixed things over fourteen years. There is an ʻaikapu for men who engage in battle. There is a hoʻokupu haka [dance offering], they will enrich the kilohana [best, highest], they will make a different kind of mist, not the ʻohu of mountains but the dust of battle. And there will be a mihi awa, where Hawaiian men forgive each other. For the ʻeha [pain], not for the joy, of being together. That's something old, something new, and something expected . . . I want to say mahalo for the first timers. I guess it would be funny to say the virgin experience. It's a dry place, it's hard place, it's a wonderful place. But that's where we have our joy and here is where we do our work. History has many stories to tell us and the standard will be set by those stories. We don't have to look; enough of our literature survived. Rapa Nui trying very hard to hold onto things. Tonga doesn't have to hold onto things, they have a living king. Hawaiʻi is diluted by many, many kinds of other mea ʻai [foods], the time of more onos [tastes]. . . . And now there is a story in Honolulu about the whole bunch of guys wearing red, and they called somebody to be a kiaʻi [guard] and speak of them very warmly, those are ma mua. Hale Mua is an organization but mua is how you go forward as a Hawaiian man. . . . Maikaʻi, it was a full year, ma mua. There's no doubt, I'm not going to say mahalo for what happened there, I'm going to say mahalo that you exist, that you danced, you made a living song; it was a whisper because the lonely one calls — *Kawaihae* means to whisper — the lonely one called from the mound of the whale and you are the voices, you weave the prayer, you are the haku [weavers] that bind men and time and space and this whole year together. Mahalo for your hana [work]. Haku is also the word for noblemen and I sit among the most noble of men, and they are Hawaiians. Mahalo ke akua no ka ʻawa.

Paʻi ka lima! (clap, clap, clap)

Kyle Nākānelua

For all of you that helped me with those children, aloha iā ʻoukou. Good investment, good payoff. . . . I heard a couple things about the Hale Mua and about a particular magic. . . . Hawaiian stuff especially like the food, very simple. ʻAwa: water, root. Very simple. Pule: mahalo [thanks], hoʻopōmaikaʻi [blessing]. Very simple. The maiʻa [banana], very simple. All very mundane things within our lives, like getting up in the morning, practicing forty times before you eat. Before you go sleep, practicing forty times, whether it be a prayer, whether it be a movement, whether it be a hand signal, whether it be a thought. The consistent mundane, boring, blah blah, ka mea ka mea, over and over again. It's what turns into the great sanctity of it all when the right moment arises for it to reveal itself. That's the mana of this Hale Mua and the fact that it is so simple it is actually that complex. One of the simplicities and its complexity at the same time is within the ʻālae text under Samuel chapter 1, verse 1 [laughter]. Ka lima, ka lima, ka lima. . . . With the hand, with the hand, with the hand you can affirm and affix anything, with the hand, with the hand, with the hand. It's what this Hale Mua spirit comes from, it's built on the lima system, four guys getting together with one guy on one side, and it present itself to somebody. So . . . in this period of rest . . . it is a time to mālama [take care of] our ʻohana, our kuleana. It is a time to *pick up* your kuleana. What is your kuleana?

NOTES
....

Introduction: Lele i Ka Pō

1. The Hawaiian comes from the Kalākaua text as included in Beckwith (1972, 187). Beckwith's translation appears on page 58. Owing to my hesitancy to translate poetry, I have used Beckwith's translation.

2. I use the terms "Kanaka ʻŌiwi," "ʻŌiwi," "Kanaka Maoli," "ʻŌiwi Maoli," and "Kanaka" interchangeably with Hawaiian and Indigenous/Native Hawaiian. The word "kanaka" means "person" and in certain contexts "man" (though it is not gendered and can refer also to women). "ʻŌiwi" is a term that associates indigeneity with the iwi, the bones. The term "maoli" means "real, true." When the word "Kānaka" takes the macron over the first ʻa,ʼ it represents the pluralized form of the term, or "people" versus "person."

3. See McGregor (2004, 219) for discussion on militarization and Hawaiian men, including participation in Vietnam. See Tengan (2008) for discussion of Nainoa Hoe, and Fainaru (2005) for the *Washington Post* article on his life and death as an American soldier. Ironically, his father, Allen Hoe, a Vietnam veteran, is also an advocate for Hawaiian independence.

4. See Eagar 2006 and the Hawaiʻi Tourism Authority Website (www.hawaiitourismauthority.org) for recent statistics. See also Blackford (2001) for a historical overview of tourism on Maui and the response by environmentalists and Native Hawaiians.

5. Despite any shortcomings, their article was an important contribution that represents one of, if not *the* first (and still one of the few) sustained treatments of Hawaiian masculinity, and its appearance in the realm of popular culture significantly helped to raise awareness and create dialogue where previously none was taking place.

6. Parallels may be (and are) drawn with the representations of Māori men in the film *Once Were Warriors* (1995). As I point to throughout this book, those are just some of the comparisons and contrasts made between Hawaiians and Māoris. See the conclusion.

7. I thank Kamika Nākānelua for reminding me that people come not only to heal themselves, but also to heal others and all Hawaiians in general.

8. Kapu's group is based in Lāhainā on Maui and played a major role in the Kūʻē ʻElua Keepers of Aloha March and Lele I ka Pō that I opened the chapter with.

9. *Nupepa Kuokoa*, December 14, 1867 (Kamakau 1992, 238–39; Kamakau 1996, 232–35).

1. Engagements with Modernity

1. Others have extensively treated the development and elaboration of the Hawaiian social system, which McGregor (2007, 23–30) summarizes in four periods (Kirch and Sahlins 1992, 2:13–17): colonization (1–600 CE), development (600–1100), expansion (1100–1650), and protohistoric (1650–1795). The stratification of society into chiefdoms, with the ʻaikapu and the heiau systems, comes in the expansion period, with the islands comparable to other emergent forms of state-level societies when Cook arrived in 1778.

2. In the conclusion, I discuss a trip the Hale Mua took to Aotearoa, during which we paid homage to Kalaniʻōpuʻu's cape, helmet, and image of Kū at Te Papa Museum in Wellington.

3. Twice Hawaiian men took up arms against the missionary-planter elite. The Wilcox Rebellion in 1889 was led by Robert Wilcox and a cohort of those who had been hand-selected by King Kalākaua to be educated abroad at leading universities of the era. Eight men were killed, 12 wounded, and 70 arrested. In the Restoration of 1895, 220 royalist men were arrested and charged as prisoners of war for treason and concealment of treason. Of these, 188 were given prison sentences, 148 of whom were sentenced to five years at hard labor. The six primary organizers — H. F. Bertlemann, W. H. C. Greig, Samuel Nowlein, W. H. Rickard, William T. Seward, Carl Widemann, and Robert Wilcox — were fined ten thousand dollars and given thirty-five-year jail sentences. The remainder were sentenced from one month to ten years and fined one hundred to five thousand dollars. Those with long sentences were incarcerated until July 17, 1898. Those with shorter sentences had been released. I thank Davianna McGregor for directing my attention to these figures.

4. Parts of this section have been previously published in two articles (Tengan 2002, 2008).

5. The interlocking directorates of the five major sugar-factor companies, Castle and Cooke, C. Brewer, American Factors (AmFac), Theo H. Davies, and Alexander and Baldwin (A&B), comprised elite white American males who effectively ran the economy and the Republican Party.

6. According to two surveys of all living graduates conducted in 1930 and 1935, most KS alumni (about 70 percent) ended up in mechanical trades and government service, though some managed to break through the "grass ceiling" (Rath 2006, 59) and become doctors, teachers, lawyers, businessmen, executives, managers, and politicians (Beaglehole 1937, 21; Hudson 1953, 593–600; McGregor 1989, 130).

7. I thank Hōkūlani Aikau for directing me to this image.

8. Thus during the infamous Massie Affair (1931–32), the beach boys were immediately (and wrongly) implicated. Numerous books, articles, and films have been produced on the pair of nationally publicized trials, the first of which ended in a mistrial of five young local men accused of raping Thalia Massie (a naval officer's wife). The second trial returned a verdict of manslaughter for the Massie gang (Massie's mother, husband, and two naval midshipmen), who murdered the "darkest" of the boys after the first trial; their sentence was commuted to a day taking photographs before being whisked back to the continent (Rosa 2000; Stannard 2005). Among other things, Hawaiian and other local Asian men became the "black peril," a trope readily deployed in colonial settings throughout the Pacific (Inglis 1974).

9. Approximately two-thirds of those identifying as Native Hawaiian in the 2000 US census were mixed-race; Hawai'i as a state also led the United States in the percentage of population (21.4) identifying with two or more races (Kana'iaupuni et al. 2005, 29; United States 2001).

10. McGregor's (2007, 249–85) recounting of the group's history presents a different picture in which both men and women are involved in all areas of organizing and leadership, though the prominence of young men and elder women was noted.

11. Despite conflation here of sexual orientation with gender, the point on inclusivity is still an important one.

12. This may have something to do with the larger feminization of the islands that occurs generally, wherein the gaze of the public eye falls constantly on the female body; thus, even women sovereignty leaders become objects to be viewed and subsequently domesticated.

13. That feeling was even more acute given the fact that his cousin Eddie Aikau was lost at sea while seeking help for the capsized *Hōkūle'a* in 1978 (Finney 1994, 77).

14. A study done by the Matsunaga Vietnam Veterans Project (n.d.) noted that more than half of the Native Hawaiian veterans surveyed experienced war-related trauma, and along with American Indians "they were more likely than any other survey group to receive combat service medals in recognition of hazardous combat duty."

15. On Maui, Leslie Kuloloio, a Korean War veteran, also took part in the PKO and later in land and burial rights efforts. Keanu Sai on O'ahu, a former captain in the Army Reserves and a classmate of Kamana'opono Crabbe of the Hale Mua, has recently become prominent in the effort to expose U.S. occupation; he has been particularly explicit in stating that his military training has better prepared him for the battles at the international front.

2. Re-membering Nationhood and Koa

1. See Pukui, Elbert, and Mookini (1974, 38, 139, 199–200) for their definitions of the names as I have used them this section. They appear to be ignorant or at

the very least neglectful of the alternate interpretations of Peleiōhōlani and Poepoe (McKinzie 1982, 290–92) and Desha (2000, 309).

2. Marion Kelly relates an oral tradition shared by E. Lāʻau and W. ʻĀkau that gives an alternative account of how Keōuakūʻahuʻula was killed and how Pelekane got its name: "Keoua is said to have been shot and killed by John Young and Isaac Davis who stood a short distance back from the water's edge below Mailekini Heiau. . . . This area now is known as Pelekani [*sic*], meaning Britain or British, because of Young and Davis' action taken there" (Kelly 1974, 7, fn**). This account agrees with that of Kamakau, who says that Keoua caught Keʻeaumoku's spear thrust and threw it back, at which point muskets were fired from the shore (though Kamakau does not identify who fired the shots), and Keoua and all the men on the canoe but two were killed (*Nupepa Kuokoa* 5/4/1867; Kamakau 1992, 157; Kamakau 1996, 111–12).

3. Kamakau's version was published in the Hawaiian language newspaper *Kuokoa* as part of a larger serial he wrote on Hawaiian history. The dates for the Puʻukoholā account appear in the April 13, May 4–May 11, 1867, issues. See also Kamakau (1992, 149–50, 154–58) for the translated version, and Kamakau (1996, 103–04, 109–13) for a reprinted Hawaiian version with modern orthography.

4. Poepoe's account of the prophecy, construction, and consecration of Puʻukoholā appears in *Ka Naʻi Aupuni* (hereafter KNA) May 17–19, June 21–July 11, 1906. His narrative drew heavily on an unpublished manuscript of Solomon Peleiōhōlani, a respected genealogist and descendant of the Hilo chief Keawemauhili (Hibbard et al. 2000, xv). See also Edith McKinzie's M.A. thesis, which includes discussion, limited translation, and full typed script of Poepoe's moʻolelo (McKinzie 1982).

5. All untranslated direct quotes from Hawaiian language newspapers are given in their original form without diacritics. Unless otherwise indicated, all translations are mine. I thank Puakea Nogelmeier for his assistance where my language skills were found lacking.

6. Desha's serial "He Moolelo Kaao no Kekuhaupio Ke Koa Kaulana o ke Au o Kamehameha ka Nui" (A tale of Kekūhaupiʻo the famous warrior of the era of Kamehameha the Great) was published in his Hilo-based weekly Hawaiian language newspaper *Ka Hoku o Hawaii (HOH)* between December 16, 1920, and September 11, 1924. The entire serial was recently republished in Hawaiian (Desha 1996) and English (Desha 2000).

7. Though he does not specifically name Gowen, his frequent use of "Napoliona o ka Pakipika" (Napoleon of the Pacific), a term that Poepoe himself did not use in his account, evidences Desha's engagement with the tenured Orientalist and his recent publication.

8. *HOH*, December 21, 1922 (Desha 1996, 2:62). Compare with Frances Frazier's translation (Desha 2000, 312): "The main idea of the writer of the story of Kekūhaupiʻo is the education of this new generation about some things pertain-

ing to the stories of the *ali'i* and their brave men of those ancient times in order for them to understand this great truth: Hawai'i Nei had very brave *ali'i*. There were also very brave warriors in his beloved race of whom the Native Hawaiian need not be ashamed." A note on the gendering of terms is also in order. In this section, Frazier translates the first instance of "kānaka koa" as "brave men" even though "kānaka" is not inherently gendered and could also be translated as "people." This is understandable, for "kanaka" sometimes takes on the masculine gender when it is used in relation to ali'i and is understood as "the chiefs' men." Also, the bulk of Desha's narrative focuses on male chiefs and their male warriors, attendants, and servants. Yet Desha is quite explicit about the need to recognize the role of female chiefs and female warriors, as in the Battle of Nu'uanu (1996, 2:211; 2000, 418). Thus I translate the next usage of "kānaka" as the nongendered "individuals" since Desha is urging his entire readership to be proud of *all* the chiefs, warriors, and brave people in Hawai'i's past. Likewise, I use "him/her" and "his/her" for the nongendered terms " 'o ia" and "kona."

9. *HOH*, December 7, 1922 (Desha 1996, 2:53; Desha 2000, 305).

10. As I did not participate in the 1991 ceremonies, the following account is based on newspaper articles (Ceremony 1991; Conrow 1991a; Conrow 1991b; Enomoto 1991; From the Past 1991; Kawaihae ritual 1991; Ward 1991), interviews (Crabbe 1999; Ka'ai 1999; Ka'ai 2003; Lake 2003; Nākānelua 1999; Nākānelua 2002b), a documentary on the event written by Meleanna Meyer and John Lake (Meyer 1998), and an unpublished conference paper by Steve Friesen (1992). I include direct citations only when I use quotes, interpretations, numbers, and other information I feel I need to attribute to a specified source.

11. See Ralston (1993) and Hoskins (2000) for debates in the Māori community around the issue of (silencing) women's voices on the marae. The protocol for speaking on the marae varies regionally, and some tribes allow women to speak.

12. *Nupepa Kuokoa*, May 4, 1867 (Kamakau 1992, 156; 1996, 111).

13. I thank John Charlot for drawing my attention to this connection.

3. Pu'ukoholā

1. Army cots and water tanks were reminders both of the military presence and that Hawaiians (especially Hawaiian men) have deep connections to the military, which allow them to use military resources for their own cultural purposes.

2. The Humboldt State class, American Indians, and NHCCS were present at the 2005 and 2006 ceremonies. The Māori contingent was there in 2006, though different Māori visitors had attended in prior years.

3. In May 2006, a ruling in favor of Kapu's family gave new hope to what was looking to be a lost battle (Appeals court 2006).

4. This event took place in 2005.

5. In 2005, one koa took a major bruise on his leg, and another received a gash in the back of his head that needed stitches.

6. This meeting took place in 1999 and was videotaped by Clifford Hashimoto; this was also the first year I had attended.

7. This process was an extremely divisive and yet (as of this writing) uncompleted one; the relevance here is that Nā Papa Kanaka became one of these claimants in 2000 and had since that time been (through its representative) quite outspoken. I had been very close to the subject, as I was member of Hui Mālama I Nā Kūpuna o Hawai'i Nei (Ayau and Tengan 2002), one of the claimant groups on the opposite side of the table as Nā Papa Kanaka.

4. Kā i Mua

1. I am likely saying too much about it and simplifying what was a very complex set of issues. Hard feelings still exist, though some bridges have been built to heal these wounds. Though I was not a member of the pā lua, I do have close relationships with members of pā lua as well as with Kapu's group. Thus, despite my desire to more fully elaborate on some of these issues, I cannot.

2. She is standing in the center of the group in figure 15. The other female member had left the group on her own because of work; it is likely that many of the other issues I discuss in this section applied equally to her, except that her departure came before the split with the pā lua. It also sounded like she was not as actively involved as the woman who stayed with Nākānelua until the split occurred, and so I discuss the latter at length.

3. This calendar is organized primarily around male gods and the chiefly religion of the 'aikapu that privileged them; women's worship, such as that of Pele on Hawai'i Island, did not adhere to this structure. For more on the Hawaiian division of the year, see Malo (1951, 30–36, 141–59; 1987, 23–26, 95–105). For a political analysis of the juxtaposition of Kū and Lono in the year, see Kame'eleihiwa (1992, 44–49).

4. Ka'ai calls this weapon the "ne'e" (literally "move"), and Nākānelua has also called it a lā'au pālau, which is a general name for a fighting club (Pukui and Elbert 1986, 189). Others have called it "ku'ia," which Pukui and Elbert (1986, 174) define as "Sharp, pointed stick, dagger, spear."

5. Gallimore et al. (1974, 194–207) argue that boys' patterns of responding to authority at home, which involved unquestioning obedience and no room for negotiation, led them to seek out freedom and equality with their peers, wherein any assertions of authority were aggressively put down. The classroom, however, required boys to respond to the teacher's authority through dialogue and discussion, which conflicted with their previously learned ways of relating to adults and was thus productive of aggressive defiance learned in peer groups. Girls, on the other hand, were socialized into a different way of relating to parents at home and also had less of a connection with peer groups.

6. Lest I give too skewed a vision of the Hawaiian education movement (Meyer 2001; 2003), I should note that at the Kanu O Ka 'Āina Hawaiian charter

school (see chapter 3), the teacher Nālei Kahakalau explained at the 'Aha Kāne 2006 (see introduction) that one of the ways they have attempted to address the different needs of the boys has been to create a hale mua for them. As the school focuses on the taro in its philosophy, their hale mua focuses on farming and planting, and it has been effective in furthering the goals of improving education for the boys.

7. Kaeppler defines ha'a as "a ritual dance performed as a sacrament on . . . *heiau*" that accompanied texts and "would have had a standardized form that ideally was performed without deviation" (since little firsthand knowledge exists, she speculates); hula, on the other hand, is defined as "formal or informal entertainment performed for a human audience" and were "composed in honor of people and places and conveyed this information in an indirect way, namely, through *kaona*, 'veiled or layered meaning' (Kaeppler 1995, 32).

8. In 1999, Kapu moved to Maui, where he had family land that was being threatened by developers seeking to assert adverse possession. He assembled a new group of Nā Koa drawn largely from young men in Lāhainā, predominantly working class. There were also young women, his wife, and the rest of his family.

9. According to Nākānelua (1999), Noelani Mahoe, the hula expert involved with the pā lua, helped put the dance together based on the pig dance from Nuuhiva.

10. In 2003, the documentary entitled *Skin Stories: The Art and Culture of Polynesian Tattoo* aired on PBS. Nākānelua and Nunes (and others from the Mua) were featured in the segment on Hawai'i. The *Honolulu Star-Bulletin* ran a story with a large image of Nākānelua's kākau (Chun 2003), and the PBS companion site for the film included his own story, which had discussion of the Hale Mua (http://www.pbs.org/skinstories/stories/nakanelua.html).

11. By "top of the lists" Haili means the top of the lists of poor life conditions resulting from poverty described in chapter 1.

12. The translation of māhū is difficult for the term is used colloquially (and not consistently) to refer to effeminate males, transgendered persons, gay men (and sometimes lesbians), and physical hermaphrodites. My usage, derived from the way men in the Hale Mua usually think of the term, is primarily in reference to effeminate males, gay men, and transgendered women (male-to-female).

13. Such appropriations do not go uncontested, though, either in Aotearoa or in Hawai'i. In a fashion that ironically mirrored the All Blacks' struggles with intellectual property rights over the "Ka Mate" haka they had traditionally performed (Jackson and Hokwhitu 2002; Tengan 2002), the University of Hawai'i football team, over half of whose players are Samoan or Hawaiian, found itself in a legal and moral quandary at the end of their 2006 season when they were forced to abandon their use of the All Blacks' new haka that had been developed and copyrighted directly in response to the Ngati Toa tribe's contestation of the All Blacks' use of their ancestor's haka (Tsai 2006). Also, the narrow definition of the

haka as a war dance is a mischaracterization; "haka" is a generic term for dances. This mirrors the misidentification of Kū as only "the god of war."

14. Such a sentiment has been repeated by others who find that the comparison to and emulation of Māori forms has gone so far that Hawaiians try to "ho'omāori" — act like a Māori. Interestingly, there is less anxiety surrounding the use of the Marquesan maha'ū; I would suggest that this has partly to do with the fact that they are not held up as the exemplars of Polynesian masculinity in the same way Māori are.

15. This section is an enactment of the difficulty and productivity of such a struggle as it has emerged primarily through discourse with Hōkūlani Aikau, an assistant professor of political science and indigenous politics at UH. We are also genealogically connected to each other and to Carl Eldridge, whom I mentioned above. To a great extent, it was precisely our familial relationship that enabled this dialogue. I also benefited from discussions with Steve Boggs, Rod Labrador, and Nandita Sharma.

5. Narrating Kānaka

1. I also interviewed two men who were not members of the group but had come with us to Pu'ukoholā that year; I do not include them here.

2. Text and translation primarily from Kamakau (1991, 141–42).

3. The Hawaiian cultural tradition of hānai, in which a relative or close friend of the birth parent(s) adopts the child, occurs regularly and differs considerably from American legal practices of adoption. See Ito (1999, 27) for a summary.

4. All direct quotes come from a July 23, 2002, interview. I initially learned of Ka'ai's dyslexia not from him in his interview but from an article written about him by Sally-Jo Keala-o-Ānuenue Bowman (2000). I also found information on specific dates in this article. Bowman does a wonderful job of conveying what it is like to "hang out" with Ka'ai and provides a nice counterbalance to my own narrative.

5. He originally designed for that stern a male chief who represented all the voyagers, including Kaha'i.

6. See McGregor (2007, chap. 3) for a cultural history of the people of Hāna to Kaupō, including Wailuanui. McGregor includes interviews with Helen Nākānelua (131, 136–37) and also talks about Kaupō and Ka'ai's Marciel family (120–23). See also Linnekin's (1985) ethnography of exchange in Ke'anae and Wailuanui in the 1970s. More recently, both Kyle and Helen Nākānelua were featured in the *Hana Hou* magazine (Wood 2006).

7. The religion professor John Charlot recalls that at the University of Hawai'i he found that many of the Hawaiian students in his classes "did not want to do well for fear of alienating themselves from the Hawaiian community and even their fellow students. In other words, the social differences and class antagonisms among Hawaiians are serious and debilitating" (pers. comm., 12/22/06).

Conclusion: The Journeys of Hawaiian Men

1. I do not address Glen's story here, as it is a complex one deserving more time and space than I am able to afford it here. His older son Lee Cooper was a point person for us in Aotearoa and coordinated most of the details for our huaka'i and was with us most of the time. I wish to acknowledge and thank him even though I do not include him in this telling. I likewise leave out descriptions of the time we spent up north in Waimate with Glen's family and the humble and gracious people that hosted us there; mahalo nui.

2. See Jolly (2001) for a more thorough analysis of the architecture of the building and the political and cultural fault lines it lies on.

3. From what I can gather in discussion with Crabbe and mere speculation, the reporter seems to have mixed up the story of Crabbe's first visit with the doctors and Koro's bestowal of a title upon him with the current visit.

4. See Mutu (2005; 2007) for a detailed discussion of these events.

5. See Kauanui (2005a; 2005b) and Cummings-Losch (2005) for discussions on the Hawaiian struggles. Notably, both articles are in the same issue of *The Contemporary Pacific* as Mutu's discussion of the Hīkoi. Our presence there linked the two discussions directly.

6. There are many, many more stories I have not told; those were just from the first half of our time spent there, and even then they don't capture all of the varied dynamics that framed our adventure (which I'll call it since we all basically saw it as such). These will have to wait for another time, another telling.

7. I recognize that this book is geared primarily to a general academic audience first, and the Hawaiian audience (academic and otherwise) second. See Tengan (2003a) for a text that addresses Hawaiian audiences equally; there, I include more Hawaiian language textual analysis (particularly on pages 91–112), additional interview segments with men of the Hale Mua, and further reflections on my positionality and practice as an 'Ōiwi anthropologist.

GLOSSARY OF HAWAIIAN WORDS

....

Definitions are taken liberally from Mary Kawena Pukui and Samuel H. Elbert's *Hawaiian Dictionary* (1986) and from my own understanding of concepts and terms, especially as they are understood and used in the context of this book, which may differ from usages elsewhere.

'ahu'ula	feather cloak or cape worn by ali'i
'ai	to eat; food, starch
'aikapu	eating with kapu, separate eating; religiopolitical system in place until 1819, which served as basis for the hale mua
'āina	land, earth (or "that which feeds")
'ainoa	to eat freely without kapu; event that ended 'aikapu system in 1819
akua	god, deity
alanui	street, road, highway, thoroughfare, waterway, course
ali'i	chief, female chief, ruler, leader
Alo Ali'i	chief's entourage; at Pu'ukoholā, the groups comprised of the chiefly descendants
aloha	love, affection, compassion, mercy, sympathy, pity, kindness, sentiment, grace, charity. The term is used with the word *'āina* to denote love of land and country.
'ano	kind, type, character, nature, disposition, sort, way
ao	light, day, world of the living, cloud, earth, realm; enlightened
'apu	coconut shell cup
a'u	swordfish, marlin, spearfish. The bill is used in the manufacture of pāhoa and other mea kaua.

ʻaumakua, ʻaumākua (pl.)	family and personal god, ancestral deity
ʻawa	kava plant (*Piper methysticum*), native to the Pacific. The root is processed to make a narcotic drink used in ceremonies and social contexts.
hā	to breathe; breath, life; four, fourth
haʻa	a bent-knee dance performed in ceremonies
hala	to pass, die; pandanus
hālau hula	hula school, troupe, group
hale	house
hale kua / hale kuku	house in which women beat kapa and carried out women's activities
hale mua	men's eating house of ʻaikapu period in which men fed the male ʻaumākua and akua and carried out men's activities
hale o Papa	women's place of worship; heiau dedicated to Papa and female akua
hānai	to adopt, care for, feed
hana kālai	carving, woodwork
haole	foreign, foreigner (now primarily signifying a white person). Various interpretations on the etymology of the word have been offered, one being that foreigners were thought to have been without breath (hā — ʻole).
heiau	place of worship, temple, shrine. Many types of heiau existed, not all of which were elaborate structures. The hale mua was a type of domestic heiau for men.
hiʻuwai	cleansing ceremony, typically done by immersing one's naked body into the ocean
hōʻailona	sign, omen
hōkū	star
honi	exchange of breath through the touching of nostrils and inhalation of the other person's hā
hoʻoikaika kino	to exercise; to strengthen the body
hoʻoilo	wet season, approximately November through April
hoʻokupu	tribute, ceremonial gift, offering
hoʻomana	worship, religion; to empower, place in authority, give mana
hoʻopāpā	contest of wits, challenge
hoʻoulu / hoʻūlu	to make grow

hua	fruit, tuber, corm, egg, seed, offspring
huakaʻi	journey, voyage, trip, mission, procession
huakaʻi mākaʻikaʻi	visit, tour, excursion, trip, from "huakaʻi" and "mākaʻikaʻi" (visit, tour, trip, voyage, sightseeing)
hui	organization, group
hula	dance, typically referring to Hawaiian dance in its various traditional (kahiko) and modern (ʻauwana) forms
hula hoʻoipoipo	a courting dance
huli	top portion of kalo used for replanting; to turn, overturn
iʻa	fish; any meat item eaten with any starch
ihe	spear
ihu	nose; bill of the aʻu
ʻimi	to search
imu	underground earth oven
ipu	gourd, calabash
iwi	bone (root word of ʻŌiwi and kulāiwi)
kā	to cast, hit, strike, thrust
kaʻau	forty
kahiko	old, ancient
kāhili	feather standard, symbolic of rank
kahu	keeper, attendant, guardian
kahului	crescent-shaped battle formation; name of Maui town that Hale Mua is based in
kahuna, kāhuna (pl.)	expert in any profession, often associated with akua specific to the kahuna's trade; priest
kahuna nui	high priest and councilor to a high chief; officiator of heiau ceremonies
kahuna pule	prayer expert
kai	ocean
kā i mua	ceremony in which young boys were initiated into the hale mua
kākālāʻau	spear fencing
kākāʻōlelo	orator, person skilled in use of language, counselor, adviser
kākau	tattoo

kālaimoku	counselor, prime minister, high official
kalo .	taro (the staple crop of Hawaiian people)
kāmaʻa	sandal, shoe
kanaka, kānaka (pl.)	person, people; Hawaiian person or people (when capitalized)
kāne	male, man
kanikapila	to play music
kānoa	bowl used for mixing and serving ʻawa
kanu	to bury, plant
kaona	a deeper, hidden meaning
kapa	tapa, barkcloth
kapu	marked with restrictions, prohibitions, and spiritual . qualities that govern interactions and behavior
kau	hot season (approximately May through October); a period of time; to place, put, hang, affix
kauhale	group of houses comprising the Hawaiian home
kaukau aliʻi	an aliʻi of lesser rank who performed service tasks
keiki	child, offspring, young taro
keiki lewalewa	young boy not initiated into the hale mua (called such because he does not wear a malo and is a "dangler")
kiaʻi	a guard
kiawe	algaroba, a thorny foreign tree found in dry areas
kīhei	a rectangular garment worn over one shoulder and tied in a knot
kiʻi	image, statue, picture, figure
kinolau	many bodies; physical manifestation and embodiment of the akua
koa	bravery, courage; someone possessing koa, warrior; a native hardwood tree
koʻihonua	genealogical chant
kuahu/ahu	altar
kūʻē	to stand apart, resist
kuʻia	"sharp, pointed stick, dagger, spear" (Pukui and Elbert). See *neʻe*
kūkākūkā	to discuss
kulāiwi	homelands, native lands, "bone plain"
kuleana	rights and responsibilities

kumu	teacher, instructor, source
kumu hula	hula instructor
kupuna, kūpuna (pl.)	elder, grandparent, ancestor
lāʻau pālau	fighting club. See *neʻe*
lāhui	people, nation, collective
lauhala	pandanus leaf
lehua	flower of the upland ʻōhiʻa lehua tree; fig., the first victim of a battle
lei	garland typically made from flowers, shells, feathers, leaves, vines, or other materials and worn around the neck or head
leina	place where the spirits leap into the Pō
lele	to jump, leap, fly
lele kawa	cliff jumping
lima	hand, five; in Hale Mua, a grouping of five individuals
loʻi	irrigated terrace, especially for the planting of kalo
lua	Hawaiian martial art focused on bone breaking, which has enjoyed resurgence since mid-1990s; two, dual; a hole
luakini	a type of heiau upon which human sacrifices were conducted
mahalo	appreciation, thanks, gratitude
mahiole	feather helmet
maikaʻi	good
makaʻāinana	commoners (as opposed to aliʻi)
makana	gift
mākaukau	ready, prepared
makua, mākua (pl.)	parent, adult; mature taro plant
malihini	guest, visitor
malo	loincloth
mana	spiritual power, potency, charisma, prestige, efficacy
manaʻo	thought, belief, conviction
maoli	real, true, authentic; indigenous Hawaiian (when capitalized or used with word "Kanaka" or "ʻŌiwi")
mea kaua	weapon
mihi	to apologize
moe	to sleep, lie down; a period of rest for the Hale Mua

moepuʻu	companion in death
mōhai	sacrifice, offering
moʻokūʻauhau	genealogy, genealogical succession
moʻolelo	story, tale, myth, history, tradition, literature, legend, narrative, account, succession of talk
moʻopuna	grandchild, offspring, descendant
mua	before, ahead, forward, in advance, first
naʻau	intestines, guts, seat of emotion and knowledge
nalu	wave
neʻe	fighting staff that is between five and six feet in height and pointed on both sides. One end is shaped to have a blade and resembles a cross between a short spear and a long club. The name, which means to "move," comes from Sam Kaʻai. Kyle Nākānelua has called it a *lāʻau pālau*, and ʻUmi Kai has called it a *kuʻia*.
niu	coconut
noa	free of kapu; unrestricted
ʻohana	family (including extended)
ʻōiwi	native, indigenous (capitalized to denote indigenous Hawaiian identity), "of the bone"
ola	life; to live
ola hou	new life; to live again
ʻōlelo	speech, language, words, a saying
ʻōlelo Hawaiʻi	Hawaiian language
ʻōlelo noʻeau	proverb, wise saying
oli	chant; to chant
ʻōʻō ihe	to hurl spears; the sport of spear throwing and dodging
pā	fence, wall, enclosure; abbreviation of *pā lua*
pāhoa	dagger
pahu	drum
pahua	spear dance
pālau	fighting club, short for lāʻau pālau. See *neʻe*
pā lua	lua school. The two most widely known pā lua in Hawaiʻi are Pākuʻialua and Pākuʻiaholo, which began, respectively, in the early and mid-1990s.
papa	flat surface, board, flats (as in the flat area below Puʻukoholā); class, rank, grade, order (as in papa aliʻi)

papa kuʻi ʻai	board for pounded taro
pāʻū	waist covering in which material is wrapped around waist and extends down at variable lengths from the upper thigh down to the ankle
pani	to close; closing ceremony
pīkai	ritual cleansing ceremony
pō	night, darkness; realm of the gods and ancestors (when capitalized)
poʻe	people
poi	pounded taro mixed with water (a staple of the Hawaiian diet)
pololū	battle pike
pono	goodness, righteousness, well-being, balance; correct or proper, just, in perfect order
poʻo	head, both of body and of an organization
poʻokanaka	heiau on which human sacrifices were conducted
pouhana	post set in the middle of each end of the hale, supporting the kaupaku; fig., support, mainstay
pū	conch shell trumpet; a gun
pule	prayer, pray
puʻu	hill, mound, promontory; a desire, need
uhi	covering, veil, solid tattoo
uku	pay, payment, fee, toll
ʻukulele	literally, "jumping flea." This is the name given to the introduced Portuguese *braguinha*, a four-stringed instrument modified slightly and made popular in Hawaiian music.
wā	period of time
waʻa	canoe
wahine, wāhine (pl.)	woman, female
wā kahiko	ancient times

REFERENCES

....

Abu-Lughod, Lila. 1991. "Writing Against Culture." In *Recapturing Anthropology: Working in the Present*, edited by R. G. Fox, 137–62. Santa Fe: School of American Research Press.

———. 2005. *Dramas of Nationhood: The Politics of Television in Egypt*. Cairo: American University in Cairo Press.

Ah Nee-Benham, K. P. Maenette, and Ronald H. Heck. 1998. *Culture and Educational Policy in Hawai'i: The Silencing of Native Voices*. Mahwah, N.J.: L. Erlbaum Associates.

Aikau, Hōkūlani K. 2005. "Polynesian Pioneers: Twentieth-Century Religious Racial Formations and Migration in Hawai'i." PhD diss., University of Minnesota.

Alakai, Cliff. 2002. Interview with the author, Honolulu. November 30.

Amaral, Hanale. 2002. Interview with the author, Wailuku, Maui. July 24.

Anderson, Benedict R. 1991. *Imagined Communities: Reflections on the Origin and Spread of Nationalism*. London: Verso.

Anzaldúa, Gloria. 1987. *Borderlands: The New Mestiza = La frontera*. San Francisco: Aunt Lute Books.

Aoudé, Ibrahim G., ed. 1999. "The Ethnic Studies Story: Politics and Social Movements in Hawai'i: Essays in Honor of Marion Kelly." In *Social Process in Hawai'i*, 39. Honolulu: Department of Sociology, University of Hawai'i at Mānoa.

Apgar, Sally. 2005. "Hawaiian Women Chart Their Own Path to Power." *Honolulu Star-Bulletin*, September 25. http://starbulletin.com.

Apio, Alani. 1998. "Kāmau A'e." Honolulu: Produced by Kumu Kahua Theater for 1997–98 season.

"Appeals Court: Hawaiians' Claim to Land Deserves a Closer Look." 2006. *Maui News*, May 5. http://www.mauinews.com. Accessed August 1, 2006.

Ayau, Edward Halealoha, and Ty Kāwika Tengan. 2002. "Ka Huaka'i o Nā 'Ōiwi: The Journey Home." In *The Dead and Their Possessions: Repatriation in Principle, Policy, and Practice*, edited by C. Fforde, J. Hubert, P. Turnbull, and D. Hanchant, 171–90. London: Routledge.

Baker, Lee D. 2006. "Missionary Positions." In *Globalization and Race: Transforma-*

tions in the Cultural Production of Blackness, edited by K. M. Clarke and D. A. Thomas, 37–54. Durham: Duke University Press.

Barnhart, Sky. 2006a. "Makua Speak: Keʻeaumoku Kapu." *Maui Weekly*, August 31. http://www.mauiweekly.com.

———. 2006b. "The Hands of Sam Kaʻai: A Son of Maui Is Recognized in a Profound New Exhibit." *Maui Magazine*, July, 10.

Basham, Leilani. 2003. Interview with the author, Honolulu. April 23.

Beaglehole, Ernest. 1937. *Some Modern Hawaiians*. Honolulu: University of Hawaiʻi.

Beckwith, Martha Warren. 1970. *Hawaiian Mythology*. Honolulu: University of Hawaiʻi Press.

———. 1972. *The Kumulipo*. Honolulu: University Press of Hawaiʻi.

Bederman, Gail. 1995. *Manliness and Civilization: A Cultural History of Gender and Race in the United States, 1880–1917*. Chicago: University of Chicago Press.

Bhabha, Homi. 1990. *The Nation and Narration*. London: Routledge.

Big Island News. 2007. *This Week Big Island*, August 1–September 3, 60–61.

Birth, Kevin. 2006. "The Immanent Past: Culture and Psyche at the Juncture of Memory and History." *Ethos* 34 (2): 169–91.

Bishop, Bernice Pauahi Paki. 1883. *Last Will and Codicils of the Late Hon. Mrs. Bernice P. Bishop*. http://www.ksbe.edu/pauahi/will.php.

Bissen, Richard Thomas, Jr. 2002. Interview with the author, Wailuku, Maui. May 2.

Blackford, Mansel G. 2001. *Fragile Paradise: The Impact of Tourism on Maui, 1959–2000*. Lawrence: University Press of Kansas.

Blaisdell, Kekuni. 2005. "I Hea Nā Kānaka Maoli? Whither the Hawaiians." *Hūlili* 2:9–18.

Blaisdell, Kekuni, and Noreen Mokuau. 1994. "Kānaka Maoli, Indigenous Hawaiians." In *Hawaiʻi: Return to Nationhood*, edited by U. Hasager and J. Friedman, 49–67. Copenhagen: International Work Group for Indigenous Affairs.

Boggs, Stephen T., with Karen Ann Watson-Gegeo and Georgia McMillen. 1985. *Speaking, Relating, and Learning: A Study of Hawaiian Children at Home and at School*. Norwood, N.J.: Ablex.

Boggs, Stephen T., and Ronald Gallimore. 1968. "Employment." In *Studies in a Hawaiian Community: Na Makamaka on Nanakuli. Pacific Anthropological Records*, no. 1, edited by R. Gallimore and A. Howard, 17–27. Honolulu: Department of Anthropology, Bernice Pauahi Bishop Museum.

Borofsky, Robert, ed. 2000. *Remembrance of Pacific Pasts: An Invitation to Remake History*. Honolulu: Univesity of Hawaiʻi Press.

Bossen, Claus. 2000. "Festival Mania, Tourism and Nation-Building in Fiji: The Case of the Hibiscus Festival, 1956–1970." *Contemporary Pacific* 12 (1): 123–54.

Bourdieu, Pierre. 1977. *Outline of a Theory of Practice*. Cambridge: Cambridge University Press.

Bourgois, Philippe I. 2003. *In Search of Respect: Selling Crack in El Barrio*. 2nd ed. Cambridge: Cambridge University Press.

Bowker, Lee H., ed. 1998. *Masculinities and Violence*. Thousand Oaks, Calif.: Sage Publications.

Bowman, Sally-Jo Keala-o-Ānuenue. 2000. "Reluctant Kahuna." *Honolulu* 35 (5): 100–07, 132–33.

Brenneis, Donald Lawrence, and Fred R. Myers, eds. 1991. *Dangerous Words: Language and Politics in the Pacific*. Prospect Heights, Ill.: Waveland Press.

Briggs, Charles L. 1986. *Learning How to Ask: A Sociolinguistic Appraisal of the Role of the Interview in Social Science Research*. Cambridge: Cambridge University Press.

———. 1996. "The Politics of Discursive Authority in Research on the 'Invention of Tradition.'" *Cultural Anthropology* 11 (4): 435–69.

Brown, DeSoto. 2002. "Colonizing the Equatorial Islands: The Bigger Picture." In *Hui Panalā'au: Hawaiian Colonists, American Citizens*, 3–4. Exhibition pamphlet. Honolulu: Bishop Museum.

Bruner, Edward M. 2005. *Culture on Tour: Ethnographies of Travel*. Chicago: University of Chicago Press.

Buck, Elizabeth Bentzel. 1993. *Paradise Remade: The Politics of Culture and History in Hawai'i*. Philadelphia: Temple University Press.

Burgess, Pualani. 1989. "Choosing My Name." In *Ho'omānoa: An Anthology of Contemporary Hawaiian Literature*, edited by J. P. Balaz, 40. Honolulu: Kū Pa'a Press.

Cabatingan, Earnest Pākī. 2002. Interview with the author, Wailuku, Maui. April 18.

Cain, Carole. 1991. "Personal Stories: Identity Acquisition and Self-Understanding in Alcoholics Anonymous." *Ethos* 19 (2): 210–53.

"Ceremony of Unification Planned at Pu'ukoholā." 1991. In *Ka Wai Ola o OHA — The Living Water of OHA*, May, 9.

Certeau, Michel de. 1984. *The Practice of Everyday Life*. Berkeley: University of California Press.

Charlot, John. 1993. *The Kamapua'a Literature: The Classical Traditions of the Hawaiian Pig God as a Body of Literature*. Laie, Hawai'i: Institute for Polynesian Studies.

Chun, Gary. 2003. "Skin as Canvas: A PBS Documentary Takes a Respectful Look at Polynesian Cultures Reclaiming Their Tattooing Heritage." *Honolulu Star-Bulletin*, May 4. http://starbulletin.com.

Clark, Hugh. 1991. "Famed Pu'ukohola Heiau to be Honored." *Honolulu Star-Bulletin*, July 28, E6–7.

Clark, Jeff. 1993. "Hawaiian Martial Art Enjoys Resurgence." In *Ka Wai Ola o OHA — The Living Water of OHA*, November, 10.

Clifford, James. 1997. *Routes: Travel and Translation in the Late Twentieth Century*. Cambridge: Harvard University Press.

———. 2001. "Indigenous Articulations." *Contemporary Pacific* 13 (2): 468–90.

Cole, Jennifer. 2001. *Forget Colonialism?: Sacrifice and the Art of Memory in Madagascar*. Berkeley: University of California Press.

Collier, W. Pūlama. 2002. "In What Ways Are Traditional Hawaiian Male Gender

Roles of Educators Relevant in a Hawaiian Immersion School?" Plan B Master's Paper, University of Hawai'i.

Connell, R. W. 2005a. "Globalization, Imperialism, and Masculinities." In *Handbook of Studies on Men and Masculinities*, edited by M. S. Kimmel, J. Hearn, and R. W. Connell, 71–89. Thousand Oaks, Calif.: Sage Publications.

——. 2005b. *Masculinities*. 2nd ed. Berkeley: University of California Press.

Conrow, Joan. 1991a. "*Hokule'a* Sails Off to Heiau Commemoration." *Honolulu Advertiser*, August 14, A3.

——. 1991b. "Hopes at a War Heiau: A Legacy of Unity, Pride." *Honolulu Star-Bulletin*, August 18, B1.

Cook, Bud Pōmaika'i, L. Tarallo-Jensen, K. Withy, S. Berry. 2005. "Changes in Kanaka Maoli Men's Roles and Health: Healing the Warrior Self." *International Journal of Men's Health* 4 (2): 115–30.

Cornwall, Andrea, and Nancy Lindisfarne, eds. 1994. *Dislocating Masculinity: Comparative Ethnographies*. London: Routledge.

Crabbe, Kamana'opono M. 1997. *Hui Kū Ha'aheo Men's Group: A Pilot Project for Adult Native Hawaiian Males Utilizing a Cultural Approach towards Healing Problems of Alcohol/Substance Abuse and Family Violence*. Conference program. Honolulu: Hale Na'au Pono and Ho'omau Ke Ola.

——. 1999. Interview with the author, Pauoa, Honolulu, O'ahu. December 11.

——. 2006. "Welcome Message." In *'Aha Kāne 2006 Native Hawaiian Men's Health Conference*. Kapālama, O'ahu: Kamehameha Schools.

Cruz, Ernie, Jr. 2001. "Where Are the Brothers?" In *Portraits*. Honolulu: Pi'inalu Music.

"Cultural Festival in Kawaihae." 2001. *Ka Wai Ola o OHA—The Living Water of OHA*, August, 9.

Cummings-Losch, Tracie Ku'uipo. 2005. "Political Reviews: Hawaiian Issues." *Contemporary Pacific* 17 (1): 203–09.

Da Pidgin Coup. 1999. *Pidgin and Education: A Position Paper*. Honolulu: University of Hawai'i. http://www.hawaii.edu/sls/pidgin.html.

Desha, Stephen L. 1996. *He Mo'olelo Ka'ao No Kekūhaup'o Ke Koa Kaulana O Ke Au O Kamehameha Ka Nui*. 2 vols. Hilo: Hale Kuamo'o.

——. 2000. *Kamehameha and His Warrior Kekūhaupi'o*. Translated by F. N. Frazier. Honolulu: Kamehameha Schools Press.

Desmond, Jane C. 1999. *Staging Tourism: Bodies on Display from Waikiki to Sea World*. Chicago: University of Chicago Press.

Diaz, Vicente M. 2002. "Fight Boys, 'til the Last . . . : Islandstyle Fooball and the Remasculinization of Indigeneity in the Militarized American Pacific Islands." In *Pacific Diaspora: Island Peoples in the United States and Across the Pacific*, edited by P. R. Spickard, J. L. Rondilla, and D. Hippolite Wright, 169–94. Honolulu: University of Hawai'i Press.

——. 2004. "To P or Not to P: Marking the Territory between Asian American and Pacific Islander Studies." *Journal of Asian American Studies* 7 (3): 183–208.

———. 2006. "Oceanic Cartographies." Unpublished manuscript in author's collection.

Diaz, Vicente, and J. Kēhaulani Kauanui. 2001. "Native Pacific Cultural Studies on the Edge." *Contemporary Pacific* (13) 2: 315–42.

Dickerson-Putman, Jeanette. 1998. "Men and the Development Experience in an Eastern Highlands Community." In *Modern Papua New Guinea*, edited by L. Zimmer-Tamakoshi, 231–52. Kirksville: Thomas Jefferson University Press.

Dominguez, Virginia. 1992. "Invoking Culture: The Messy Side of 'Cultural Politics.'" *South Atlantic Quarterly* 91 (1): 19–42.

Eagar, Harry. 2006. "Residents' Negative Perceptions Rise—Survey." *Maui News*, December 14. http://www.mauinews.com.

Elliston, Deborah A. 1997. "En/Gendering Nationalism: Colonialism, Sex, and Independence in French Polynesia." PhD diss., New York University.

———. 2004. "A Passion for the Nation: Masculinity, Modernity, and Nationalist Struggle." *American Ethnologist* 31 (4): 606–30.

Enloe, Cynthia H. 1990. *Bananas, Beaches and Bases: Making Feminist Sense of International Politics*. Berkeley: University of California Press.

Enomoto, Catherine Kekoa. 1991. "Healing Is Gift as Heiau Marks 200." *Honolulu Star-Bulletin*, August 19, B1, B3.

Erai, Michelle Frances. 1995. "Maori Soldiers: Maori Experiences of the New Zealand Army." M.A. thesis, Victoria University.

Fabian, Johannes. 1983. *Time and the Other: How Anthropology Makes Its Object*. New York: Columbia University Press.

Fahim, Hussein, ed. 1982. *Indigenous Anthropology in Non-Western Countries*. Durham: Carolina Academic Press.

Fainaru, Steve. 2005. "On Campaign Trail, a Single Shot." *Washington Post*, January 28, A1.

Farnell, Brenda. 1999. "Moving Bodies, Acting Selves." *Annual Reviews of Anthropology* 28:341–73.

Ferguson, Kathy E., and Phyllis Turnbull. 1999. *Oh, Say, Can You See? The Semiotics of the Military in Hawai'i*. Minneapolis: University of Minnesota Press.

Finney, Ben. 1979. *Hokule'a: The Way to Tahiti*. New York: Dodd Mead.

———. 1994a. *Voyage of Rediscovery: A Cultural Odyssey through Polynesia*. Berkeley: University of California Press.

———. 1994b. "The Other One-Third of the Globe." *Journal of World History* 5:273–97.

———. 2003. *Sailing in the Wake of the Ancestors: Reviving Polynesian Voyaging*. Honolulu: Bishop Museum Press.

Finney, Ben R., and Karen Ann Watson-Gegeo. 1977. *A New Kind of Sugar: Tourism in the Pacific*. Santa Cruz, Calif.: Center for South Pacific Studies.

Fornander, Abraham. 1996. *Ancient History of the Hawaiian People to the Times of Kamehameha I*. Honolulu: Mutual Publishing.

Foster, Robert John. 2002. *Materializing the Nation: Commodities, Consumption, and Media in Papua New Guinea*. Bloomington: Indiana University Press.

Foucault, Michel, and Colin Gordon. 1980. *Power/Knowledge: Selected Interviews and Other Writings, 1972–1977*. New York: Pantheon Books.

Foucault, Michel, and Paul Rabinow. 1984. *The Foucault Reader*. New York: Pantheon Books.

Friesen, Steven J. 1992. "Puʻukohola: Something Old and New in Hawaiian Spirituality." Paper presented at 1992 International Congress, Melbourne, July 15.

———. 1996. "The Origins of Lei Day: Festivity and the Construction of Ethnicity in the Territory of Hawaiʻi." *History and Anthropology* 10 (1): 1–36.

"From the Past." 1991. *West Hawaiʻi Times*, August 16, 1A.

Fujitani, Takashi, Geoffrey M. White, and Lisa Yoneyama. 2001. *Perilous Memories: The Asia-Pacific War(s)*. Durham: Duke University Press.

"Fun Things to Do on the Big Island." n.d. Website of the Mauna Kea Beach Hotel, Prince Resorts, Hawaiʻi. http://www.princeresortshawaii.com/big-island-recreation.php.

Gallimore, Ronald, Joan Whitehorn Boggs, and Cathie Jordan. 1974. *Culture, Behavior, and Education: A Study of Hawaiian-Americans*. Beverly Hills, Calif.: Sage Publications.

Gallimore, Ronald, and Alan Howard. 1968. "Studies in a Hawaiian Community: Na Makamaka on Nanakuli." *Pacific Anthropological Records*, no. 1. Honolulu: Department of Anthropology, Bernice Pauahi Bishop Museum.

Gardiner, Wira. 1992. *Te Mura o te Ahi: The Story of the Maori Battalion*. Auckland: Reed.

Gennep, Arnold van. 1960 [1908]. *The Rites of Passage*. Translated by M. B. Vizedom and G. L. Caffee. London: Routledge and Kegan Paul.

Gillis, John R. 1994. "Memory and Identity: The History of a Relationship." In *Commemorations: The Politics of National Identity*, edited by J. R. Gillis, 3–24. Princeton: Princeton University Press.

Ginsburg, Faye D. 1989. *Contested Lives: The Abortion Debate in an American Community*. Berkeley: University of California Press.

Glenn, Evelyn Nakano. 2002. *Unequal Freedom: How Race and Gender Shaped American Citizenship and Labor*. Cambridge: Harvard University Press.

Goodyear-Kaʻōpua, Jennifer Noelani. 2005. "Ku i ka Mana: Building Community and Nation Through Contemporary Hawaiian Schooling." PhD diss., University of California, Santa Cruz.

Gordillo, Gaston. 2006. "The Crucible of Citizenship: ID-Paper Fetishism in the Argentinean Chaco." *American Ethnologist* 33 (2): 162–76.

Gowen, Herbert H. 1919. *The Napoleon of the Pacific, Kamehameha the Great*. New York: Fleming H. Revell Company.

Graburn, Nelson H. H. 2001. "Secular Ritual: A General Theory of Tourism." In *Hosts and Guests Revisited: Tourism Issues of the 21st Century*, edited by V. L. Smith and M. Brent, 42–50. New York: Cognizant Communication Corporation.

Greene, Linda W. 1993. *A Cultural History of Three Traditional Hawaiian Sites on the*

West Coast of Hawai'i Island: Pu'ukoholā Heiau, National Historic Site, Kawaihae, Hawai'i, Kaloko-Honokōhau, National Historical Park, Kaloko-Honokōhau, Hawai'i, Pu'uhonua o Hōnaunau, National Historical Park, Hōnaunau, Hawai'i. Denver: National Park Service, Denver Service Center. http://www.nps.gov.

Gupta, Akhil, and James Ferguson. 1997. "Culture, Power, Place: Ethnography at the End of an Era." In Culture, Power, Place: Explorations in Critical Anthropology, edited by A. Gupta and J. Ferguson, 1–29. Durham: Duke University Press.

Hale, Constance. 2004. "Giving Voice." Honolulu Magazine, November, 104–7, 146, 148.

Hall, Lisa Kahaleole. 2005. "'Hawaiian at Heart' and Other Fictions." Contemporary Pacific 17 (2): 404–13.

Halualani, Rona Tamiko. 2002. In the Name of Hawaiians: Native Identities and Cultural Politics. Minneapolis: University of Minnesota Press.

Handy, E. S. Craighill, Elizabeth Green Handy, and Mary Kawena Pukui. 1972. Native Planters in Old Hawai'i: Their Life, Lore, and Environment. Honolulu: Bishop Museum Press.

Handy, E. S. Craighill, and Mary Kawena Pukui. 1972. The Polynesian Family System in Ka'ū, Hawai'i. Rutland, Vt.: C. E. Tuttle.

Haraway, Donna Jeanne. 1991. Simians, Cyborgs, and Women: The Reinvention of Nature. New York: Routledge.

Hargrove, Ermile, Kent Sakoda, and Jeff Siegel. n.d. Hawai'i Creole English, Vol. 2003: School of Languages, Cultures, and Linguistics.

Harper, Phillip Brian, 1996. Are We Not Men? Masculine Anxiety and the Problem of African-American Identity. New York: Oxford University Press.

Harrison, Faye V. 1997. "Anthropology as an Agent of Transformation: Introductory Comments and Queries." In Decolonizing Anthropology: Moving Further Toward an Anthropology for Liberation, edited by F. V. Harrison, 1–15. Arlington, Va.: Association of Black Anthropologists.

Hartwell, Jay. 1996. Nā Mamo: Hawaiian People Today. Honolulu: 'Ai Pōhaku Press.

Hasager, Ulla, and Jonathan Friedman, eds. 1994. Hawai'i: Return to Nationhood. Copenhagen: International Work Group for Indigenous Affairs.

Hasager, Ulla, and Marion Kelly. 2001. "Public Policy of Land and Homesteading in Hawai'i." Social Process in Hawai'i 40:190–232.

Hau'ofa, Epeli. 1993. "Our Sea of Islands." In A New Oceania: Rediscovering Our Sea of Islands, edited by E. Waddell, V. Naidu, and E. Hau'ofa, 2–16. Suva: School of Social and Economic Development, University of the South Pacific.

Hereniko, Vilsoni, and Rob Wilson, eds. 1999. Inside Out: Literature, Cultural Politics and Identity in the New Pacific. Oxford: Rowman and Littlefield.

Hibbard, Don, Holly McEldowney, and Nathan Napoka. 2000. "Introduction." In Kamehameha and His Warrior Kekūhaupi'o, xiii–xx. Honolulu: Hawai'i.

Ho, Wayne Puka. 2002. Interview with the author, Wailuku, Maui. April 18.

Hokowhitu, Brendan. 2004. "Tackling Maori Masculinity: A Colonial Genealogy of Savagery and Sport." *Contemporary Pacific* 16 (2): 259–84.

———. 2008. "The Death of Koro Paka: 'Traditional' Māori Patriarchy." *The Contemporary Pacific* 20 (1): 115–43.

Holt, John Dominis. 1964. *On Being Hawaiian.* Honoluluu: Topgallant Publishing.

Hoskins, Te Kawehau Clea. 2000. "In the Interests of Māori Women? Discourses of Reclamation." In *Bitter Sweet: Indigenous Women in the Pacific,* edited by A. Jones, P. Herda, and T. M. Suaalii, 33–48. Dunedin, NZ: University of Otago Press.

Howard, Alan. 1974. *Ain't No Big Thing: Coping Strategies in a Hawaiian-American Community.* Honolulu: University of Hawai'i Press.

Hudson, Loring. 1953. *The History of the Kamehameha Schools: 1887–1950.* 2 vols. Honolulu: Kamehameha Schools.

Hutchinson, John. 1987. *The Dynamics of Cultural Nationalism.* London: Allen and Unwin.

Ihimaera, Witi. 2002. "Masculinity and Desire: Rewriting the Polynesian Body." In *Joseph Keene Chadwick: Interventions and Continuities in Irish and Gay Studies,* edited by J. Rieder, J. O'Mealy, and V. Wayne, 122–31. Honolulu: University of Hawai'i Press.

Imada, Adria L. 2004. "Hawaiians on Tour: Hula Circuits through the American Empire." *American Quarterly* 56 (1): 111–49.

Inglis, Amirah. 1974. *Not a White Woman Safe: Sexual Anxiety and Politics in Port Moresby, 1920–1934.* Canberra: Australian National University Press.

Ishiwata, Eric. 2002. "Local Motions: Surfing and the Politics of Wave Sliding." *Cultural Values: Journal for Cultural Research* 6 (3): 257–73.

Ito, Karen L. 1999. *Lady Friends: Hawaiian Ways and the Ties that Define.* Ithaca: Cornell University Press.

"It's Festival Weekend at Pu'ukohola Heiau." 1998. *Honolulu Advertiser,* August 13, B2.

Jackson, Steven J., and Brendan Hokowhitu. 2002. "Sport, Tribes, and Technology: The New Zealand All Blacks *Haka* and the Politics of Identity." *Journal of Sport and Social Issues* 26 (2): 125–39.

Jacobs-Huey, Lanita. 2002. "The Natives Are Gazing and Talking Back: Reviewing the Problematics of Positionality, Voice, and Accountability Among 'Native' Anthropologists." *American Anthropologist* 104 (3): 791–804.

James, Kerry. 1994. "Effeminate Males and Changes in the Construction of Gender in Tonga." *Pacific Studies* 17 (2): 39–69.

Jolly, Margaret. 1992. "Specters of Inauthenticity." *Contemporary Pacific* 4 (1): 49–72.

———. 1997. "Woman-Nation-State in Vanuatu: Women as Signs and Subjects in the Discourses of *Kastom,* Modernity and Christianity." In *Narratives of Nation in the South Pacific,* edited by T. Otto and N. Thomas, 133–62. Amsterdam: Harwood Academic Publishers.

———. 2001. "On the Edge? Deserts, Oceans, Islands." *Contemporary Pacific* 13 (2): 417–66.

Jolly, Margaret, and Nicholas Thomas. 1992. "The Politics of Tradition in the Pacific." *Oceania* 62 (4): 241–48.

Ka'ai, Sam Kaha'i. 1991. *A Presentation by Sam Ka'ai.* Videocassette (20 minutes). Honolulu: Na Maka o ka 'Āina.

———. 1999a. Interview with the author, Makawao, Maui, November 7.

———. 1999b. Papa ku'i 'ai workshop. Pukalani, Maui, November 6. Transcript in author's collection.

———. 2002. Interview with the author, Pukalani, Maui. July 23.

———. 2003. Interview with the author, Makawao, Maui. March 30.

———. 2006. Interview with the author, Pukalani, Maui. July 21.

Kaeppler, Adrienne L. 1995. "Visible and Invisible in Hawaiian Dance." In *Human Action Signs in Cultural Context: The Visible and the Invisible in Movement and Dance*, edited by B. Farnell, 31–43. Metuchen, N.J.: Scarecrow Press.

Kahapea, Alexander N. 1990. *Alika, the Hawaiian.* 2 vols. Hilo, Hawai'i: ALFLO RONCO.

Kaholokula, Joseph Keawe'aimoku. 2007. "Colonialism, Acculturation, and Depression among Kānaka Maoli of Hawai'i." In *Penina Uliuli: Confronting Challenges in Mental Health for Pacific Peoples*, edited by P. Culbertson, M. N. Agee, and C. Makasiale, 180–95. Honolulu: University of Hawai'i Press.

Kajihiro, Kyle. 2000. "Nation Under the Gun: Militarism and Resistance in Hawai'i." *Cultural Survival Quarterly* 24 (1): 28–33.

———. 2007. *A Brief Overview of Militarization and Resistance in Hawai'i.* Honolulu: DMZ-Hawai'i/Aloha 'Aina. http://www.dmzhawaii.org/overview_military_in_hawaii.pdf.

Kamakau, Samuel Mānaiakalani. 1991. *Tales and Traditions of the People of Old = Nā mo'olelo o ka po'e kahiko.* Translated by M. K. Pukui and D. B. Barréere. Honolulu: Bishop Museum Press.

———. 1992. *Ruling Chiefs of Hawai'i.* Honolulu: Kamehameha Schools Press.

———. 1996. *Ke Kumu Aupuni: Ka mo'olelo Hawai'i no Kamehameha Ka Na'i Aupuni a me kāna aupuni i ho'okumu ai.* Honolulu: 'Ahahui 'Ōlelo Hawai'i.

Kamau'u, Māhealani. 1996. "Native Hawaiian in Prison." In *Nā Mamo: Hawaiian People Today*, edited by J. Hartwell, 173–74. Honolulu: 'Ai Pōhaku Press.

———. 1998. "Host Culture (Guava Juice on a Tray)." *'Ōiwi: A Native Hawaiian Journal* 1:135–36.

———. 2002. "Bereaved Daughter-in-Law." *'Ōiwi: A Native Hawaiian Journal* 2:219–20.

Kame'eleihiwa, Lilikalā. 1992. *Native Land and Foreign Desires: How Shall We Live in Harmony? = Ko Hawai'i aina a me na koi puumake a ka poe haole: Pehea la e pono ai?* Honolulu: Bishop Museum Press.

———. 1996. *He Mo'olelo Ka'ao o Kamapua'a, A Legendary Tradition of Kamapua'a, the Hawaiian Pig-God: An Annotated Translation of a Hawaiian epic from* Ka Leo o ka Lāhui, *June 22, 1891–July 23, 1891.* Honolulu: Bishop Museum Press.

———. 1999. *Nā Wahine Kapu: Divine Hawaiian Women*. Honolulu: 'Ai Pohaku Press.

Kana, Jacob. 2002. Interview with the author, Waihe'e, Maui. June 28.

Kanahele, George S. 1986. *Kū Kanaka, Stand Tall: A Search for Hawaiian Values*. Honolulu: University of Hawai'i Press.

———. 1982. *Hawaiian Renaissance*. Honolulu: Project WAIAHA.

Kana'iaupuni, S. K., N. Malone, and K. Ishibashi. 2005. *Ka Huaka'i: 2005 Native Hawaiian Educational Assessment*. Honolulu: Kamehameha Schools, Pauahi Publications.

Kann, Mark E. 1991. *On the Man Question: Gender and Civic Virtue in America*. Philadelphia: Temple University Press.

Karpiel, Frank J., Jr. 2000. "Mystic Ties of Brotherhood: Freemasonry, Ritual, and Hawaiian Royalty in the Nineteenth Century." *Pacific Historical Review* 69 (3): 357–97.

Kauanui, J. Kēhaulani. 1998. "Off-Island Hawaiians 'Making' Ourselves at 'Home': A [Gendered] Contradiction in Terms?" *Women's Studies International Forum* 21 (6): 681–93.

———. 1999a. "Imaging Hawaiian Struggle and Self-Determination Through the Works of Na Maka o ka 'Aina." *Pacific Studies* 22 (2): 131–39.

———. 1999b. "'For Get' Hawaiian Entitlement: Configurations of Land, 'Blood,' and Americanization in the Hawaiian Homes Commission Act of 1921." *Social Text* 17 (2): 123–44.

———. 2000. "Rehabilitating the Native: Hawaiian Blood Quantum and the Politics of Race, Citizenship, and Entitlement." University of California Santa Cruz.

———. 2002. "The Politics of Blood and Sovereignty in Rice v. Cayetano." *PoLAR* 25 (1): 110–28.

———. 2004. "Asian American Studies and the 'Pacific Question.'" In *Asian American Studies After Critical Mass*, edited by K. A. Ono, 123–43. Malden, Mass.: Blackwell.

———. 2005a. "Precarious Positions: Native Hawaiians and U.S. Federal Recognition." *Contemporary Pacific* 17 (1): 1–27.

———. 2005b. "The Multiplicity of Hawaiian Sovereignty Claims and the Struggle for Meaningful Autonomy." *Comparative American Studies* 3 (3): 283–99.

———. 2007. "Diasporic Deracination." *Contemporary Pacific* 19 (1): 138–60.

Kauanui, J. Kēhaulani, and Ty P. Kāwika Tengan. n.d. "Mana Wahine, Mana Kane: Decolonizing Hawaiian Gender." Unpublished manuscript in author's collection.

"Kawaihae Ritual Aims to Mend Old Fences." 1991. *West Hawai'i Today*, August 19, 6A.

Keesing, Roger. 1989. "Creating the Past: Custom and Identity in the Contemporary Pacific." *Contemporary Pacific* 1:19–42.

Kelly, John D. 1995. "The Privileges of Citizenship: Nations, States, Markets, and Narratives." In *Nation-Making: Emergent Identities in Postcolonial Melanesia*, edited by R. Foster, 253–73. Ann Arbor: University of Michigan Press.

Kelly, John Dunham, and Martha Kaplan. 2001. *Represented Communities: Fiji and World Decolonization.* Chicago: University of Chicago Press.

Kelly, Marion. 1974. *E Hoolono i ke Kai Hawanawana: Listen to the Whispering Sea. Historical Survey of the Waimea to Kawaihae Road Corridor, Island of Hawaiʻi.* Honolulu: Department of Anthropology, Bernice P. Bishop Museum.

Kent, Noel J. 1993. *Hawaiʻi: Islands Under the Influence.* Honolulu: University of Hawaiʻi Press.

Kiʻili, Keoki. 2002. Interview with the author, Wailuku, Maui. December 5.

King, Samuel P., and Randall W. Roth. 2006. *Broken Trust: Greed, Mismanagement and Political Manipulation at America's Largest Charitable Trust.* Honolulu: University of Hawaiʻi Press.

Kirch, Patrick Vinton, and Marshall David Sahlins. 1992. *Anahulu: The Anthropology of History in the Kingdom of Hawaiʻi.* 2 vols. Chicago: University of Chicago Press.

Kolb, Michael. 2006. "The Origins of Monumental Architecture in Ancient Hawaiʻi." *Current Anthropology* 47 (4): 657–65.

Lake, John Keola. 2003. Interview with the author, Honolulu. January 20.

Lamphere, Louise, Helena Ragone, and Patricia Zavella, eds. 1997. *Situated Lives: Gender and Culture in Everyday Life.* New York: Routledge.

Lassiter, Luke E. 2005. *The Chicago Guide to Collaborative Ethnography.* Chicago: University of Chicago Press.

Lederman, Rena. 2005. "Challenging Audiences: Critical Ethnography in/for Oceania." *Anthropological Forum* 15 (3): 319–28.

Linde, C. 1993. *Life Stories: The Creation of Coherence.* New York: Oxford University Press.

Lindholm, Charles. 2002. "Culture, Charisma, and Consciousness: The Case of the Rajnaeeshee." *Ethos* 30 (4): 357–75.

Linnekin, Jocelyn. 1985. *Children of the Land: Exchange and Status in a Hawaiian Community.* New Brunswick. N.J.: Rutgers University Press.

———. 1990. *Sacred Queens and Women of Consequence: Rank, Gender, and Colonialism in the Hawaiian Islands.* Ann Arbor: University of Michigan Press.

———. 1992. "On the Theory and Politics of Cultural Construction in the Pacific." *Oceania* 62:249–63.

———. 1997. "Consuming Cultures: Tourism and the Commoditization of Cultural Identity in the Island Pacific." In *Tourism, Ethnicity, and the State in Asian and Pacific Societies,* edited by M. Picard and R. E. Wood, 215–50. Honolulu: University of Hawaiʻi Press.

Linnekin, Jocelyn, and Lin Poyer. 1990. *Cultural Identity and Ethnicity in the Pacific.* Honolulu: University of Hawaiʻi Press.

Lopes, Kūkona. 1999. Interview with the author, Kailua, Oʻahu. December 3.

Lucas, Carolyn. 2006a. "Precarious Puukohola. Legendary Heiau Faces Extensive Repairs After Earthquake Damage." *West Hawaiʻi Today,* November 30. http://www.westhawaiitoday.com.

———. 2006b. "Recapturing a Culture: Festival Gives Visitors a Chance to See the Glory of Old Hawai'i." *West Hawai'i Today*, August 13. http://www.westhawaii today.com.

Lynch, Russ. 2001. "The Economics of Aloha." *Honolulu Star-Bulletin*, August 12, E1, E12.

MacCannell, Dean. 1999. *The Tourist: A New Theory of the Leisure Class.* Berkeley: University of California Press.

Malo, Davida. 1951. *Hawaiian Antiquities (Moolelo Hawai'i).* Honolulu: The Museum.

———. 1987. *Ka Moolelo Hawai'i: Hawaiian Antiquities.* Edited by M. N. Chun. Honolulu: Folk Press Kapiolani Community College.

Manalansan, Martin F. 2003. *Global Divas: Filipino Gay Men in the Diaspora.* Durham: Duke University Press.

Manderson, Lenore, and Margaret Jolly, eds. 1997. *Sites of Desire, Economies of Pleasure: Sexualities in Asia and the Pacific.* Chicago: University of Chicago Press.

Mankekar, Purnima. 1999. *Screening Culture, Viewing Politics: An Ethnography of Television, Womanhood, and Nation in Postcolonial India.* Durham: Duke University Press.

Marcus, George E., and Michael Fischer. 1986. *Anthropology as Cultural Critique: An Experimental Moment in the Human Sciences.* Chicago: University of Chicago Press.

Marshall, Mac. 1979. *Weekend Warriors: Alcohol in a Micronesian Culture.* Palo Alto, Calif.: Mayfield.

Marshall, Wende Elizabeth. 1999. "Recovering Nation: Disease, Decolonization and Healing in Wai'anae, O'ahu." PhD diss., Princeton University.

———. 2006. "Remembering Hawaiian, Transforming Shame." *Anthropology and Humanism* 31 (2): 185–200.

Matsunaga Vietnam Veterans Project. n.d. "The Legacy of Psychological Trauma of the Vietnam War for Native Hawaiian and American of Japanese Ancestry Military Personnel." United States Department of Veterans Affairs Website, http://www.ncptsd.va.gov/ncmain/ncdocs/fact_shts/fs_hawaiian_vets.html.

Mattingly, Cheryl. 1998. *Healing Dramas and Clinical Plots: The Narrative Structure of Experience.* Cambridge: Cambridge University Press.

McClintock, Anne. 1995. *Imperial Leather: Race, Gender, and Sexuality in the Colonial Conquest.* New York: Routledge.

McGregor, Davianna Pōmaika'i. 1989. "Kūpa'a I Ka 'Āina: Persistence on the Land." PhD diss., University of Hawai'i.

———. 1990. "'Āina Ho'opulapula: Hawaiian Homesteading." *Hawaiian Journal of History* 24:1–38.

———. 2003. "Constructed Images of Native Hawaiian Women." In *Asian/Pacific Islander American Women: A Historical Anthology*, edited by S. Hune and G. M. Nomura, 25–41. New York: New York University Press.

———. 2004. "Engaging Hawaiians in the Expansion of the U.S. Empire." *Journal of Asian American Studies* 7 (3): 209–22.

———. 2007. *Nā Kuaʻāina: Living Hawaiian Culture*. Honolulu: University of Hawaiʻi Press.

McGregor-Alegado, Davianna. 1980. "Hawaiians: Organizing in the 1970s." *Amerasia* 7 (2): 29–55.

McKinzie, Edith Kawelo Kapule. 1982. "An Original Narrative of Kamehameha the Great Written in Ka Naʻi Aupuni (1905–1906) by Joseph Poepoe: Hawaiian Text with English Translation and Brief Comparative Reviews of Earlier Historical Biographers of Kamehameha I." Master of Education, University of Hawaiʻi.

Merry, Sally Engle. 2000. *Colonizing Hawaiʻi: The Cultural Power of Law*. Princeton: Princeton University Press.

———. 2006. "Transnational Human Rights and Local Activism: Mapping the Middle." *American Anthropologist* 108 (1): 38–51.

Merry, Sally Engle, and Donald Brenneis, eds. 2003. *Law and Empire in the Pacific: Fiji and Hawaiʻi*. Santa Fe: School of American Research Press.

Meskin, Kelli. 1997. "Native Hawaiian Inmates: They Are the Majority in Hawaiʻi Prisons, a Minority in the State." In *Ka Wai Ola o OHA—The Living Water of OHA*, January, 1, 6.

Messner, Michael A. 1997. *Politics of Masculinities: Men in Movements*. Thousand Oaks, Calif.: Sage Publications.

———. 1998. "The Limits of 'The Male Sex Role': An Analysis of the Men's Liberation and Men's Rights Movements' Discourse." *Gender and Society* 12 (3): 255–76.

Meyer, Manulani Aluli. 2001. "Our Own Liberation: Reflections on Hawaiian Epistemology." *Contemporary Pacific* 13 (1): 124–48.

———. 2003. *Hoʻoulu: Our Time of Becoming: Collected Early Writings of Manulani Meyer*. Edited by M. Meyer. Honolulu: ʻAi Pohaku Press.

Meyer, Meleanna Aluli. 1998. *Hoʻokuʻikahi: To Unify as One*. Videocassette (47 minutes). Honolulu: Native Books and Beautiful Things.

Mookini, Esther T. 1974. *The Hawaiian Newspapers*. Honolulu: Topgallant.

Morley, David, and Kuan-Hsing Chen, eds. 1996. *Stuart Hall: Critical Dialogues in Cultural Studies*. London: Routledge.

Mutu, Margaret. 2005. "Political Reviews: Māori Issues." *Contemporary Pacific* 17 (1): 209–15.

———. 2007. "Political Reviews: Māori Issues." *Contemporary Pacific* 19 (1): 233–40.

Myerhoff, Barbara. 1982. "Life History Among the Elderly: Performance, Visibility, and Re-membering." In *A Crack in the Mirror: Reflexive Perspectives in Anthropology*, edited by J. Ruby, 99–117. Philadelphia: University of Pennsylvania Press.

Nāhale-ā, Kīhei. 2002. Interview with the author, Hilo. November 26.

Nākānelua, Kyle Kaʻohulani. 1999. Interview with the author, Lākini, Wailua, Maui. November 26.

———. 2002a. Interview with the author, Wailuku, Maui. November 4.

———. 2002b. Interview with the author, Kahului, Maui. December 29.

———. 2006. Interview with the author, Kahului, Maui. July 19.

Nā Papa Kanaka o Puʻukoholā. 1999. "Puu Kohala Heiau Na Papa Kanaka Mission Statement, Na Oli Pono O Ka Heiau." Copy available at Hamilton Library, University of Hawaiʻi, Mānoa.

Niezen, Ronald. 2003. *The Origins of Indigenism: Human Rights and the Politics of Identity*. Berkeley: University of California Press.

Nunes, Keone, and Scott Whitney. 1994. "The Destruction of the Hawaiian Male." *Honolulu Magazine* July, 43, 59–61.

O'Nell, Theresa DeLeane. 1996. *Disciplined Hearts: History, Identity, and Depression in an American Indian Community*. Berkeley: University of California Press.

Ochs, Elinor, and Lisa Capps. 1996. "Narrating the Self." *Annual Reviews of Anthropology* 25:19–43.

OHA. 2006. "Native Hawaiian Data Book." An Office of Hawaiian Affairs Publication. Prepared by the Office of Board Services. Lea K. Young, Research Specialist. Honolulu: OHA. http://www.oha.org.

Okamura, Jonathan. 1998. "The Illusion of Paradise: Privileging Multiculturalism in Hawaiʻi." In *Making Majorities: Constituting the Nation in Japan, Korea, China, Malaysia, Fiji, Turkey, and the United States*, edited by D. C. Gladney, xv, 350. East-West Center Series on Contemporary Issues in Asia and the Pacific. Stanford: Stanford University Press.

Ortner, Sherry B. 1996. *Making Gender: The Politics and Erotics of Culture*. Boston: Beacon Press.

Osorio, Jonathan Kamakawiwoʻole. 2001. "'What Kine Hawaiian Are You?' A *Moʻolelo* about Nationhood, Race, History, and the Contemporary Sovereignty Movement in Hawaiʻi." *Contemporary Pacific* 13 (2): 359–80.

———. 2002. *Dismembering Lahui: A History of the Hawaiian Nation to 1887*. Honolulu: University of Hawaiʻi Press.

———. 2003. "Kūʻē and Kūʻokoʻa: History, Law, and Other Faiths." In *Law and Empire in the Pacific: Fiji and Hawaiʻi*, edited by S. E. Merry and D. Brenneis, 213–38. Santa Fe: School of American Research Press.

Paglinawan, Richard Kekumuikawaiokeola, Mitchell Eli, Moses Elwood Kalauokalani, and Jerry Walker. 2006. *Lua: Art of the Hawaiian Warrior*. With Kristina Pilahoʻohauʻoli Kikuchi-Palenapa. Edited by S. K. Bowman and T. L. Moan. Honolulu: Bishop Museum Press.

Pao, Franklin. 2006. "Puʻukohola Heiau." Personal Website, http://kaimi.home stead.com/PUUKOHOLA.html.

Parker, Andrew, et al., eds. 1992. *Nationalisms and Sexualities*. New York: Routledge.

Peacock, James L., and Dorothy C. Holland. 1993. "The Narrated Self: Life Stories in Process." *Ethos* 21 (4): 367–83.

Peirano, Mariza G. S. 1998. "When Anthropology Is at Home: The Different Contexts of a Single Discipline." *Annual Reviews of Anthropology* 27:105–38.

Perkins, 'Umi. 2006. "Teaching Land and Sovereignty — A Revised View." *Hawaiian Journal of Law and Politics* 2:97–111.

Perry, Kekailoa. 2002. "It's Time to Kick Myth of Crabs in a Bucket." *Honolulu Advertiser*, January 27. http://the.honoluluadvertiser.com.

Phillips, Susan U. 1972. "Participant Structures and Communicative Competence: Warm Springs Children in Community and Classroom." In *Functions of Language in the Classroom*, edited by C. B. Cazden, V. P. John, and D. Hymes, 370–94. New York: Teachers College Press.

Pierce, Lori. 2004. " 'The Whites Have Created Modern Honolulu': Ethnicity, Racial Stratification and the Discourse of Aloha." In *Racial Thinking in the United States: Uncompleted Independence*, edited by P. R. Spickard and G. R. Daniel, 124–54. Notre Dame: University of Notre Dame Press.

Poepoe, Joseph Mokuohai. 1905–1906. *Kamehameha I. Ka Nai Aupuni o Hawaii. Ka Liona o ka Moana Pakipika.* Published serially in *Ka Nai'i Aupuni* (newspaper), Nov 25, 1905–Nov 16, 1906.

Pratt, Mary Louise. 1992. *Imperial Eyes: Travel Writing and Transculturation.* London: Routledge.

Pukui, Mary Kawena, and Samuel H. Elbert. 1986. *Hawaiian Dictionary.* Honolulu: University of Hawai'i Press.

Pukui, Mary Kawena, Samuel H. Elbert, and Esther T. Mookini. 1974. *Place Names of Hawai'i.* Honolulu: University Press of Hawai'i.

Pukui, Mary Kawena, E. W. Haertig, and Catherine A. Lee. 1972. *Nānā i ke kumu (Look to the Source).* 2 vols. Honolulu: Hui Hānai.

Ralston, Caroline. 1984. "Hawai'i 1778–1854: Some Aspects of Maka'ainana Response to Rapid Cultural Change." *Journal of Pacific History* 19 (1): 21–40.

——. 1993. "Maori Women and the Politics of Tradition: What Roles and Power Did, Do and Should Maori Women Exercise?" *Contemporary Pacific* 5 (1): 23–44.

Rath, J. Arthur. 2006. *Lost Generations: A Boy, a School, a Princess.* Honolulu: University of Hawai'i Press.

Reed-Danahay, Deborah E., ed. 1997. *Auto/ethnography: Rewriting the Self and the Social.* New York: Berg.

Robertson, Carol E. 1989. "The Mahu of Hawai'i." *Feminist Studies* 15 (2): 312–26.

Rosa, John P. 2000. "Local Story: The Massie Case Narrative and the Cultural Production of Local Identity in Hawai'i." *Amerasia Journal* 26 (2): 93–116.

Sahlins, Marshall David. 1981. *Historical Metaphors and Mythical Realities: Structure in the Early History of the Sandwich Islands Kingdom.* Ann Arbor: University of Michigan Press.

——. 1985. *Islands of History.* Chicago: University of Chicago Press.

Sai, David Keanu. 2004. "American Occupation of the Hawaiian State: A Century Gone Unchecked." *Hawaiian Journal of Law and Politics* 1:46–81.

——. 2005. "Kahana: How the Land Was Lost (review)." *Contemporary Pacific* 17 (1): 237–40.

Said, Edward. 1978. *Orientalism.* New York: Vintage Books.

Salmond, Anne. 1975. *Hui: A Study of Maori Ceremonial Gatherings.* Wellington: A. H. and A. W. Reed.

Sandoval, Chela. 1991. "U.S. Third World Feminism: The Theory and Method of Oppositional Consciousness in the Postmodern World." *Genders* 10:1–24.

Sato, Charlene J. 1991. "Sociolinguistic Variation and Language Attitudes in Hawai'i." In *English Around the World: Sociolinguistic Perspectives*, edited by J. Cheshire, 647–63. Cambridge: Cambridge University Press.

———. 1993. "Language Change in a Creole Continuum: Decreolization?" In *Progression and Regression in Language: Sociocultural, Neuropsychological, and Linguistic Perspectives*, edited by K. Hyltenstam and A. Viberg, 122–43. Cambridge: Cambridge University Press.

Schwalbe, Michael L. 1996. *Unlocking the Iron Cage: The Men's Movement, Gender Politics, and American Culture.* New York: Oxford University Press.

———. 1998. "Mythopoetic Men's Work as a Search for *Communitas.*" In *Men's Lives*, edited by M. S. Kimmel and M. A. Messner, 565–77. Boston: Allyn and Bacon.

Silva, Noenoe K. 2004a. *Aloha Betrayed: Native Hawaiian Resistance to American Colonialism.* Durham: Duke University Press.

———. 2004b. "I Ku Mau Mau: How Kanaka Maoli Tried to Sustain National Identity Within the United States Political System." *American Studies* 45 (3): 9–32.

Sinha, Mrinalini. 1995. *Colonial Masculinity: The 'Manly Englishman' and the 'Effeminate Bengali' in the Late Nineteenth Century.* Manchester: Manchester University Press.

Smith, Anthony D. 1991. *National Identity.* Reno: University of Nevada Press.

Smith, Linda Tuhiwai. 1999. *Decolonizing Methodologies: Research and Indigenous Peoples.* London: Zed Books.

Sodetani, Naomi. 2003. "Way of the Warrior." *Hana Hou! Magazine of Hawaiian Airlines*, April–May, 26–33.

Stannard, David E. 2005. *Honor Killing: How the Infamous "Massie Affair" Transformed Hawai'i.* New York: Viking.

Stauffer, Robert H. 2004. *Kahana: How the Land Was Lost.* Honolulu: University of Hawai'i Press.

Stillman, Amy Ku'uleialoha. 1994. "'Nā Lei O Hawai'i': On Hula Songs, Floral Emblems, Island Princesses, and *Wahi Pana.*" *Hawaiian Journal of History* 28:87–108.

———. 2001. Re-membering the History of the Hawaiian Hula. In *Cultural Memory: Reconfiguring History and Identity in the Postcolonial Pacific*, edited by J. M. Mageo, 187–204. Honolulu: University of Hawai'i Press.

Stirling, Amiria Manutahi, and Anne Salmond. 1976. *Amiria: The Life Story of a Maori Woman.* Wellington: A. H. and A. W. Reed.

Stirling, Eruera, and Anne Salmond. 1980. *Eruera, the Teachings of a Maori Elder.* New York: Oxford University Press.

Stoler, Ann Laura. 1995. *Race and the Education of Desire: Foucault's History of Sexuality and the Colonial Order of Things.* Durham: Duke University Press.

———. 2002. *Carnal Knowledge and Imperial Power: Race and the Intimate in Colonial Rule*. Berkeley: University of California Press.

Stromberg, Peter G. 1993. *Language and Self-Transformation: A Study of the Christian Conversion Narrative*. Cambridge: Cambridge University Press.

Swain, Jon. 2005. "Masculinities in Education." In *Handbook of Studies on Men and Masculinities*, edited by M. S. Kimmel, J. Hearn, and R. W. Connell, 213–29. Thousand Oaks, Calif.: Sage Publications.

Swora, Maria Gabrielle. 2001. "Commemoration and the Healing of Memories in Alcoholics Anonymous." *Ethos* 29 (1): 58–77.

Tamura, Eileen H. 1996. "Power, Status, and Hawai'i Creole English: An Example of Linguistic Intolerance in American History." *Pacific Historical Review* 65 (3): 431–54.

Tapsell, Paul. 2002. "Marae and Tribal Identity in Urban Aotearoa/New Zealand." *Pacific Studies* 25 (1–2): 141–71.

Teaiwa, Katerina. 2004. "Multi-Sited Methodologies: 'Homework' in Australia, Fiji, and Kiribati." In *Anthropologists in the Field: Cases in Participant Observation*, edited by L. Hume and J. Mulcock, 216–33. New York: Columbia University Press.

Teaiwa, Teresia K. 1999. "Reading Gauguin's *Noa Noa* with Hau'ofa's *Nederends*: Militourism, Feminism and the 'Polynesian' Body." *UTS Review* 5 (1): 53–69.

———. 2001. "Militarism, Tourism and the Native: Articulations in Oceania." PhD diss., University of California, Santa Cruz.

Tengan, Ty P. Kāwika. 1997. "The Architecture of Canoes and Nations: A Case Study in Hawaiian Cultural Nationalism." B.A. Honors Thesis, Dartmouth College.

———. 2002. "(En)gendering Colonialism: Masculinities in Hawai'i and Aotearoa." *Cultural Values: Journal for Cultural Research* 6 (3): 239–56.

———. 2003a. "Hale Mua: (En)gendering Hawaiian Men." PhD diss., University of Hawai'i at Mānoa.

———. 2003b. "Ke Kūlana He Māhū: Remembering a Sense of Place (review)." *Contemporary Pacific* 15 (1): 231–33.

———. 2004. "Of Colonization and Pono in Hawai'i." *Peace Review* 16:157–67.

———. 2005. "Unsettling Ethnography: Tales of an 'Ōiwi in the Anthropological Slot." *Anthropological Forum* 15 (3): 247–56.

———. 2008. "Re-membering Panalā'au: Masculinities, Nation, and Empire in Hawai'i and the Pacific." *Contemporary Pacific* 20 (1): 27–53.

Tengan, Ty P. Kāwika, and Jesse Makani Markham. n.d. "Performing Polynesian Masculinities in American Football: From Rainbows to Warriors." Unpublished manuscript in author's collection.

Timmons, Grady. 1989. *Waikiki Beachboy*. Honolulu: Editions Limited.

Tobin, Jeffrey. 1994. "Cultural Construction and Native Nationalism: Report from the Hawaiian Front." In "Asia/Pacific as Space of Cultural Production," edited by R. Wilson and A. Dirlik. Special issue, *Boundary 2* 21 (1): 111–33.

Trask, Haunani-Kay. 1984. *Fighting the Battle of Double Colonization: The View of a Hawaiian Feminist*. East Lansing: Office of Women in International Development.

——. 1991. "Natives and Anthropologists: The Colonial Struggle." *Contemporary Pacific* 3:159–67.

——. 1994. "Refusal." In *Light in the Crevice Never Seen*, 26–29. Corvallis: Calyx Books.

——. 1999. *From a Native Daughter: Colonialism and Sovereignty in Hawai'i.* Honolulu: University of Hawai'i Press.

Trask, Mililani. 2001. "A Question of Sovereignty." *Landrights Queensland*, online newspaper of FAIRA, March 2001. http://www.faira.org.au/lrqarc.html.

Tsai, Michael. 2003. "Is Surfer Sunny Garcia a North Shore Reality?" *Honolulu Advertiser*, June 26. http://www.honoluluadvertiser.com.

Tsai, Stephen. 2006. Warriors Making Over Haka. *Honolulu Advertiser*, November 29. http://the.honoluluadvertiser.com.

Tsutsumi, Cheryl Chee. 2001. "King's Spirit Lives at Big Island Festival." *Honolulu Star-Bulletin*, August 12, D6.

Turner, Terence. 1994. "Bodies and Anti-Bodies: Flesh and Fetish in Contemporary Social Theory." In *Embodiment and Experience: The Existential Ground of Culture and Self*, edited by T. Csordas, 27–47. Cambridge: Cambridge University Press.

Turner, Victor. 1969. *The Ritual Process: Structure and Anti-Structure.* Chicago: Aldine.

United States, Census Bureau. 2001. "The Two or More Races Population." Census 2000 Brief, http://www.census.gov/prod/2001pubs/c2kbr01–6.pdf.

Valeri, Valerio. 1985. *Kingship and Sacrifice: Ritual and Society in Ancient Hawai'i.* Chicago: University of Chicago Press.

Vanderpoel, Peter. 2006. Interview with the author, Kula, Maui. July 20.

Visweswaran, Kamala. 1994. *Fictions of Feminist Ethnography.* Minneapolis: University of Minnesota Press.

Walker, Isaiah Helekunihi. 2005. "Terrorism or Native Protest? The Hui 'O He'e Nalu and Hawaiian Resistance to Colonialism." *Pacific Historical Review* 74 (4): 575–601.

——. 2008. "Hui Nalu, Beachboys, and the Surfing Boarder-lands of Hawai'i." *Contemporary Pacific* 20 (1): 89–114.

Wallace, Anthony F. C. 1956. "Revitalization Movements." *American Anthropologist* 58:264–81.

Ward, Deborah L. 1991. "Puukohola Ceremony Meant to Heal, Unite." In *Ka Wai Ola o OHA*, 13— *The Living Water of OHA*, November, 13.

Watson-Gegeo, Karen Ann, and Geoffrey M. White, eds. 1990. *Disentangling: Conflict Discourse in Pacific Societies.* Stanford: Stanford University Press.

Wendt, Albert. 1999. "Afterword: Tatauing the Post-colonial Body." In *Inside Out: Literature, Cultural Politics, and Identity in the New Pacific*, edited by V. Hereniko and R. Wilson, 399–412. Lanham: Rowman and Littlefield.

Wertsch, James V. 2002. *Voices of Collective Remembering.* Cambridge: Cambridge University Press.

White, Geoffrey M. 1991. *Identity Through History: Living Stories in a Solomon Islands Society*. Cambridge: Cambridge University Press.

———. 1997. "Museum/Memorial/Shrine: National Narrative in National Spaces." *Museum Anthropology* 21 (1): 8–27.

———. 2000. "Histories and Subjectivities." *Ethos* 28 (4): 493–510.

———. 2001. "On Not Being a Theme Park: Pearl Harbor and the Predicament of National Memory." Unpublished manuscript in author's collection.

———. 2004. "National Subjects: September 11 and Pearl Harbor." *American Ethnologist* 31 (3): 293–310.

Willard, Michael Nevin. 2002. "Duke Kahanamoku's Body." In *Sports Matters: Race, Recreation, and Culture*, edited by J. Bloom and M. N. Willard, 13–38. New York: New York University Press.

Wilson, Christie. 2006. "Anthropologist Dates Maui Heiau to Early 13th Century." *Honolulu Advertiser*, August 18. http://www.honoluluadvertiser.com.

Wong, Laiana. 2002. "He ʻai pala maunu na haʻi." *Honolulu Star-Bulletin*, December 8, A2.

Wood, Houston. 2006. "Three Competing Research Perspectives for Oceania." *Contemporary Pacific* 18 (1): 33–55.

Wood, Paul. 2006. "Hawaiian Roots: Maintaining the Mana in Maui's Koʻolau." *In Hana Hou* 9:60–73.

Young, Kanalu G. Terry. 2004. "An Interdisciplinary Study of the Term 'Hawaiian.'" *Hawaiian Journal of Law and Politics* 1:23–45.

Yuval-Davis, Nira, and Flora Anthias, eds. 1989. *Woman-Nation-State*. London: Macmillan.

Zisk, Janet. 2002. "Kamehameha Schools and the Panalaʻau Colonists." In *Hui Panalāʻau: Hawaiian Colonists, American Citizens*, 5–6. Exhibition pamphlet. Honolulu: Bishop Museum.

....

Dedman, Palikapu, 59, 61
deities. *See* akua
Delos Reyes, Hoaka, 219, 226
Desha, Stephen L., 70–72, 232 nn. 6–7
Diaz, Vicente, 24
discourse, 16–17, 23, 166, 216; aloha, 73; colonial, 97, 140, 144; historical, 14, 66–67; of identity, 22, 66, 116. *See also* moʻolelo
disease, 36–37, 146, 203
duality, 35, 98, 100–101, 188; gendered, 142–44, 157. *See also* balance

economy, subsistence, 43–44. *See also* capitalism
education: colonial, 45–47; gender and, 139–40, 156, 234 nn. 5–6, 236 n. 7; Hawaiian cultural, 98, 103, 107, 135–36, 169, 185, 189–90, 232 n. 8; Māori cultural, 205–6; status and, 62–63
Eldridge, Carl "Kale Boy," 61, 169, 189, 219–20, 236 n. 15
emasculation, 3, 8–11, 45, 144; colonialism and, 58, 130, 215. *See also* feminization; masculinity
emotion, shared, 19, 88, 120, 164
employment. *See* occupations
Establishment Day, 72; Festival, 98–99, 107

family: breakdown of, 38, 177–78; responsibility for, 52, 60, 183–84
Farm, Kyle Elama, 132, 222
feminist critique, 8, 10, 15, 185; reaction against, 13–14, 156, 159
feminization, 132, 140; of Hawaiʻi, 8, 12–13, 50, 144, 152, 213, 231 n. 12; of men, 50–51, 90, 202. *See also* emasculation
Festival of Pacific Arts, 76
fighting arts. *See* lua
film: Hawaiian characters in, 8–9

Finney, Ben, 55, 62
Flores, Elaine, 79
Forbes Cave, 121–22
Fornander, Abraham, 70
Freemasons, 39–40
Friesen, Steve, 82, 84
Fujimori, Rose, 79

gender: balance, 35–36, 156–162; duality, 58–59, 142–43; imperialism and, 34, 38, 200; occupations, 23–24, 35, 42–44, 129, 158; roles, 9–13; as social practice, 16, 33–34; transgender, 152, 161, 206, 235 n. 12
genealogy: in chants, 25, 178; gender politics and, 159; for indigenous anthropology, 25; in moʻolelo, 178, 186; Oceanic/Polynesian, 29–30, 201–3; performed, 95, 208–9
Gibson, Glen Puhi, 119, 203
Gibson, Manu, 219, 225
Gon, Sam, 94
Gora, Kealiʻi, 81
Gora, Keōua, 81
Gowen, Herbert, 71

haʻa: hula vs., 235 n. 7
Haili, Kaʻiana, 150
haka, 127, 153, 206–7, 235 n. 13
Halekiʻi-Pihana Heiau State Monument, 141–42, 188
Hale Mua: Aotearoa visit of, 202–13, 215–16; calendar, 132–33; camaraderie, 119, 134, 168–69, 188–89, 196; changes in, 216–17; as community, 177, 194, 196; egalitarianism of, 132, 141, 166, 191, 194, 214; at Hīkoi protest march, 210–12, 214; male space of, 104, 128, 141, 156; of Maui, 202, 217; membership of, 2, 62, 119, 133, 145, 151, 167–69, 171–72, 235 n. 6; model of, 130–31, 149–

13; in Hale Mua, 119, 133; Hawaiian influences on, 202–4, 208–9, 211; Hīkoi protest march, 210–12; influence on Hawaiians, 12–13, 48–49, 76, 127, 175, 201, 235 n. 13, 236 n. 14; as kindred, xii, 203; Party, 211; performance, 205–6; at Puʻukoholā, 103, 110, 233 n. 2

marae, 76–77, 129, 177, 233 n. 11; Koraunui, 208, 210–11

Marble, Roger, 119

marches: Battle of Nuʻuanu, 199, 214; Hawaiʻi Loa Kū Like Kākou, 64; Hīkoi, 210–12, 214; Keepers of Aloha, 3, 5, 214, 230 n. 8; Kū i ka Pono, 211; ʻOnipaʻa, 63–64

martial arts. *See* lua

Martinson, Martin, 119, 168

masculinity, xi, 10–16, 45–52, 140, 157, 202; dance and, 152–55; military and, 6, 47–48; modern, 38–39; ritual and, 64–65, 97, 144; violence and, 148–51; warrior, 66, 115, 137. *See also* emasculation; gender

Massie Affair, 231 n. 8

material culture, 125, 205; carving, 132–39, 175–78, 191–92

Māui(akamalo), 202–3

Māuiroto, 82, 203, 208

Meinecke, Fred Kalani, 78, 82

memory, 66–68, 74–78, 83, 98, 116; narrating, 178, 186–87. *See also* moʻolelo

men, Hawaiian: absent, 10, 48, 58, 60, 76, 80, 84, 127, 215; as beach boys, 8, 51–52, 231 n. 8; disempowered, 3, 5, 8, 37, 130; as film characters, 8–9, 51; imprisonment of, 11, 61–62; as leaders, 13–14, 21, 39, 114, 159–60; roles and responsibilities of, 6, 52, 60, 134, 142, 159, 166, 184–85; status of, 62, 86, 129, 157, 159, 167. *See also* gender; masculinity

men's movements, 156, 159

Merrie Monarch Festival, 152, 154, 206

Meyer, Meleanna, 88

military: Hawaiian men in U.S., 6–7, 21, 46–47, 180, 188, 233 n. 1; KSB and, 46–47; occupation of land, 43, 49, 61; Stryker brigade, 6; veterans, 48–49, 61, 229 n. 3, 231 n. 14–15

Million Man March, 156

missionaries, Calvinist, 36–37

Mitchell, Kimo, 61

modernity, 60–62; alienation and, 33, 193, 196; gender and, 38, 131, 159–60; maoli vs., 101, 136; violence of, 147–51

Molitau, Kaponoʻai, 5, 94

Mollar, Earl Mo, 181

monarchy, 2; Hawaiian Kingdom, xiii, 2, 35–42, 56, 64, 69

moʻolelo, 14, 66, 71, 78, 186–87, 218; community and, 28, 74, 138, 170; contesting dominant narratives, 14–15, 66–67; contexts for, 120, 163–65; of Hawaiian culture, 135–36, 185; interviews as, 27, 164, 171; socialization via, 165–67, 170; subjectivity and, 18–20, 25; talk-story, 19, 163–64, 196, 219–27. *See also* under individuals' names

Mound of the Whale. *See* Puʻukoholā

mythopoetic movement, 156

Nā Alo Aliʻi. *See* Alo Aliʻi

Nā ʻElemākua, 103

NAGPRA (Native American Graves Protection and Repatriation Act), 121

Nāhale-ā, Kīhei, 13

Nākānelua, Debbie, 127

Nākānelua, Helen, 181

Nākānelua, Kamika, 119, 167

Nākānelua, Kyle, 5, 22, 147; at ʻawa, 219, 227; on dance, 152–53, 155; Hale

177; embodied, 87, 132; gendered knowledge of, 10, 60, 169; lost, 5–6, 72, 76, 131, 169, 178, 185; masculine, 12, 64, 84, 126, 158; neocolonialism vs., 22, 136, 157–58; revitalized, 6, 13, 53, 76, 190. *See also* material culture

training, physical, 125, 128–29, 145–47, 151. *See also* dance; lua

Trask, Haunani-Kay, 10, 23, 58–59, 140

treaty of reciprocity, 41

Turia, Tariana, 211

Turner, Victor, 85–87, 89–90

unity. *See* ho'oku'ikahi

University of Hawai'i: ethnic studies, 54; Hawaiian studies, 55, 57, 59, 140

urban status, 44, 184, 188, 206

Vaituulala, Mike Luatangi, 224

Vanderpoel, Peter Lupe, 168, 215–16, 223

veterans, 48–49, 61, 229 n. 3, 231 n. 14–15. *See also* military

violence: gendered, 9, 11, 52, 59, 125, 129, 131, 141; modernity and, 147–51; repudiation of, 6, 144–45, 149–51; statistics on, 147–48

voyaging, 54–55, 57, 172–73, 176; in Aotearoa, 209; as metaphor, 24, 78, 189–90. See also *Hōkūle'a*

Waimea Hawaiian Civic Club, 72, 74, 98

war: dance, 153; god, 144, 236 n. 13;

Iraq, 6; Vietnam, 61; World War II, 2, 47–49. *See also* military

warriorhood. *See* koa

warriors: colonial discourse on native, 144; gendered, 11–12, 233 n. 8; modern Hawaiian, 4, 6, 18; Polynesian, 49, 154, 202; repudiating violence, 6, 150–51. *See also* koa; military; Nā Koa

weapons, 110, 118, 142, 145, 234 n. 4; carving, 134–39, 191–92; spear dance, 155; Māori weaponry school, 203, 211

Wehe Kū, 141, 145

whaling, 38

"Where Are the Brothers?" (song), 11, 204

Wilcox Rebellion, 230 n. 3

women, Hawaiian: as bearers of tradition, 34, 60, 76, 80, 84; bodies of, 8, 90, 231 n. 12; hula and, 50, 127, 152–54; as leaders, 10, 21, 59, 96, 140, 159–60; lua and, 127–29; as Nā Koa, 126, 129; power and, 13, 96, 158–59; at Pu'ukoholā, 96, 115, 157; status of, 36, 39; Western culture and, 9, 36. *See also* gender

Wong, Hinaleimoana, 161

work, 183–85, 188–91. *See also* occupations

Yano, Rodney, 48

Young, John (Olohana), 68, 232 n. 2

Ty P. Kāwika Tengan is an associate professor of anthropology and ethnic studies at the University of Hawai'i, Mānoa.

Library of Congress Cataloging-in-Publication Data
Tengan, Ty P. Kāwika, 1975–
Native men remade : gender and nation in contemporary Hawai'i /
Ty P. Kāwika Tengan.
p. cm.
Includes bibliographical references and index.
ISBN 978-0-8223-4338-7 (cloth : alk. paper)
ISBN 978-0-8223-4321-9 (pbk. : alk. paper)
1. Hawaiians — Government relations. 2. Hawaiians — Social life and customs.
3. Hale Mua (Organization) 4. Men — Hawaii — Social conditions.
5. Masculinity — Hawaii. 6. Hawaii — Government relations. 7. Hawaii —
Social life and customs. I. Title.
DU624.65.T46 2008
305.3109969 — dc22   2008019637